STRENGTH & ENCOURAGEMENT

SO YOU CAN PRAISE ME IN THE MIDST OF THE FIRE

366 Daily Devotions

by
Debra Stuart Sanford

CCB Publishing
British Columbia, Canada

Strength & Encouragement:
So You Can Praise Me in the Midst of the Fire 366 Daily Devotions

Copyright ©2013, 2014 by Debra Stuart Sanford
ISBN-13   978-1-77143-152-1
Second Edition

Library and Archives Canada Cataloguing in Publication
Sanford, Debra Stuart, author
Strength & encouragement : so you can praise me in the midst of the fire
366 daily devotions / by Debra Stuart Sanford. -- Second edition.
Issued in print and electronic formats.
ISBN 978-1-77143-152-1 (pbk.).--ISBN 978-1-77143-153-8 (pdf)
Additional cataloguing data available from Library and Archives Canada

Book design by Kevin O'Keefe.

This book may be ordered from: **www.AlephTavScriptures.com**

Publisher: CCB Publishing
                 British Columbia, Canada
                 www.ccbpublishing.com

I want to personally thank my husband, William Sanford, for his love and support while creating this book. Without his encouragement this book would not have been published.

This book is dedicated to my dad and mom, Grover and Betty Stuart, who taught me the Truth and how to walk in faith. They are a daily inspiration to me through their faithful, consistent, unbending example of walking in love, compassion, and righteousness. This book is also dedicated to my children who bless me daily: Jennifer, Jessica, Jason, Jordan, Justin, and also those children that Father has added to me: Josh, Michael, Joshua, Chloe, Madelyn, and Tobey Samuel. I am so thankful to have been blessed so richly with such a loving and caring family.

Praising God in the Midst of the Fire

Many times you find yourself in the midst of a fiery test and you need extra strength to help you stand firm. If you seek strength from the scriptures and listen to the voice of your Heavenly Father, then you will be strengthened and become much stronger than you were before. Your Heavenly Father knows what tests you need to become the person He can use for His Kingdom. We are here for only one purpose - to conform to His Image. Knowing this you must realize that your life will take you through times when He will perfect your faith and your perseverance. "Count it all joy" when you enter these times of testing knowing that your Father loves you enough to prepare you for His Eternal Kingdom of Light. This life you live is temporary, but He is preparing you for eternal life where you will rule with Him. Do not look at the details of your life and the situations that you find yourself. Look at the bigger picture- how must you change to become that being of light that rules nations once you have finished your short existence here on earth. You must view all things as temporary and possessions as fleeing. As you let go of the material things and long for the spiritual things, then you will see through the eyes of your Father.

This book is designed to help you learn to carry on a conversation with your Loving Heavenly Father. Read this book as if your Father is speaking directly to you. Converse with Him through this conversation and He will manifest Himself to you and reveal to you hidden things from His Words. The tests you are facing will be unveiled to you and you will have understanding and be able to overcome with new found faith and perseverance. Be strong. Be brave. You are an overcomer!

Without battles there are no victories! Without victories you do not become strong-you do not overcome!

Psalms 1

My Beloved, praise Me in the midst of the wickedness of others. Praise Me when others are walking in wickedness all around you. They will suffer loss and you will gain the eternal rewards from My Kingdom. They will go into the Lake of Fire and will be no more, but you will live eternally in My Kingdom of Light. Rejoice and be glad when others persecute you for the sake of righteousness. Rejoice and be glad when the wicked mock you. They cannot stand to see you walk in righteousness. They cannot stand to see you do what is right, because your righteousness exposes their sins. They want to see you sin and walk in darkness, so they do not have to see their sins. They walk in the shadows and are happy, but the light of your righteousness exposes their sins and make them see that their life is one of misery and darkness. Rejoice that you do not have to walk in the shadows, but you walk in the Light. There are those around you that see your light and rejoice with you in all you do. I will bring success to what you put your hand to. I will bless all your ways, because you want to serve Me and walk in My ways. Rejoice and be glad that I love you so much.

Strength And Encouragement

Psalms 2

My Beloved, rejoice in Me. Fear Me and walk in my ways. Fear Me and I will bless you. Do not fear man, because he is a mere mortal. Fear Me, because you love Me and want to serve Me. I want you to rejoice and be glad and know that I AM YHUH. Fear Me in all you do. Fear Me in the midst of oceans and the rise of the seas. Take Me by the Hand and rejoice in all circumstances. I will open My Hand to you and help you through all your troubles. There are times when you will have to praise Me and not know what I Am doing. You will have to have faith that I know what I AM doing and trust in Me to help you find your way. I always have a plan for you. It is laid out clearly before Me, so you can see your path ahead. My angels go before you and make your pathway straight. When all is ready to move forward, then you will go forward. What if this takes time? Then you must wait and stand firm and do not waiver. You must be like a mighty oak with its roots going deep into the ground-well anchored and unbending. You will never fall or be embarrassed, if you put your trust in Me. You are a Light to the nations-a mighty warrior. You will fear Me and walk in strength and dignity among the nations. Rejoice that I love you so much.

Psalms 3

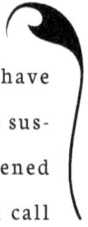

My Beloved, victory comes from Me. If you have success, it is because I have given it to you. If you have the ability to overcome, it is because I have sustained you. If you have the ability to see clearly, it is because I have opened your eyes and allowed you to see. All good things come from Me. If you call on My name, I hear you. If you are walking in righteousness and keeping My ways, then I will answer you quickly. If you are in sin, then I must deal with your sin first, and then I will answer you. If you are in sin, then repent quickly, because it hinders My blessings from coming to you. If you are suffering with bad health, then repent so I can heal you. If you are not prospering financially, then repent so I can bless you. If you know what you are doing wrong, then change your ways. If you do not know what you are doing wrong, then seek Me and I will show you the way to go. I will bless you and help you, so you can have victory. If you are being tested for your faithfulness, then stand firm and do not waiver and I will give you victory in your test, and you will receive even more blessings than before. You must know that I love you, and My ultimate purpose for you is to shape you into the person that I want you to become. You must emerge from your body strong and mighty, so you can serve Me in My Kingdom of Light.

Strength And Encouragement

Psalms 4

My Beloved, come to Me when you are angry or upset, and I will deliver you from this oppression. Come to Me and tell Me about your problems. If a man has tried to harm you or take from you, then come to Me and I will counsel you. You can be angry and not sin, if you come to Me and allow Me to help you see clearly about what actions you should take. I will deliver you from the anger and oppression and set you free, so you do not sin against your fellow man. If your enemy that hates you rises up against you, I will give you the strength and courage to stand firm. I will deliver you and keep you in a strong tower, so no one can hurt you. If many come against you to mock you and ridicule you and dishonor your name, I will close the mouth of the oppressor and I will lift you up and put him to shame. If you walk in righteousness, I will bless you and raise you up above the others around you. I will keep you safe from the trap of those that hate you. Do not be afraid, but rejoice that I love you so much. I will deliver you from your anger and fill you with joy when I manifest My faithfulness to you. You will know that I have heard your prayers and acted on behalf of you, because you are Mine and I love you so much.

Psalms 5

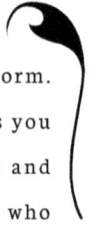

My Beloved, rejoice and be glad, because I am your shelter from the storm. I am the One who holds you- the One who keeps you -the One who wraps you in My arms of love. I am the One who is with you and guards over you and keeps you safe. There is no man that you should fear. There is no man who can harm you. I keep you safe in My arms of protection. There are many men around you. They do not know Me like you know Me. You know the One who created you -the One who formed you- the One who knows what you need at any moment in time. I made time and I will take time away. I created time as a device, so you would know when to keep My feast days and My timetable, so you would know My coming and going while you live in this fleshy body. When you are released from your flesh, then you will see Me face to face and you will not be tormented by the flesh. You see others around you, and you are grieved by their sins. You stand upright in My Presence, and you do not bend. You will be rewarded for your faithfulness. I will prove My faithfulness to you and make your way straight, so you can see clearly and be at one with Me. Rejoice and be glad that I love you so much and that I keep you hidden in My wings.

Strength And Encouragement

Psalms 6

My Beloved, when others come against you and cause you to become angry, it only brings darkness to you so you cannot see clearly. Your anger is a like a cloud surrounding you, so you cannot see the light. You cannot see the way to go. You cannot know what is right and wrong, because your anger overshadows the way before you. You must cry out to Me concerning all those who cause you to become angry. Why are these people making you angry? Is it you that is at fault? Is it them that are at fault? If it is others that are in sin and they try to draw you into their sin or they belittle you because you are righteous, then I will take care of those people. You must love them in the midst of their sin. Do not fall into sin because of them. Instead overcome the situation by loving them and developing a higher walk of righteousness, so they can see it clearly. If it is you that is in sin, then you must admit that you are at fault and confess your sins. If you cannot admit that you are in sin, then you will continue to become angry. If you cannot repent, then the weight of your sin will continue to weigh on you and can mislead you into further sin. Repent at the first sign of sin, and then you will not grow angry and sullen. Call on My name and I will help you repent and be at one with Me.

Psalms 7

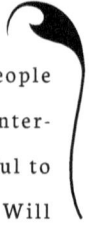

My Beloved, I test the hearts and minds of the righteous. I test all My People who call on My name to see if they are worthy of bearing My name and entering My Kingdom of Light. I test the righteous and find out who is faithful to Me even in the midst of troubles. Will they call on My name for help? Will they look to the world for their help? What will they do? The righteous will call on Me quickly and find shelter under My wings. They will be safe from those who try to bring them harm. If you are in sin, repent quickly, so that My judgment will not come upon you. If you continue not to repent, then My weapons of death will come upon you and carry you down to the grave. There you will sin no more and be saved from eternal destruction. I will save the faithful from impending danger. My faithful will not even know what is coming, but My messengers will come to redeem them from the trouble at hand. You do not have to fear any man or any problem. You must only fear Me and walk in My ways. You must know that I AM King of the universe and all things are in My hands. Is there anything too hard for Me to do for you?

Strength And Encouragement

Psalms 8

My Beloved, praise Me for My mighty works. I placed the sun, moon, and stars in the sky. I hung all the planets. I made a universe for you to live in. I spread out the skies, so that it continues to expand and makes room for all My Children. I will fill the universe with My Children and they will spread My love throughout all the worlds that I have created. I look to the seed that I have placed here on earth-My righteous seed. I have placed them and they prosper and bloom. They are ready for the harvest. They have spread their flowers, so all the seed have traveled around the earth and many men have been touched by their presence. I have kept My Children in a safe place. I have kept My Children in My Hands, so that I can feed them and clothe them and love them tenderly. You are here to be tested and found faithful to Me. You are here to spread the good news about Me to those who do not know Me, so they can be saved from eternal destruction. I want My universe to be filled with the faithful-the righteous. I want My universe to be filled with praises for Me and all my works that I have done for My Children. I will bless those who bless Me and curse those who curse Me. Those who call on My name will be saved in the last day of judgment.

Psalms 9:1-10

My Beloved, Give thanks to Me for all my works. I have blessed you in ways that you do not know. I have lifted up your countenance when you were weak and sad, and I comforted you in the midst of you trial-your test- your troubles. I have heard your prayers. I have not abandoned you. I have looked from My Highest Dwelling Place and looked upon you and had mercy on you and I pushed back your enemies from you and saved you. I have saved all your ancestors-those that loved Me. I have fought on behalf of them. I have gone to war with them. I have stood beside them in times of trouble. I have remembered your seed and I have remembered My Covenant with you. I will not forget My promises to you. I will not forget that I made you in My image and I will bless you according to your deeds. Raise your eyes to Me to the heavens and see what I have in store for you. Do not cry and mourn in your situation for it will change as if over night. All you have to do is be obedient to Me and walk in My ways and I will bless you -you and your entire house. I will visit you and dwell with you and walk close to you. I will speak to you and bring you healing. I AM the One who made you and I will continue to form you and make you My own.

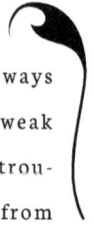

Psalms 10

My Beloved, I have stood up for the righteous. I have lifted My Hand against your enemies and thrown your enemies aside. I have kept you in My Hand and your enemies are scattered away from you. The wicked are all around you, but they cannot touch you. The wicked despise Me and mock Me and say that I am dead. They say that there is no Elohim. They believe that they are Elohims, and they serve themselves. They do not desire to serve Me. You serve Me and love Me and I will count it to you as righteousness. If your enemy scorns you, I hear his words and I will repay him for his wickedness. I will hear him in his arrogant state, and I will humble him and bring him low. The humble man asks Me what he can do for Me to please Me. The humble man is My delight and I long to have the humble men close to Me. If you are arrogant and do whatever you want to do and say that I will forgive you, then you will be surprised. I will forgive you if you turn from your sins, but you will have to pay for each of your sins. You will have to pay the penalty for your sins. You must not be deceived. You will pay for all your sins.

Psalms 11

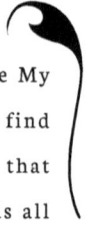

My Beloved, I test the righteous, and if they pass the test, they will see My face and dwell with Me in My eternal Kingdom. If you seek Me, you will find Me. If you come into My presence, then you will hear My voice. You say that you do not know My voice or you do not hear My voice, but My voice is all around you. Look at nature. Look at the weather. Look at the Light in My people's eyes. Look at the animals that I created. Look and see the signs that I give you all around you. Look and see and notice what I do for you. If you see what I AM doing, then you will be able to see things the way I see things. You cannot understand your life until you see things the way that I see them. For the sake of My Children, I reveal Myself to them and let them know what I expect of them. If you do not understand My laws, then you cannot understand how to please Me. You must study carefully My laws and walk in them daily, so you can please Me. Then you will stay in my refuge and be safe. I will keep you humble under My continuous testing, and the fire will develop you into the person I want you to become. Rejoice that I love you so much!

Strength And Encouragement

Psalms 12

My Beloved, I know you see the wicked all around you. Everywhere you look you see the sins of men. You want to remain pure and not be touched by the world. Even where you work or study, there are those who do not know Me and do not want to know Me. They love the world and want to be a part of the world. They want to have wealth, fame, power, and glory. They do not seek after Me, but they want to have all the money that they can get. They are greedy and selfish and not filled with loving kindness. They are vile and full of murder in their hearts. My Children are filled with love, and they will be upheld even in the darkest of days. When the storm comes, the wicked will be washed away, but My Children will stand firm and rejoice that I love them so much. I see the poor and needy, and I will open My Hand to them. I will not allow the wicked to torment them for long. I will arise and scatter the wicked and place the poor over them, so the wicked will be their slaves. I can do all things. You must trust Me to do what is best for you and your family. You must trust Me to fulfill the purpose that I have for you. I will stand by and uphold you all the days of your life.

Psalms 13

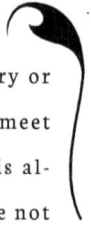

My Beloved, I give you more than you ever need. You should never worry or be afraid. You must trust Me to take care of you. You must trust Me to meet all your needs. You may not see a way out of your situation, but there is always a way and I will guide you to the path to take. If you feel like you are not getting answers to your questions and you have asked Me many times, then wait and be patient. Sometimes I want you to trust Me, and wait, and I will work it out. If you are asking for specific instructions on which way to go, the instructions will come and I will guide you. When the time comes for Me to open a door, I will open the door and show the way to go. Do not worry or be afraid. I am always with you no matter what situation you are in. If you have sinned, then repent and turn from your evil ways, so you can hear My voice clearly. If you are following the traditions of man and not My laws, then repent and follow My laws. Where are My laws? My laws are in My words-the scriptures. Look carefully and follow each of My laws, and you will be greatly blessed-you and your entire house. Give generously to those around you, and you will be greatly blessed. I look at your heart. Do you want to give to others? Do you want to be greedy? Only I know your heart.

Strength And Encouragement

Psalms 14

My Beloved, I will restore My People's fortunes. I will bring all my people back to My Land and restore what has been taken from them. You will see how I miraculously open doors for My People that only I can open and shut doors that hinder them from going forward and prospering. My Children are greatly blessed. Your ancestors have cried out to Me for redemption, but you will receive the profit of all their prayers. They did not see My Hand move on behalf of them, but you will see My Hand move on account of you and all My People that return to the Land. Only those who are called will come. Only those who have understanding into Me and My ways will come. Others will mock you and say that you are foolish for doing such a thing. Do not listen to them, but listen only to Me and I will guide you. Wicked men are all around you trying to lead you astray. They do not know My ways, yet they say that they have wisdom. They say they have understanding, but they know nothing. You know Me and have seen glimpses of Me at every corner-every turn you make. You are led by Me. You know My presence and My peace. You know which way to turn by My spirit. You are blessed by Me and I will never abandon you. I will always remain beside you and lovingly guide you into all My promises.

Psalms 15

My Beloved, who can dwelt in My presence? Who can stand before Me? Whose prayers will I hear? I will hear the prayers of those who obey My command-ments-those who follow in My Ways-those who want to please Me by keeping all My laws. If you walk blamelessly before Me, not doing as you please, but doing as I desire you to walk, then you will stand before My presence and see My face. You will know Me and I will know you as a husband and wife know each other-intimate with each other. If you do not want to come out of the world, then you are not worthy of standing before Me. You must love Me with your heart, soul, mind, and strength. If you speak evil towards others, then repent. Let all your words be filled with love and kindness towards others. Do not take bribes to harm others. Do not take interest from a loan, and if it has been years and the person cannot pay you back, then forgive the loan and let the burden be taken off your brother. Be kind to your neighbors helping them whenever you can. Do not love evil, but scorn the evil doers and have no part with them. Do not desire to look into the things of the world, but look into the things of Me. Desire to learn more about Me than the things of the world, and I will bless your hands and feet and all that you do.

Strength And Encouragement

Psalms 16

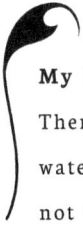

My Beloved, come rest in my refuge. There is nothing good outside of Me. There is only the dry desert wasteland of the world-not a place to find living water in which to drink. Come close to Me and know Me-know who I AM. Do not think that you can talk to Me once a week and still draw closer to Me? When you come close, I am close. I love you so much and want you to know Me and remain in My Presence. Go into Me and find the answers to all your questions. They will come. Just be looking for Me in all you do and say and you will find Me. Look for Me when you are kind to others. Blessings will come back to you. Even in times of trouble, give to others and I will give back to you. Everyday someone needs an encouraging word or a hug. You can give to others from your heart and bless so many people. Arise above your problems, and be loving and kind to others. Only then can you see My ways. Your eyes will be filled with Light and you will be a light to those around you- a beacon to a lost and dying world.

Psalms 17

My Beloved, I have probed your heart, I have visited you in your dark days- when all seems lost. Have you turned from Me or do you continue to praise Me for all My blessings that I have given you? Why do you serve Me- because other men serve Me or because you feel like this is the way to go or because you love Me and want to please Me? Only if you love Me with all your heart, soul, mind, and strength will you ever know Me and really serve Me. If you serve Me, I will protect you like I protect the pupil of My eye-like I shelter you with My wings-like I hold you in My Hand and fill you with My love. Do not be deceived. You can feel like you should do something, but still not receive My instruction to do this thing, because you serve yourself and not Me. Listen to My voice and love Me and want only Me. There are many who say they want to serve Me, but they do not know how to serve Me. You can make people smile by showing them My love for you. Let Me radiate through you, so they can see My Love. You must lift up your eyes to Me and allow Me to guide you every step of the path. I AM your strength and shield-your high tower in times of trouble. I will not leave you or forsake you all the days of your life.

Strength And Encouragement

Psalms 18:1-27

My Beloved, call upon My name when you are troubled-when darkness overtakes you-when you are lost in darkness and fear overtakes you. Call upon My Name and I will be a shelter to you-a high tower so no one can reach you-a shield to protect you from your foe-a fortress that cannot be penetrated. I will protect you and keep you, because you trust in Me to keep you safe-because you walk in My Ways-because you want only to please Me. I will come to you and scatter the darkness. I will come to you and break the back of your enemy. I will send My messengers to clear the way for you. You will not be forgotten in your time of need. You will be cared for by your Elohim. No one will be able to defend you, but Me. Do not run to man to help you, but run to Me and I will send you help. I will send you a helper-someone who can give you just what you need. Be strong. Be brave. I AM close at hand. I AM near. Do not be afraid. Call on Me and wait. I will answer. Be patient. I will move mountains for you. I will bless you greatly.

Psalms 18:28-50

My Beloved, I AM your shield from all those who try to harm you. I AM your fortress-your high tower-where no one can touch you. I AM the shield that keeps you close to Me -a shelter in times of trouble. I will care for you and keep you close to My bosom. You are My beloved and I want you to see My ways, so I will unveil them to you because you call on Me day and night and you keep My Ways. I will light your path and make your pathway straight, so you will always know the way to go, and you will not stumble and fall in the darkness. You will not fall before your enemies and be humiliated. I will prosper everything that you put your hands to, because you are led by Me. My messengers will come to you and guide you. I will open doors for you and close doors for you, so you are always on the right path. Do not be afraid of the future. I hold the future in the palm of My Hands. If you are in sin, then you should be afraid, because punishment will come to you. If you are walking in righteousness and loving those around you, then rejoice because your future is full of blessings. Why do I afflict My righteous? So they can be humbled and I can raise them up to do the work of the Kingdom. If you are being afflicted, rejoice that I love you so much to use you greatly in My Kingdom of Light.

Strength And Encouragement

Psalms 19:1-11

My Beloved, look at the sky. Look to nature. Look to the animals. Look at the universe. Do you see my design in all of it? I have formed and placed everything in motion. You are man and you are finite. I AM YHUH and I AM infinite. I AM always and forever. I AM never ending without beginning. Who are you that you could compare Me to you? Who are you to question Me? Who are you that you think you know the path for your life? I have chosen you and guarded you all your life. I have been beside you and protected you and kept you in the path that I have for you. I have sent messengers to help you and show you the way to go. You need to open your eyes and see the signs of My presence all around you. You need to see how I AM guiding you in the little things you do. You are My beloved, and I am preparing you for the days ahead by the situations that you are enduring at this present time. You must look to My words and find strength. If you read My words, you will be healed, and you will find joy. If you read and mediate on My words, you will find wisdom and enlightenment. If you read My words and think on them, you will be able to apply them to your life and walk in righteousness. You will be able to love and help those around you. You can be My Hands and Feet. You must see the bigger picture. This life is not just about you, but how you can love and help others around you. Show My love to others and give them the strength that they need to have to endure until the end. You are strong, because I have given you strength. If you are weak, call on My name and I will come to you and strengthen you. You need only call on Me, and I will come to you and minister to you in all that you do, because I love you.

Psalms 19:12-14

My Beloved, be careful not to sin in ways that you know are wrong, and be careful not to sin in ways that you do not know are wrong. Ask Me to help you see the sins that you are unintentionally doing, so you will be blameless before Me. I will reveal to you the hidden sins, so you can repent and walk upright before Me. Even if you do not know that you are in sin, I still hold you accountable for your sins. I will punish you mildly for those sins that you do not know about, but I will punish you harshly for those sins that you know and continue to walk in. You must pay for all your sins-known and unknown sins. You must be balanced before Me, so that your good deeds outweigh the sins. You must reach out to others and be loving and kind, and watching very carefully over your mouth, so that you will not say any words to hurt others. You must say words that uplift and encourage those around you. You must be the one to stop others from saying ugly hurtful words. You must confront them in love and compassion, because only then will they listen to your words of rebuke. You must bring peace wherever you go. You must spread love to others. Listen to others and comfort them in their pain. The world is a desolate place, and you need each other to stand firm and not waiver. Be bold and be strong and endure to the end. Guard over the meditations of your heart, so you only meditate on Me and My ways, and then you will be able to know the path I have for you and discern what is right and wrong and stand blameless before Me.

Strength And Encouragement

Psalms 20

My Beloved, I will hear you in times of distress. I will hear you in times of trouble. When you think that I do not hear, I always hear your voice and I will answer you. I will provide a path for you to take. I will show you the way. I will bring you a light to your eyes, so you can see. I will prove Myself faithful to you. I will remember all your good works -all your acts of kindness. I will remember all your tithes and offerings that you have given to Me. I will remember your obedience. If you are in sin, then I will point out your sin to you when you call on My name, so you can be cleansed and depart from your sinful ways. If you repent, I will hear your voice. If you rebel against Me, then I will not listen, but I will wait until you repent and follow My ways. I will show you the way that is best for you to go. You must trust Me. You must know that I know what is best for you and I will only give you the best. Sometimes you beg Me to give you something, but I know it is not best for you, so in my loving kindness and compassion for you, I do not listen to your prayer and do not give you what you desire. If what you ask Me to do is good for you, then I will give you your heart's desires. First you must pray and seek Me for what I desire for you to do and as you do this, then I will prosper your hands and you will have success in all you do, because I love you so much.

Psalms 21

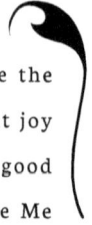

My Beloved, I find great joy when you are strong- when you overcome the darkness around you. I find great joy in seeing you blessed. I take great joy in seeing you obey Me and worship Me and praise Me for all the many good things that I have given you. I take great joy in knowing that you love Me and want to serve Me. I will never turn My face away from you. I will hear the words of your mouth and I will listen to you and help you in all that you ask Me to do. I will give you the desires of your heart knowing that you only want to serve Me in all your ways. I will lift you up above the others and I will help you to find the path I have for you. I have chosen a straight path for you. I have chosen a path of prosperity. I have chosen a path where you can love others and greet them lovingly and give them compassion in the midst of their trials. I have given you a heart to love others and reach out to them with open arms of love and make sure that they are sheltered with your love. All the things I do for you will conform you into My image and lift you up, so you can be a vessel of honor chosen for My House. Rejoice and be glad that I have chosen you as My own and I will bring you by the hand to My eternal kingdom. Do not give up, but be strong and mighty and stand firm in the midst of the fire.

Strength And Encouragement

Psalms 22:1-24

My Beloved, you ask me why I have abandoned you. You ask me why I have turned my face from you. You ask me why I do not hear your prayers anymore, but I do hear your prayers. I am always with you-always beside you. I placed you in your mother's womb to carry you safely until you were ready to emerge into this world. I gave you hope to live while you were lying on your mother's breasts. I gave you the strength you needed to survive. I held you in my arms and showed you the way to grow and prosper. I have sent my messengers to you to watch your way and care for you. You are precious in my sight and I love you deeply. Even when the dark times come, I AM still with you and will never leave you. You may look at the situation at hand and wonder what will happen to you, but look only to Me and trust Me and I will bless you. I will show you the way. I will allow you to see the future for you and your family. You must trust Me in every detail of your life. Do not look and focus on all the details of the situation, but pray and ask Me to help you. Call on My name and I will not turn My face from you, but I will help you in all ways. I will have a clear path for you and prove Myself faithful to you, so you can walk in strength not bending or wavering but mighty and powerful-full of faith and able to stand against all who come against you. I AM.

Psalms 22:25-31

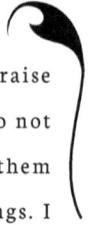

My Beloved, praise Me among your brothers and sisters of the faith. Praise Me in the midst of your family. Praise Me with those of the world who do not know Me. Lift up My name and let them know of My faithfulness. Let them know who I AM and who I can became to them. I AM Creator of all things. I AM King of the universe. I know all things and I hold all things in My Hands. I move and I know and I see and you will be touched by Me, if you call on My Name. I know you, and I formed you, and I AM always with you. I have no beginning or end. I AM and I AM. You cannot understand, because you have a finite mind. I AM infinite and eternal and I want you to live with Me eternally. Those who serve Me will live in My kingdom eternally, but those who rebel against Me will be cast into outer darkness and will be no more. You must set your eyes on Me and not waiver. Darkness grows stronger, and this land will become covered by it. If you keep your eyes on Me, you will not waiver or bend and you will be able to be led out of the darkness and into the Light. I will bring you to a safe haven and keep you there while all the rest of the world is in peril. You should rejoice and be glad that I love you so much to hear your prayers and bring you safely out of the danger and into a place of rest and peace. Rejoice and be glad this day!

Strength And Encouragement

Psalms 23

My Beloved, you will lack nothing, if you follow in My ways. I will guide you down the right paths, so you should not fear that any evil will overtake you. You will be protected from disasters, so you should have no fear. You should trust only in Me. I AM faithful to you. I AM always beside you and know exactly what you need. What you think you need and what you really need may be totally different. That is why you have to trust Me to give you what is best for you. This is just like a child who cries for candy, and you know that is not what the child needs. The child needs warm nourishing food to help him grow and prosper. I know what you need to grow and prosper in Me. You should be concerned about your spirit growing, not your flesh. You should be concerned about sacrificing your flesh, so your spirit can grow and become strong. You must be self-disciplined and have self-control. You must not desire the things of the flesh, but the things of the sprit. If you overcome the things of the flesh and follow after Me, I will bring you to my wedding supper and you will sit at My Table and feast with Me and we will become as one. You will be heirs to My kingdom and rule over many. You will be given the universe as your inheritance, and I will fill the universe will new life, and you will teach many My ways and how to walk in love. Look beyond your flesh and look to Me, so I can show you hidden things not of this world.

Psalms 24

My Beloved, the world is Mine and all the people who live in it are Mine. Few are chosen to be My own children. Few are adopted by Me into My kingdom of Light. Who can stand before Me and worship Me? Who can stand before Me and hear My voice? Those who have clean hands and a pure heart-who do not desire the things of the world-the vanities of this world-pride, lust, power, fame, money. Those who desire to serve only Me do not want the things of the world, but they want to know Me and walk in My ways. They are My Children who love Me and want to be in My presence. They want to be in control of their flesh and not sin against others. They want to control their tongue, so that they bless others and not curse or humiliate others. They want only to bring love and kindness to others. Those who are full of hatred and revenge will not come into My Kingdom of Light. Those who have murder in their hearts and want to see others come to ruin and destruction will not enter into My Kingdom. Those who are filled with light and love and want only good things to come to others are the ones who know who I AM. I AM Love. I AM Truth. I AM Light. I AM Salvation to a lost and dying world. Soon this world will end, but My Kingdom will not end. I have an eternal kingdom and I want you to live with Me eternally and be at one with Me.

Strength And Encouragement

Psalms 25:1-11

My Beloved, I AM good and fair. I AM mericiful and compassionate. I AM beside you always-all day long and all night long. I hear your prayers, because you love Me. I AM near. I AM never far away. If you feel that I AM far away, then you must look at your life and see how you have moved from My presence. You must judge yourself fairly. Are you in sin? What must you do to change? What good things must you do to help others? You must look to Me, and I will give you understanding into My ways. I will give you the path to take to draw closer to Me. I will listen to you as you repent, and I will remember your sins no more. I will be merciful to you in your punishment for your sins. I know that you are seeking Me and want to change. I must always punish you for your sins, because I AM fair and just. I AM the judge, so I disperse the punishment. I choose what the punishment will be, so pray for My mercy, and grace upon you. I will listen to your pleas. I will help you to look at your past and see how I have changed you through the sins you have committed against Me. I have punished you for your sins with a punishment that has changed you for good. Only I know what you need to change you. I know what you need to help you become a kinder and loving person. I AM always forming you everyday into My image, so rejoice in this. Do not look to your past and grieve. The past has changed you into what you are today.

Psalms 25:12-22

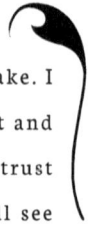

My Beloved, if you fear Me, I will guide you and show you the path to take. I will make you prosperous in all your ways. I will show you My Covenant and how to keep it. I will protect you, because you call on My Name and you trust in Me as your refuge. If you fear Me and worship only Me, then you will see the desires of your heart. You will long for Me and I will bring you what you desire. My desires for you will become your desires. You do not have to be afraid. You need only trust in Me. Your enemies will fall down beside you. You will not be disgraced or brought to ruin by your enemies, but I will lift you up and your enemies will scatter and suffer loss. The world is cruel and only wants to have victory- no matter who it harms to get what it wants. The world will take everything from you and overtake you unless your faith is in Me, and then I will not allow your enemy to conquer you. I will give you the integrity and wisdom to overcome. You need not be afraid. What can man do to you? Only what I will allow him to do to you. If you desire to serve Me, then you can walk through the fire and not be burned. You can walk through adversity and danger and not be harmed. If you look at your enemy in fear, then you do not trust Me. You must look at your enemy and know that I will help you overcome. I will show you a way to bypass your enemy or outwit your enemy. I will show you a hidden way to overtake your enemy. I AM King of the Universe. Everything is in My Hands. I hold all things and I move all things. There is nothing that I cannot do for those who believe in Me. There is nothing that I cannot do for those who call upon My Name and trust in Me. Lift up your head! Look on Me for your strength! I AM and I AM.

Strength And Encouragement

Psalms 26

My Beloved, live a blameless life before Me. Look to Me and trust Me with all your heart, soul, mind, and strength. I will test you and examine you and you will be clean before Me. Walk in My truth-in My commandments-in My ways of loving kindness and tender mercies towards others. Praise Me for all My wonders around you. Praise Me in the midst of others for all the good things that I have done for you. Let only thanksgiving be on your tongue. Thank Me all the day for all My many blessings on you. Stand firm and do not bend to temptations. Stand firm and do not bend to the things of the world. If you will turn your face towards Me and do not long for the things of the world, then you will be at peace and your spirit will rest and you will be at one with Me. Arise! Stand up! Do not be lazy any longer. Lift up your eyes and trust in Me to guide you and to protect you. You do not have to turn to men for healing. Call on My name and I will heal you. You do not have to run to men for money or loans. Call on My name and I will provide you with the money that you need. I will provide a job for you and you can work hard and earn a living for your family. Every man should work hard and this will heal his soul and give him strength and heal his body. If a man is lazy and does not work, then he will not prosper. He will become ill and lazy and his mind will diminish. You long to have days where you don't work and these are good days of rest, but you should never long to not work at all. You should always want to use your body for good things, so you can help others and help your family have all they need. If you are ill and cannot work, ask Me to heal you so you can work again. Rejoice that you have so much already and I will bless you with more. If you do these things, you will be blameless before Me, and I will bless you in all you do.

Psalms 27:1-3

My Beloved, I AM a light for your path. I will show you the way. I AM your salvation. I will protect you from all evil. I AM your stronghold. I will make you strong, so you can stand firm in the days ahead. I will guard over you and protect you, because I love you. Praise Me in all things. Rejoice that I have made you to serve Me. You can only be happy and complete when you are serving Me. You are fulfilled when you are seeking Me in all your ways. You know that I love you and care for you daily, because all around you are My fingerprints on the things I do for you. You are being prepared for the future-for My future kingdom. You must arise and be strong and endure until the end. I will bring you into My house singing and dancing. You will worship Me in the midst of many, and rejoice that I have been faithful to you in all things. You must continue to serve Me in spirit and truth. You must not give up or give in to temptations. You must be strong and mighty. You must be strong and brave. You are My child-My heir to the kingdom. You must know that many watch you and you prove to those around you your faithfulness to Me by your acts of loving kindness-no matter if it is towards your family or friends or strangers-those you do not know. As long as your heart is bent towards serving others and giving your love towards them, then you are My Hands and My Feet. Open your eyes and see what you must do every day to help others. When you focus on others, you do not focus on yourself, and your life will be much happier. Rejoice in the wisdom that I give you.

Strength And Encouragement

Psalms 27:4-6

My Beloved, you should only seek to dwell in My Presence all your days. You should praise Me and shout for joy at all my wondrous works that I have done for you and all your ancestors. I have saved them from danger, so that you can exist today and carry on their seed of righteousness. You are greatly blessed to be called My child-My heir to the throne-My first born. You will inherit the kingdom but you first must be prepared-be ready to rule over others. You must be wise and have understanding and tender mercies. You must be able to show love to others. I rule in love and compassion, but justly and fairly. I always do what is right for others. If someone wrongs you, I will make them pay for their sins against you. I will bring back to you what has been lost. I will keep you from evil men. I will shelter you and protect you. I will keep you in My tent-wrapped in the folds of the tent, so you are hidden from danger. I will cover you in the last days, and keep you safe from danger. I will protect you and keep you in My Hands, so no one can touch you. Rejoice and be glad that I will keep you close to Me and protect you from the evil ones. You are greatly blessed. You are held in the Hands of the Creator-the one who made you. I am still forming you in My Hands as you live this life on earth. You will emerge from your fleshy body fully formed and ready to stand before Me. You will emerge a glorious being ready to inherit My Kingdom of Light. Rejoice and be glad that I AM giving you so much!

Psalms 27:7-14

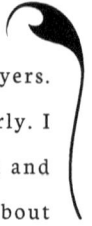

My Beloved, seek My face and I will show you favor and answer your prayers. Seek My face and I will bless you. I will lift you up, so you can see clearly. I will allow you to see the path ahead of you. There are many around you and they need to hear about My love and kindness. Sometimes all they hear about is My justice and My discipline. I want them to know that I give them Truth, and I expect them to walk in it, but if they do not want in Truth, then I will have to repay measure for measure for their rebellion against Me. They say they love Me, but if they love Me they will obey Me. They will desire to obey Me and only want to do My will for them- knowing that My will for them is the best for them. If you will seek My face, your children will seek Me also. Let your children see you fast and pray and draw close to Me. Draw them in with you, and they will be blessed. See what I do for you, if you serve Me with all you heart. I will add to your family children, husbands, and wives. I will bless the womb of your wife and the hands of your husband. I will lift up your eyes, so you can see My face. Fast and pray and seek Me with all your heart, so your heart can turn to Me and I will see how you humble yourself towards Me. I honor a humble servant. David was a humble servant and I blessed him greatly. Notice when he writes songs to Me that he always asks for mercy, because he knows that he sins, but he is quick to ask to be forgiven. Repent quickly. Do not hold onto your sins, but remain in right standing with Me, and I will bless you.

Psalms 28

My Beloved, I AM a Rock in the midst of a dry barren desert. When you think that you are all alone. I AM there. When you think that you can go on no longer, I AM there. When you think that you want to give up. I AM there. I AM a Rock in that dry barren place. Speak to the Rock and I will bring water gushing forth just like I did for Moses in the desert. I gave to My People generously even in a dry barren place. I AM your shield from the heat. Come close to Me. I will protect you from evil men. I will set you free from them. They will not overtake you as long as you as doing My will. As long as you are righteous before Me, you will not be swept away with them. You will be preserved and protected. You will be lifted to a high place, so you can breathe. You are My beloved. I would not leave you lacking or without. I AM always there. I AM always besides you. I will never leave you or forsake you. If you think I AM distance and do not hear your prayers, it is because you have your eyes on the situation and not on Me. I can do all things. Nothing is impossible for Me. Sometimes what you want Me to do is not My will. You must accept My will for you and know that I only give you the best. Accept My gift as the best, and I will bless you greatly.

Psalms 29

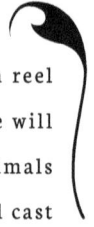

My Beloved, My Voice is mighty and powerful and will make the earth reel and rock. My Voice will shatter the trees and uproot the land. My Voice will make the earth split and the trees take blaze. My Voice will quake the animals and make them give birth. My Voice is mighty and powerful when it will cast upon the earth. My Voice is kept silent on earth, so you only hear Me in a whisper. You have to be quiet and still and focus your eyes on Me. The entire outside world must stop in your head, and you must worship Me and know that I love you and want to hold you close. You must seek Me, and you will find Me. Do not expect a loud booming voice to come at you. Do not expect to hear My Voice overtake you and bring you to your knees. I AM found in the silence and in the stillness and I whisper to you, so your sprit receives My Voice and you are filled with My Presence. As you focus on Me and worship Me then My Voice becomes clearer, so you can discern My Will. Most of the time you ask Me for signs to guide you along the way-sign posts so you will not be lost as you walk down the path of life. You talk to Me and you hear Me, but you want a sign to follow. I give you the signs, but really all you have to do is follow My Peace that I give you. I will give you strength to stand firm and peace to guide Me. Look for these two things in your life. Where does your strength come from? Where is your peace leading you? If you are sad and lonely, then you are out of My peace. Come closer to Me, and I will redeem you from all your troubles. I will show you who I AM.

Strength And Encouragement

Psalms 30:1-5

My Beloved, you cried to Me and I heard your prayer. You lifted your voice up to Me and I heard you, and you lifted your requests up to Me. When you call upon My name, I will hear you and I will heal you. I will heal your broken heart. I will heal your broken body. I will deliver you from all sickness and diseases. I will show you a way out. I will show that I AM your Healer. Look to Me in times of need. Do not look to man, but listen to My Voice and I will show you what to do. I will show you the path to take. I will deliver you from your pool of tears. Tears will no longer stain your face. You will rejoice and be glad. The night may be dark, but light comes in the morning. You will be glad and rejoicing when the light comes to you and heals you and restores you to good health. You will dance and sing and rejoice in your Maker. I fashioned you and made you, and I know what you need before you ever ask. I just want you to learn to come to Me and ask Me for everything just like a child comes to a parent and asks the parent for good gifts. I will only give you good gifts, because I love you so much. Rejoice and be glad that I have chosen you to be My Child. I have chosen you to be heir to My Kingdom. Rejoice and be glad, and do not weep any longer for your victory draws near.

Psalms 30:6-12

My Beloved, you may remember your prosperous days when you thought nothing would ever change. You think that you would go on forever and never have any hardship. You were ripe for affliction. You were fat and prosperous and heavy. You did not need to turn your face towards Me. You were brought down low. You were taken to your knees, so that you could cry out to Me Your Maker-Your creator. Do you have need for Me now? Do you want to call on My Name now? You can be moved. You can be shaken. You are not as strong as you thought. You are only human. You are nothing in My presence. You are flesh and your flesh will burn away in the midst of Me. You guarded carefully and sheltered with my Hand, so you will not perish. You are kept in My palm. You are My Beloved. If I see you becoming haughty or if I see you becoming too fat, then I afflict you and make you humble, so you can serve Me. It is far better for you to be afflicted and serve Me, then to have much and do not serve Me. You are My beloved, and I guard over you so carefully. I watch over you all the day. I send My angels to care for you. I give you only good gifts. I will not allow you to become haughty and lazy. I will not allow you to be fat and full of ambition. You will desire to serve only Me, and you will love only My ways, and if you do not follow close to Me then I will rearrange your path so you will. You will be molded into My Hands. You will become at one with Me. You will be aflame with Me and walk only in righteousness. You will have victory, and I will bless you.

Strength And Encouragement

Psalms 31:1-5

My Beloved, I AM your fortress and your strength. I hide you by My Hand from your enemies. I keep you safe from all calamities. I hold you close to Me like a mother holds her baby close to her breast. I AM always close to you. I hear your every breathe. I want you to lean on My bosom and hear My voice as I tell you hidden things. I Am Truth. Come to Me and you will hear the Truth and it will set you free from the bondage of the world and break the traps that have been set for you. Your enemies want to entangle you, so you do not have time to spend with Me. If you do not know My Voice, then you can be misled very easily. If you do not know My voice, then you can be led astray and get off the path I have for you. You must know My Voice. How do you learn to hear My Voice? You quietly listen for Me to speak and you quietly answer Me and hear My replies. You should have this quiet place with you all the time, so I can guide you here and there. If you have no quiet time, then you miss out on knowing who I really am. What happens if you are playing music all the time or if you are watching TV all the time or if you are on the computer all the time? How can you ever hear Me speak to you? You cry out to Me, but do you listen for Me to answer. You think that when you ask Me in your prayers that there will never be a respond. You must always wait for a respond, and know that I want to talk to you and guide you. Be strong and mighty and wait upon Me, and you will be blessed.

Psalms 31:6-18

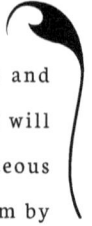

My Beloved, I will turn My face towards you, if you call on My name and trust in Me to save you. I will not allow your enemies to overtake you. I will not allow unrighteous men to over shadow you. All those who are righteous and trust in My name will be redeemed from the wicked. I will cover them by My Hand and keep them in My shelter. You may grow weary in your struggles everyday with your flesh. You may grow weary in your battles to subdue the flesh. You may feel as if you cannot go on. You may want to stop and not endure, but I encourage you this day to turn your face towards Me and trust Me to lift you up in the midst of conflict. I AM your strength, and I will help you even when men seek you and try to kill you. My servant David spend many nights running from his enemies-those who hated him, and he called on My Name and I delivered him from his enemies. I lifted him up as My righteous one and made him ruler over many. I will do the same for you and lift you up, and give you dominion over many. This life passes quickly, and soon you will emerge from this body into a glorious being of light. You will be finished with your earthly struggles, and you will receive the reward for all your travail. Do not give up the fight, but call on Me for strength, and I will give to you generously because I love you.

Strength And Encouragement

Psalms 31:19-24

My Beloved, praise Me for the goodness-the good things-that I have given you and your family. Praise Me in the midst of others. Lift up My Name and tell others of My faithfulness. Lift up My Name and show others that I AM the one who upholds you and strengthens you. I will bless you for your faithfulness and your courage to stand up and proclaim My Name in the midst of others. I will reward you, because you love Me and because you fear Me and obey My commands. I will conceal you in the shelter of My wings. I will cover you like a mother bird covers her young from harm and protects them and shields them. I will cover you and keep you from the evil plots of man. I will conceal you and keep you from the slander of men, and give you favor with those around you. Lift up your head and be brave and strong and I will talk with you and guide your path. Do not fear anything, but rest in My Presence. Do not worry about any danger. I will keep you in My Hands, and nothing can touch you. I will give you the wisdom you need to make decisions, so you can go forward wisely. I will give you what you need to rest and be at peace with Me. The world is dark, but I AM Light and I can guide you directly. The world will pass away, but I will never pass away. Cling to Me and I will keep you close to My bosom. I will nourish you and keep you safe. I will hold you in My arms of love, and you will be strong.

Psalms 32

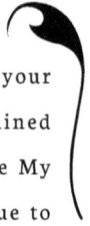

My Beloved, when you turn your face away from Me and do not confess your sins, you dry up like a withered piece of wood. All the life force is drained from you. My Hand is heavy upon you and you cannot breathe, because My Spirit is on you. You are grieved and moan all the day, but you continue to want to cling to your sin, or your pride will not allow you to confess to Me and allow Me to cleanse you. You must find your way to Me. You must see how you are not at peace within yourself. You are at war with yourself. You know you have done wrong or you are still doing wrong. You know that you have turned away from Me. You are not connecting to Me. Your prayers are fleeing from Me, because you will not confess your sins to Me. You must lift up your heart to Me, and sacrifice your flesh. Once you have confessed your sin to Me, then you will feel the liberty of repentance, and I will forgive you from the wrong that you have done. Holding onto sinful ways will cause you more grief down the road. You may be able to cover it for a while, but soon your sin will be exposed and you will be humiliated. Strike down your pride while you can, or I will have to strike it down for you, and the entire world will see your humiliation. Come to My arms and cling to Me. I am calling to you to come to Me in a time where I can be found. If you wait too long, the raging waters will overtake you and you will suffer for all your sins. You will have to pay the full measure of your sins, because you did not repent when I called you to repent. Come. Come quickly to Me. Bear your soul to Me, so you can be cleansed by My Spirit and be clean before Me.

Strength And Encouragement

Psalms 33:1-9

My Beloved, sing to Me for I AM good. Lift up your voice and shout your praises. Lift up your voice and sing songs about your thankfulness to Me. Make a new song from your heart! Give of yourself in your song. Dance and sing and rejoice, because I have been so good to you. I have given you all you need. I watch over every breath that you take. I cover you with My Hand. Nothing can harm you unless I allow it to touch you, and then only in My judgment for past sins. You are ripe for punishment only if you have deviated from My path for you. I AM Creator of all things. I spoke and there it was. I spoke and there it stood. I breathed life and there was Creation. I breathed life and there was my heavenly host. I AM the giver of life and I take away the breath of life from you. I give and I take. I show mercy and compassion, but I AM also fair and just. I love you deeply, but I AM forming you into My image preparing you for the days ahead when you will reign with Me in My Kingdom. You are My Children heirs to the promises of eternal life with Me. You are My beloved, and I rejoice in your praises and shouts of joy. I know you live in exile, but soon I will take you by the hand and lead you into the land I promised to Abraham, Isaac, and Jacob- a rich fertile land filled with many treasures. You will be blessed above all the nations of the world, and all will know I AM the only wise Elohim-the only true Elohim. I will bless you and keep you all the days of your life on this earth. Rejoice in this.

Psalms 33:10-22

My Beloved, I see all men. I watch the whole earth filled with men going in all directions. I know who fears Me and wants to serve Me. I know who truly loves Me. I know those who want to obey Me. I have fashioned all the hearts of men. I know each of their hearts, because I have created them. I know how they are. They do not know Me and who I AM. They know Me, if they love Me and have become intimate with Me. They know Me, if they call on My Name and commune with Me. A man cannot count on his strength to save him. A nation cannot count on its army to save them. I have taken small armies and conquered large armies, because it pleased Me to humble them and bring them down off their throne of power. I have taken small men to overcome giants. All things are in My Hands. Nothing is impossible with Me. You must look to Me for salvation. Call on My Name, and I will be your strength and shield. I will carry you through the darkest of times. I will be the One who saves you in famine. When enemies come to your borders, I will make an escape for you. I will show you the way and you will be delivered from all things that may harm you. Just trust in Me in all your ways, and you will see your deliverance.

Strength And Encouragement

Psalms 34:1-7

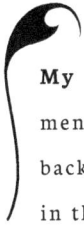

My Beloved, praise Me with your whole heart. Praise Me in the midst of men. Boast about Me and all the things that I have done for you. Do not hold back your praises about Me when in the presence of men. Rejoice over Me in the midst of others, and I will count it as righteousness to you. I will lift up your voice and let all the men around you hear your praises about Me. If you are fearful, come to Me and I will bring you deliverance from what you fear. There is no room for fear when you trust in Me. There is no need to fear any man. How can man harm you? No one can touch you unless I allow it to happen. Even then I will hold you in the palm of My Hand and protect you from all evil men. I will lift you up, so you can see clearly what men are doing around you, so you can guard your steps and steer away from those who hate you. Listen to My Voice of guidance, so you will not be entrapped by evil men. If you listen to my direction, then I will guide you away from those who want to harm you. If you praise Me in the midst of all your situations, I will hear your prayers and deliver you. I will surround you with My Presence. I want to grow close to a man who praises Me and does not complain against Me. I will send My angel to encamp around you and deliver you. I will hold you next to Me, and no one will be able to harm you even in the most dangerous situation. Praise Me in all you do and say. Let your lips be filled with praises about Me. Let laughter be on your lips and not sadness. Rejoice that I love you so much and I AM preparing you for the days ahead to be strong and overcome.

Psalms 34:8-14

My Beloved, taste and see that I AM good. Come closer to Me and see that I AM satisfying. Look into Me. Draw close to Me. I AM a consuming fire. I will draw you close to Me like a moth to the flame, but I will burn away your flesh and conform you the closer you draw to Me. Do not resist Me, but draw closer to Me. Learn to fear Me. A man that fears Me will lack nothing. How can you fear Me? Keep My laws and love them with all your heart. Desire to serve Me, and yearn only to please Me. You must want to do what is right. You must want to turn your head away from evil and not turn your head towards it. You must want to depart from worldly things, and only walk in righteousness. You must want to guard your tongue, and only say pleasing things to others. You must want to spread loving kindness and tender mercies around to others, so they can rejoice over your kind words of healing. Pleasing words can uplift the soul of a man. You must want to uplift others and pull them up from despair. You must want to be a guiding light of righteousness to others. You must want to be the life preserver that you throw out to those who are sinking. Do not allow your brother to walk in sin when you know that you can help him. Encourage him and strengthen him, and I will bless you. I will make you stronger, so you can support others in your walk on this earth. Give to others, and I will give to you in abundance. Rejoice and be glad that I love you so much.

Strength And Encouragement

Psalms 34:15-22

My Beloved, My eyes are always on you watching you. My ears are always listening for your cries. My hands are on you and you should never be fearful. You should never be afraid. You should always trust in Me. If you are righteous, then suffering will come your way, but if you call on My Name I will answer you and help you overcome those who oppose you. Your enemies are nothing in My sight. You should never be afraid of them. I will bring angels to fight on behalf of you. I will lift you up above the circumstances and keep you so no man can harm you. What can he do to you if you are in My Hands? The evil man will prosper and try to take what is yours, but he will take nothing from you. I give to whom I want to give, and I take from whom I want to take. I am King of the Universe, so all decisions are in My Hands. No matter how far you think I AM away, I AM near. You need to repent and draw near to Me in all your ways-not just a few. You must guard your tongue and speak words of kindness to others, so you can show others by your example who I AM. I AM an Elohim of kindness towards those who serve Me and want to be obedient. I will bless those who serve Me with all their heart.

Psalms 35:1-10

My Beloved, I will fight on behalf of you. I AM your salvation in times of trouble. Those who oppose you will be put to shame. I will bring only success to your door, and those who oppose you will not have success. I will make a path way for you, so that those who hate you will not be an obstacle for you. I will make war against them, and they will vanish from the face of the earth. No man can stand against Me. No one can rise up against Me, because I will shatter them with one blow. What is man to Me? A mere breathe that I can take away at any second. I hold you in My Hands, so no man can harm you. Rejoice and be glad that I love you so much. I will give to you exactly what I want you to have-no more and no less. If you feel that you have less than what you need, then do not complain but call upon My Name and we will reason together. You can be content with much less. You can be content with little. You must turn away from your lusts of the world and only rely on Me and My Ways. When others call on the world for healing and help from their enemies, they will not receive My help. If they call on Me for their healing, needs, and protection from their enemies, then I will hear their prayers and act on behalf of them. I AM always listening. Obey My commandments and love me and serve Me, and I will give to you freely. Be a humble servant-quick to obey and willing to act at a moment's notice.

Strength And Encouragement

Psalms 35:11-28

My Beloved, I will not allow your enemies to gloat over you-to rejoice when your fall. I will pay back to them what they wanted to happen to you. I will see if they are happy when you fall, and I will be angry with them and put My Hand upon them and make them pay with many lashes on their backs for their wickedness against you. Do not be happy when someone falls or is punished. Do not rejoice over the hardship or pain of others. Instead pray for them and stand beside them and support them through their hardship. Even if they were not there for you, you must be there for them. I will count it as righteousness towards you. I will lift you up and bless you. If others are mean to you, then be kind to them. If others turn their face away from you in times of need, then you turn your face towards them in times of suffering. I will bless you for your kindness. It will be like hot coals cast upon their head, when you pour your love upon them and treat them in kindness when they treat you with hatred. You must rise above the others and not be like the world. You must be kind and tender to all men no matter how they treat you. I will bless you greatly for all your acts of kindness.

Psalms 36

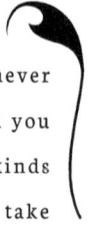

My Beloved, I AM the Fountain of Life. I will water you, so that you never thirst again. I will shelter you with My Wings of protection. I will hold you fast, so no man can harm you. Man lays in his bed at night and plots all kinds of evil-how he can make money at the cost of someone else-how he can take revenge on someone he hates-how he can murder someone and get away with it. I see him and I laugh. He thinks that all his wicked deeds are hidden, but I know them every one. I know what he thinks and how he plots, and I will bring him down low. I will disgrace the wicked and bring them humiliation, or I will kill them and take their evil schemes far away from the righteous. You do not have to be concerned about men. If a man is trying to harm you, listen for My Voice and I will guide you. Sometimes I say to go away from the evil ones and find a new residence. Sometimes I say to pray and fast and I will alter the situation. Sometimes I change the heart of a man towards you, or I bring in other men to help you who have power over the man. There are many things that I can do. All things are temporary and they can change overnight. I hear your prayers, and I will help you in all situations that you find your-self. Just call on My Name for help.

Strength And Encouragement

Psalms 37:1-11

My Beloved, trust in Me and do good. Trust in Me and be faithful, and then you will flourish and I will give you your heart's desires. Why will I give you your heart's desires? At this point your heart will be bent on serving Me and your desires will be My desires. You will want to do My will in all areas of your life, and you will long to do what is good in My eyes. You will want to walk a straight upright path before all those around you, so you will be a light to those willing to see the Light. Commit yourself to Me in all your ways. Act in righteousness. Do not waiver when you see the wicked being rewarded. Their fortunes will quickly vanish, and they will fall before your eyes in a tragic end. You will see the "stars" of the world and how quickly they vanish, and then no one can remember who they are. Those who do good things and help others will be remembered for a long time after they are gone. Many will honor the name of the righteous. After the righteous ones have died, those left behind will speak their names and tell of the goodness they brought to this world. You are planting good seeds. You are building a house. What kind of house are you building-one that will stand even after you die or one that will collapse and fall? You must build a stable house for your family-one that will stand for years after you are gone and continues on in your children and grandchildren, so I can pour out blessings on your family for years to come.

Psalms 37:12-24

My Beloved, the wicked may prosper, but not for long. They may laugh at the righteous, but in the end they will suffer great loss. The wicked try to gather in as much money, property, power, and wealth as they can. They want to run the world or the land where they dwell. They cannot do anything unless I allow them to do it. I use wicked men to punish the wicked. My judgment is poured out on the wicked by the wicked. They will be repaid for their wickedness. The righteous I hold by the hand, and I guide your step. If you fall, I keep you from harm. I guard over you, so you get up quickly and draw closer to Me. The wicked will die and be no more, but the righteous will live eternally with Me and receive their inheritance as My Firstborn Children. You must remember to always give generously to others. Give as I give. I give to all men, and I want you to give to all those in need. Show them that you are loving and kind, and you serve a loving and kind Elohim. They will see your light and be touched by you. You do not have time to delay, but you must listen to all I tell you to do. I will not allow you to suffer during difficult times, and I will feed you during famine. I will give you an escape to another place, so you can be fed. You do not have to fear. The wicked may have wealth, but you have Me to guide you into all prosperity. You have Me to show you the way to escape danger. If you call on My Name and listen to My Voice, you will always be cared for and be safe.

Strength And Encouragement

Psalms 37:25-40

My Beloved, I care for My People who love Me and want to walk in My Name. I care for those who call on My Name and want to serve Me with all their heart. I never abandon My Children and leave them without food or water. I give them shelter and make a clear path for them, so they do not stumble and fall. I guarded them from the Evil One, and I guard them so they can see clearly ahead. I strengthen them. I AM a refuge for them in times of trouble. They stay within Me, and I keep them from all the troubles around them, and they walk in My peace. The man who walks in My peace will live long and prosper and his children will live long and prosper. If a man worries and is afraid of the future, then he has no faith in Me. He has no faith in the One who forms him and he does not know Me. If he knew Me, then he would know that I will always stand beside him and protect him from loss. A righteous man has faith in Me and does not worry about tomorrow. He trusts Me to care for him and meet all his needs. You must also trust Me and know that I will lift you up above the circumstances. I will lift you up and make you whole in My arms of love. Many trials come upon the righteous, but I will help you use all these trials to transform you into a being of light. You must look ahead to what I AM doing in you and not what is happening around you. I AM forming you into the glorious being that you need to be for My Kingdom of Light. You must trust Me in all I do for you. You must accept My Will for you.

Psalms 38:1-22

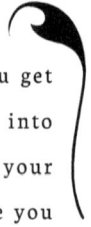

My Beloved, I see you all the day. I know when you fall and when you get up. Call on My Name to give you strength to stand firm and not fall into temptation. I will give you the strength you need. If you do not confess your sins to Me and turn away from your sins, then your guilt will overtake you and you will become sick and ill and your body will be sluggish, tired, worn, heavy, because you are resisting Me and My repentance. Do not give into your flesh, but stand firm and resist all evil. Fast and pray and ask Me to help you overcome whatever it is that makes you weak and vulnerable. I will help you, so the sin will not overtake you. You must close your eyes to the things of the world-the lust of the eyes, the pride of life. You must always focus on the things of the spirit-joy, love, truthfulness, patience, longsuffering, per-severance. You must try to walk in My ways and be like your Father. Look to Me and see how I walked on this earth. I laid down My life for others, and you should do the same. Your life is not your own. Your life is My life, and I give you life every day. When I am ready, I take the breath of life away from you. You are here only to be My servant and to be My Hands and Feet. You must listen to My directions and be obedient, and then I can bless you in all your ways. I can pour blessings into your house and give you abundance. I can cover your body with My presence and you will not become ill, but your strength will be renewed.

Strength And Encouragement

Psalms 39:1-7

My Beloved, your life is but a breath. You are temporarily living on this planet in your fleshly body. You are temporary, and yet you are eternal. You are an eternal being living that is forming and being shaped inside of a temporary fleshy body. The flesh wars against you and forms you like a bird slowly pecking against his shell, so he can emerge a stronger bird. You are struggling with the flesh daily. You tell yourself that you will guard your tongue and not speak, yet you see the wicked around you and all they do, and you are so grieved. You wonder how much longer you will have to endure their presence, and see all they do to harm others. They do not walk in love and compassion, but they are greedy and immoral. They want only to do what they want to do. They do not care about others. They seek material possessions, and they do not understand the things of the spiritual realm. They are blind and lost dying slowly and going to their graves in ignorance. They are a pathetic group of people, but you arise from among them victorious, because you know the Truth and you see clearly and you walk in righteousness. Do not allow them to sway you. Do not give up your good fight of faith. Continue to be strong and brave and fight against your flesh daily. You will become stronger and be able to subdue your flesh and overcome.

Psalms 39:8-13

My Beloved, you are a traveler just passing through this Earth. This is not your home. This is a land made of dirt, but you are made of the spirit. You do not belong here. You are a foreigner living in an alien place. You are enclosed in flesh and you war against it daily. I use your flesh to punish you and help you walk in a life of righteousness. You must not turn to evil, but run away it and be free of the heavy blows of My Hand. If My Children do not listen to My Voice, then they will be judged according to their deeds. They will be judged according to how they help others and how they give sacrificially to others not thinking of themselves. You must know that I will align your flesh and spirit, so you will walk with Me on this Earth, or you will never walk in peace and have comfort in My Presence. Hold onto Me and love Me with all your heart. Hold onto Me and My ways and walk in them, so you can be righteous as you travel through this life. Men will stop you and ask you what you are doing to live the way you do. They will see your light and rejoice that there are some who know Me and know how to be seen in the darkness of this world. They will rejoice over your goodness and how you treat your fellowman. Do not give up or yield to temptation, but continue to stand strong, and I will bless you until the day that your travels on this Earth is over.

Strength And Encouragement

Psalms 40:1-5

My Beloved, call on My Name when you are slipping away from Me, and I will put you on a solid Rock. I will give you firm footing, so you will not slip and fall. Do not allow for sin to consume you, but call on Me for strength and comfort. I will give you peace. I will put a new song in your heart, so you will rejoice instead of mourn. I will lift you up, so you can sing praises to Me, and rejoice in the midst of your brethren. You will strengthen them and encourage them and help them as they stand in the way of faith. You will only need Me in this life. Do not look to arrogant or worldly men, but look only to Me and know the One who created you and be fulfilled in My Presence. I will help you overcome in all areas of your life, if only you allow Me to help you. Sometimes you want your own ways and you are selfish and do not think of how your actions will effect others. You only think of how your actions will benefit you. Sometimes what benefits you will harm others, so you must look with eyes of gold-My eyes-and see the world through a new perspective. Take a step back and see the world the way I see it. You are here only temporarily and you are here with one sole purpose: to glorify My Name and bring Light to a lost and dying world- to be transformed into a new being full of light and love- ready to inherit My Kingdom. You must look ahead into the future and see what I want you to see, so you can be wise and caring and at one with Me.

Psalms 40:6-10

My Beloved, I do not demand sacrifices of animals anymore, but I do demand you allegiance-your devotion-your commitment to serve Me. I do demand your obedience-willing ears-ready to listen. I do demand your whole heart-edness-loving Me with all your heart, soul, mind, and strength. You would be lost and dying, but I have saved you-lifted you up-called you My own. I have saved you from destruction. I have guided your feet and if you choose to listen, I will lead you into the eternal gates of salvation in my Kingdom of Light. You may not see the way clearly, but if you walk in faith and trust Me to guide you, then I will deliver you. I will hear you as you call on My Name. If you bend your ears to Me and listen to My Voice and obey, then you will ride above the others and see with eyes of gold-illuminated with My wisdom. You will see ahead of the others and understand that the way ahead is one of trial and suffering, because you will be tested and found faithful before you enter My Kingdom. You must prove yourself to be called one of My own-My heir-My chosen. All is written about you in the scroll of The Book of Life. Your days are numbered and accounted for and your deeds will be listed, because I already know what you will become. I know all things, because I AM the Creator. You are created and you are lacking in knowledge. I yearn to be at one with you, so I can teach you the secrets of the universe. I long to have you close to Me, and soon I will return and take you home. I will end all this pain and suffering, and you will receive the crown of life-the crown given only to the righteous-the crown saved for the Children of the Eternal Father-the Great I AM.

Strength And Encouragement

Psalms 40:11-17

My Beloved, I AM your helper and rescuer. I will have mercy on you and pull you up from the darkness that surrounds you and tries to engulf you. There are men everywhere that hate you and want to harm you, but I will not let them touch you. I will keep you in the palm of My Hand. I will hold you close. I will hear your prayers- your every whisper. I will hold you and you will know I will save you. I will uphold you, and you will see clearly. The path is dark ahead for those who do not seek Me. If you cannot see ahead, then you have failed to hear my Voice. I will always guide you and let you know what is up ahead. You will always know. I will not keep My secrets from you. I will tell you all the things that I will do for you. I will tell you secret things, if you long for My voice and want to hear My Words. I will tell you the traps ahead, so you will be careful. I will tell you about the victories. I will show you a way around the obstacle that you will encounter. You must listen in the quietness. You must listen in the still moments. You will find My Voice, and you will recognize My Words as Truth. You will know and feel who I AM. You will not be deceived in the darkest of days. You will know the Eternal One and know My substance. I will give you light and strength. I will give to you generously, so you can see the way ahead and not be harmed by anyone. Your enemies will say, "let's take them here", but you will not go there, because you will be one step ahead of their traps. You will be ahead of all their deception. They will know that you are not to be touched -that you are Mine. Rejoice and be glad in this!

Psalms 41

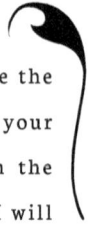

My Beloved, blessed is the man who takes care of the poor. This may be the poor in spirit or the poor in finances. If you give to the poor through your gifts, then you will be blessed. If you give generously to the poor in the land who are lacking in food, clothes, or shelter, then you do well and I will bless you greatly. If you bring light to the poor in spirit so they receive the Truth, then I will bless you greatly. As you live, you should do both. Your light should reflect Me wherever you go, and your words should always bring healing to others. You should also have your hands open to those in need. If you love Me, you will be blessed with good things. Those who love Me want to be My Hands and Feet. They want to obey Me and give generously. I will keep these children well and no sickness will overtake them. I will give them victory over their enemies. I will show My faithfulness to them by how I treat them. I will show My Children that I stand beside them and always give to them. There will be no doubt in their mind that I have given them favor. There will be no doubt in their mind that I have poured out My blessings on them. If you doubt Me and where I AM, then you must draw closer to Me by repenting and doing My will- not your will. You can easily see the faults of others, but do you see your own faults? Call on My Name so I can reveal your hidden faults, so you can repent and be blessed in My Presence.

Strength And Encouragement

Psalms 42:1-5

My Beloved, you call upon Me day and night and I see your tears as you long to draw close to Me. You long for Me as a thirsty deer longs for water. You long for Me and My Land where you can be delivered from exile and live among My People again. You want to sing and dance among My People, but there are none among you that want to sing and dance, because they are sad and their soul longs to return to their home and live in My Presence. You have been placed in exile, because of the sins of your ancestors. Those around you taunt you and say, "Where is your Elohim? Where is the One who delivered you from Egypt and brought you out with a mighty Hand and now has turned you over to your enemies? Where is the one who cast you into the nations and has left you there?" Arise, My People, because your salvation is near. I will call you home to Me, and it will be soon. You will be able to sing and dance among My People and praise Me with the crowds of My Children returning to enjoy My Festivals once again. They will keep My Festivals the way I wanted My Children to keep My Festivals-not the way they are kept now. The people living on My Land now are struggling to keep some form of My ways and hold onto some form of My Laws and Truth. They are in error, but I will correct their ways. I will send teachers to them to tell them how to keep My ways. I will choose men who love Me to reveal the error in their ways, and they will bring Truth to the eyes of My People. I love My People and I have not deserted you. I will bring you home to the Land that I have given you as I have promised.

Psalms 42:6-11

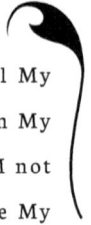

My Beloved, when you are so downcast, remind yourself of Me and all My creation. I have stretched Myself across the sky and I hold all things in My Hands. Do you think that I have forgotten you? Do you think that I AM not mindful of you? No. I love you deeply. You are My chosen one. You are My child. You are heir to My Kingdom of Light. You are joint heir with Me in My Kingdom. You are My beloved and I think of you all the day. You are My bride. You are My intimate lover. You are the apple of My eye. I have not forgotten you. I know your every breath. I know all you do and say. I am beside you all during the day. When you are sad, call on My Name and rejoice that I love you so much. Do not be concerned about men or anything that they do or say. Do not be concerned about the future. I will take care of you. If you are in need of healing, call on My Name and I will direct your path and show you the way to get healed. You may need to repent and put aside all your worldly ways. Do not cling to the world, because in the world is no joy. Hold onto Me and My ways and you will find great joy. You will find pleasure in Me that you will never find in the world. The things of the world glitter and you think that you will be happy if you have them, but they are only a mirage. They are fleeing. They are temporary. The things of Me are eternal and you earn great rewards by seeking out and obtaining these things. Rejoice and be glad that I have given you so much. Rejoice and be glad that the world is a better place because of your presence-because your love is among men-because your compassion is present in the midst of a very dark world. Rejoice and be glad that I have given you so many gifts, and lift up your eyes to Me and focus on Me, so you will not ever have to be downcast again.

Strength And Encouragement

Psalms 43:1-5

My Beloved, I AM your Savior. I Am the One you must turn to in times of trouble. If there are those who are trying to deceive you and mislead you, then open your eyes and look to Me and know that I will help you stand firm and not be moved. Just call on My Name and be free from their deception. They want to pull you away from Me, so you will not keep My ways, because they are convicted by your righteousness. They want you to stay far away from them, so they will not see the Light. I Am the Light and I will guide you along the way. Many are those who have lost their way, but if you rely on Me to strengthen you and be your strength, then you will help them be strong and overcome. You must be a Light to others, because they need to see your righteousness. Many are those who are lost along the way. They become bitter and angry over the things that befall them. You must trust Me to deliver you from all of them and set your heart free, so it can rejoice again. You must lift up your voice and praise Me, so you can be free and not surrounded by hate and deception. Many are those who want to lead you astray and keep you from Me. Lift up your eyes, so you can see Me and walk in My ways, so you can be blessed by My Right Hand. Many are those who want to find a way out of the sin they are in, but there is no one to help them. Be the one who helps them find their way, and I will bless you greatly. If you have saved one of my lost little ones from destruction, then you will receive a great reward.

Psalms 44:1-8

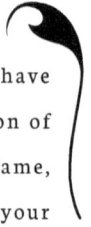

My Beloved, I have given you My Name to wear and you are My Child. I have given you favor and protect you by My Right Hand. You are an extension of My Arm. You have been given My Authority in the Land. Call on My Name, and I will send My messengers to help you. I will help you overpower your adversaries by My Right Hand. No man can harm you. You should not trust in money. You should not trust in attorneys or doctors. You should not trust in other people to help you, but you should trust in Me to overcome those who come against you. You should overshadow yourself with My Words and remain in My strong high tower, so that no one can touch you. When you walk away from Me and turn your face away from Me, then you are open to harm. You must not walk in sin, but walk in the Light and I will bless you. I will open doors for you. Many are the men who look for riches and power and fame. My Children look for Me and I raise them up, so that they have great riches-not as the world gives, but as I give to My Children. The things of the world will not bring you happiness, but the things given by Me will bring you great satisfaction. Draw close to Me and I will draw close to you and show you hidden things.

Strength And Encouragement

Psalms 46:1-3

My Beloved, I AM your refuge and strength-an always present help in times of trouble. I AM near to you always. I always hear your words and the meditation of your heart. I draw near to those who meditate on Me all day and night and do not enter into frivolous worldly meditations. I look for the one who meditates on Me and is lifting up prayers to Me for those around them. I look for the one who is righteous in all his ways, and I will bless him and lift him up. I will bless you and keep you close to Me. I will overshadow you and lift you to high places, so you can see ahead and know the way you are walking. You will need only Me to guide you. I AM the Light in the midst of the darkness. I help you when you think no one can help you. I open doors for you that no one can open for you. I look around and pull to you those who can help you when you are in times of need. I grasp their hearts and turn their hearts toward you, so they will show you favor and help you in your difficult situations. You do not walk alone in this world, but you walk with many who are always close to you yet they are not seen. You walk in the physical but the spiritual realm is so close to you, so that many can lend their hands to you. Watch carefully and see how the helpers bring you strength and courage by opening doors for you, so you can prosper and be delivered from difficult situations. Do not be afraid.

Psalms 46:4-7

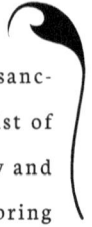

My Beloved, come to My city-the place that I love. Come to My beloved sanctuary and dwell in My Presence. My river of life flows through the midst of My city-the city promised to My People. I will always watch over My city and care for My People. I will make them glad in the darkest of days. I will bring rejoicing to them-singing and dancing. I will lift up their heads, and when the dawn comes they will not be moved. They will stand firm and not be shaken. The kingdoms will crumble around them and fall. The earth will shake and melt away at the sound of My Voice. I will shout and the foundations of the earth will falter and the earth will collapse, but My Children will be safe in My Bosom-close to Me, and will see Me create a new heavens and earth around them. They will rejoice over their new home in the midst of Me. They will never bend, but always stand firm and upright. They will not falter and lose faith, but they will be mighty and powerful knowing that I AM faithful. Do you be as the heathen and lose sight of Me, but stand firm everyday and dwell close to Me, so I can guide you down the path that leads to righteousness. I will help you as you dwell within Me and know Me and My Ways. Do not be ashamed to bear My Name. You are My child, and I will redeem you on the last day.

Strength And Encouragement

Psalms 46:8-11

My Beloved, come before Me and know that I Am the all-knowing and only wise Elohim. I know the beginning and the end. I know what will happen before it ever happens. You wonder how I can take care of you, but I have made the path before you. I have carefully carved it with My Hand to tailor you and fashion you and make you into the supreme glorious being that will take over My kingdom and have authority over many. Not all who call me Father or YHUH will enter into My kingdom. Not all that call me Master or Jehovah will enter into My Kingdom. Not all that call me the only Elohim will enter into My kingdom. They must serve Me whole heartedly and obey My commandments. They must know that I AM in control of all things. All nations will bow to Me. All nations will know that I AM. All nations will fall to My power. I will bring all nations to peace. I raise up armies and I cast armies down. I bring men to power and I overtake men and cast them down. They are all pawns in My Hand. None can run away from My authority. None can run from My greatness. They all say that they are in control. If they believe this, then they do not know Me. They do not understand who I AM. If through faith you endure to the end and cling to Me even in the darkest of days, then I will help you overcome and be counted worthy to become a part of My Kingdom of Light.

Psalms 47:1-9

My Beloved, shout unto Me. Shout praises to My Name. Shout to Me in one ac-cord. Shout to Me and hear My Mighty voice in the midst of you. I enter into your praises. I come to My People who praise Me. I enter into the midst of My People who love Me and shout to Me. Praise Me as King of the Universe-Maker and Creator of all things. Sing unto Me with musical instruments. Sing unto Me with your voices and let Me know that you honor Me with your songs. Sing unto Me about all the miracles that I have done for you. Shout aloud all the blessings that I have brought to you. You are My People-the ones I love. I have set aside a land for you-chose from all the earth-chosen just for you to bless you. Many have tried to rob you of your blessing, but I will bring you all back to your land and you will be filled with My Presence there. I raise up nations, and I destroy nations with one blow of My Hand. No man can do this. I will raise up the nation of My People in one swoop, and you will fill My Land. You will rejoice and be glad, and no man can stop you or what I have planned for you. You will have victory and you will once again be powerful in the earth.

Strength And Encouragement

Psalms 48:1-14

My Beloved, praise Me for I AM King of the Universe. I AM Creator of all things. I have established Jerusalem as My City- the city of the great king. I rule her and I watch over her and I know all that happens to her. I know her great decline, and how she has crumbled since My People have gone into exile. I have groaned over her and wait for the day when I will restore her once again. I will hold her in My Hand until then. I will make her strong in the days to come against her enemies. Look at her how she is bent down low. Look at her how the surrounding nations hate her and want to destroy her. They fire their missiles at her and I deflect them. I protect her now even in her crumbled state. Soon she will arise like a mighty warrior and she will destroy all her surrounding enemies and take over their land because it is My Land and it is not their land. They mock and yell and shout to no avail. They can say what they want, but the Land is still Mine and I give it to whom I choose. The time of judgment is also over and soon I will be able to arise and bring My People home. I will be able to bring My Children home singing and dancing and shouting victory. They will dance in the streets of My City-the city of the great king. They will know that I have given them victory. The Elohim of Judah has arisen. The Elohim of Israel has given them victory. Rejoice and be glad that I have not forgotten you or the promises that I have made with your ancestors. I have not forgotten our covenant, but I will keep you safe in My arms of love and return you to My Land, so you can serve Me once again.

Psalms 49:1-20

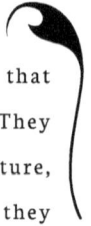

My Beloved, there are many evil men around you that mock you and say that they are better than you because they have wealth or power or fame. They think that they will live forever and never die. They do not see the future, but only today and how great they are. Their life quickly vanishes, and they are no more. They go to the grave and they rot away like every other man who has ever lived. This is the way of the flesh. The flesh will go back to the earth from which it was made. My People are eternal beings. They will sleep in the grave, and then they will be taken up at the last trumpet and return to Me. It will be a day of great rejoicing. It will be a great Day of Judgment for men who will be denied My Presence and will be thrown into the Lake of Fire and be no more. They will no longer exist. They will be judged for their deeds. The books will be read and the scales will be balanced. The verdict will be given and all that are Mine will be at My side to watch the wicked burn and become no more. My Children will not be tormented by the wicked any longer. At this time all the angels that have rebelled against Me will also be judged and they will be cast into the Lake of Fire and become no more. I take their spirit from them, and they no longer exist just like they never existed. There will be no trace of them-only a memory. They will no longer be able to torment My Beloved Ones. They will only be able to remember them as in a fog so long ago. Soon even this memory will become lost and their memory will no longer exist. Men build great houses and give their estates their name so they can last for generations, but I come by and destroy their houses and their name no longer exists. I give and I take away. I build up and I destroy. All men are in My Hands and I bless who I please. I bless My Children, because I love them and want to see blessings overflowing into their houses.

Strength And Encouragement

Psalms 50:1-6

My Beloved, I call to the heavens and I call to the earth for all My Helpers to gather My Children from the east to the west and gather them for judgment, so I can free them from the sins of the earth and they can be free to live with Me eternally. I judge My Children while they are on earth, and they pay for their sins while they are on earth, so that the scales are even and they will be found righteous before Me and worthy of entering My Kingdom. Whatever sins you do against Me, you must pay for those sins while on earth. It may be in the form of restitution in money, in time, in possessions taken from you. It may be in the form of grief, disappointment, and sadness. It may be in the form of people who mock and torment you. It may be in the form of physical ailments. It may be in the form of your family causing you grief by their lack of walking in My ways. You will suffer everyday for your sins. Everyday you will be tested and tried and found faithful in My sight. You must realize that I watch over you all day long and I tell you to do certain things and I see if you will be obedient to do it. All my faithful servants will be blessed on this earth and their blessings will be great. Choose. Do you want to walk in righteousness and be blessed, or do you want to go the way of the world and pay for your sins day after day? I want to bless you, so be righteous in all your ways.

Psalms 50:7-15

My Beloved, the earth is Mine and all that lives on the earth. I know all the animals, because I made all of them. I know all their movements and how they migrate and what they eat. I know the number of every species. I know where each creature lives, because I fill all things and know all things. I know the hearts of men and I search for the man who wants to serve Me-the heart that is bent towards Me and longs to do My Will. I look across the earth and I find the faithful and the righteous. I look and see who wants to obey Me and follow My laws. My People use to bring Me animal sacrifices, but I came and walked among you and died for you so you would no longer have to sacrifice animals, but only believe in Me and be received by Me. You have been covered with the blood-not of animals, but the blood that I shed at the hands of evil men. I laid down My life, so you would no longer have to be in the bondage of sin, but you are free to walk in My ways and follow Me. If you want to know what sacrifice to bring to Me, then lift up your voice in thanksgiving to Me. I have given you so much that you should never complain as My People complained in the wilderness. You should call on My Name, if you need something. If you have troubles (and the world will always have troubles), call on Me and I will deliver you from all your troubles. If you have promised Me to do something, then do as you have said that you will do. Praise Me every day for all the blessings that I have given you. Walk in faith and remain at peace. Love those around you and do good things for others. This is the life that I desire for you.

Strength And Encouragement

Psalms 50:16-23

My Beloved, why do you act like the wicked? Why do you slander the members of your own family or your neighbors? Why do you say words of deceit and steal from others? You may not steal their possessions, but you definitely steal their peace and contentment by your evil words. If you truly love someone, you will forgive their offenses and overlook their weaknesses and put aside all hatred and unforgiveness. If you truly love someone, you will understand that they are just flesh and they do make mistakes. You will forgive and forgive and forgive. You will only keep love in your heart and not bitterness or resentment. You will want to help others and not take from others by your evil words. You may want a person to hurt, because you are hurting. It is called revenge. You should guard over your mouth and say pleasing words to others-words that will build up and not tear down. You will comfort and heal the person with your words and lift them up from their dark place. You must be very careful to put your flesh aside and walk in My Spirit. Who are you to judge others? You do not know their heart or their hurts or their struggles. You must look at your own faults and allow Me to help you become strong enough to overcome them. You must call on Me, and I will help you forgive and forget. This is My way of love and this is how I want My Children to walk-hand in hand with Me -not allowing unforgiveness to hinder your walk. You must be able to put aside your feelings and think about what others are feeling. Be at peace and rest in My Presence, and you will do well.

Psalms 51:1-9

My Beloved, when you sin, you sin against Me, so I AM the one who judges you. If you hurt someone, you hurt Me. If you cheat someone, you cheat Me. If you lie to someone, you lie to Me. All your sins are against only Me, so I judge you with a fairness that you do not understand but only seek to understand. My judgments are fair and just and no man can judge like I do. I see and know all things. I know the heart of every man. I know the intention of the heart, and know if the sin was a deliberate act of rebellion against Me or unknow-ingly committed in ignorance. I know how to judge the man based on his heart. Is his heart turned towards Me or against Me? I can judge a righteous man in one way and judge an unrighteous man in another way, but both ways are just. I balance the scales with man. I give him a way to compensate for his sins, because I know that he lives in flesh. All his sins are on one side of the scale, and when he makes restitution and loves others on the other side of the scale. When the scale tips in the side of sin, then I bring punishment to offset the scales, so he will be balanced and learn to serve Me fervently. The world cannot understand these things. I AM teaching My Children to be loving and kind and compassionate. I want My Children to also be just and fair. I made you to be creatures of righteousness and to love others. The hurts in your life keep you from showing love to others at all times. Come to Me and I will heal you and set you free from the bondage of sin. Release all your bitterness and unforgiveness and be free to love others. This is My way. Walk in My way.

Strength And Encouragement

Psalms 51:10-13

My Beloved, I will create in you a clean heart. I will give you an unyielding spirit. I will cleanse you and heal you of all your past sins. You do not have to carry the burden of past sins. Once you pay for the sins, then they are forgiven and the price has been paid. I gave My blood to cover your sins. I will not have your enemies trample My blood. I will restore Jerusalem and rebuild her walls. I will destroy her enemies. I will overcome all those who have tried to prevail over Me. I will lift up My People and I will sustain them. I will make them strong and mighty. I will make them invincible. I will not allow them to be vulnerable any longer. They will be able to defeat their enemies with the judgment of My Right Hand. I will defeat them with My breath. I will not take My Spirit from you. I will not take My Presence from you. I will not take from you any longer, but I will give to you and reinforce My ways within you. I will create in you a righteousness that you have never known. You will be brought up high, and you will stand above other men in your thought and actions. You will know that I have delivered you from the things of man, and I will give generously to you in all your ways. You will know that I have blessed you and lifted you up, so you can serve Me with all your heart. Rejoice and be glad that I love you so much.

Psalms 51:14-19

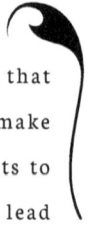

My Beloved, I long for My Children to repent. I look for a willing heart that wants to be in right standing with Me. I look for a man who wants to make things right with his enemies and do what is right for all men. He wants to treat everyone just and fair. Only look towards Me, so I can guide you to lead a life like this. If you have sin in your life, then repent and turn aside from it. Do what is right in My eyes and not in the eyes of men. Look to Me and watch how I change you from glory to glory as I slowly guide you in the right direction. I will help you give up the works of the flesh, and look towards the works of the spirit. If you have a broken contrite heart that has repented and is willing to obey, then you will receive Me and know Me. A man who is humble in My sight is a man who bends to My will for him. A proud arrogant man is one who wants to go his own way and do as he pleases. If you know that you are not right before Me, then pray and fast and get your heart right so you can hear My voice and obey My words. After this you will know that you are aligning yourself with Me and My will. Once you have aligned your will with My will, then you will walk hand in hand with Me. Rejoice that I do not delight in burnt sacrifices, but I delight in a heart that is bent towards Me and wants to serve Me with his whole heart. There are men that try to walk in the grey areas and live right on the edge of the world. You cannot do this for long, because the world will suck you into it. You have to walk in the Light and turn your face towards Me and not look into the things of the world. This will keep your heart pure and broken towards Me.

Strength And Encouragement

Psalms 52:1-9

My Beloved, many men are liars and want to deceive others. They have a sharp evil tongue that they use to do evil and not good. They speak evil to harm others and to benefit themselves. They tear down with their words and they bring dishonor to the names of others. I want My Children to lift up the names of others and encourage others with their words-not to ever tear down other believers. You must know that your tongue has the gift of healing in it. If you draw from Me, I will bless you and give you the words you need to speak to others, so that they will be healed whether they are broken hearted, fearful, lacking in faith, or physically ill. Your words will pierce deep into the soul and restore the soul of man. You must realize that the best way to help others around you is to walk in a righteous life style and be able to hear My Voice and obey Me. You will then be able to give of yourself to others. You will be like a leafy olive tree with oil to anoint others and shade for others to rest under. Your oil will refresh and cleanse and give repentance by the words you speak, because it is I that speaks through you and not yourself. You are the vessel and I fill the vessel with oil and you pour it out to others. The more that you allow Me to fill your vessel, the more you can give to others. If you seek the things of the world, then you will not receive from Me. If you sacrifice yourself and walk in the path of righteousness, then you will be able to be a light to others and a vessel poured out giving life to all around you through the healing presence that I pour through you. Rejoice and be glad that I can use you so much in this life. Just focus on Me, and I will show you how to be at one with Me and be able to give freely to others.

Psalms 53:1-6

My Beloved, I look out among the seas of people on this planet, and I look to see if I can find a righteous man-a man to whom I can cast My favor on. I look upon the sea of men, and I cannot find one man who is totally righteous in all his ways. Man is marred by his flesh and he struggles daily, but soon My Spirit will pass over the men of this world and My People will arise and awaken and will walk in My ways. I will take the dead bones and breathe life into them. They will arise and stand up and fight against the darkness until it leaves My Land, and then My People will rest in My Presence. Many men will die in deception thinking that there is no Elohim. They will not know Me and will end. Only the few-the chosen-the seed of righteousness will see Me and know Me and want to walk in My Ways and do what is right in My Sight. My Children are hidden among the weeds, but I will send My angels to find them as My Spirit passes over them, and they will be brought back to My Land and under My wing. The end of exile is soon. Some of My Children are already waking up and preparing for the others who will need to know My Ways. You must be listening to My Voice, so when I speak to you, you can go to Jerusalem, My sacred mountain. You must be with My People in the last days, or you will be destroyed by your enemies. Arise, My Children! Arise and march forward, because the end is near! Arise and be brave and strong, because I love you so much and I will stand beside you and make you stand firm. I will restore My People's fortunes.

Strength And Encouragement

Psalms 54:1-7

My Beloved, I AM your support. I hold you all day. Even in the midst of trouble I hold you and support you and protect you from your enemies. Your enemy may come in various different forms. You may not have a man with a weapon coming against you, but you do have enemies of your flesh. You have weak areas in your flesh that war against you all day long. You have weaknesses that keep you from being victorious. You have fleshly desires or fears that keep you from being righteous. If you fear, then you sin. You should trust in Me in all things. You should not be fearful of man or anything. You should trust in Me to deliver you from all things. If you have a fear, then attack it with your entire mind. Go at your fear straight on never giving into it. If you fear man, then call on Me and I will allow you to see in a different light, so you will not fear man but only Me. If you fear heights or elevators or any such thing such as this, then call on My Name and I will give you the courage to overcome. Fear is not from Me, but it is bondage and should be broken. You should stand against the fear, and I will help you be able to overcome. If you are facing fleshly desires, then you must resist the temptation and trust in Me to help you overcome. Do not put yourself in a place where you are vulnerable. Do not put yourself in places of wickedness. You should stay in a quiet place- a place of peace, so you can rest and focus on Me until you have your fleshly desires under control. I will reward you for your self-control and your self- discipline. I will give generously to you for wanting to stand firm and obey Me in all your ways.

Psalms 55:1-23

My Beloved, I know when men come against you to do evil. They may say kind words to you, but their heart is at war with you and wants to harm you, because they are jealous of what you have. They want what you have and what you stand for, or either they detest the light within you and they hate you without a cause. They do not know why every time you enter a room that they despise you. You have love within your heart and you are happy, because you are content in Me. They cannot stand this joy and light being around them, because they are so miserable with their life and they cannot stand to see someone content and happy. They look for ways to make you unhappy by finding fault with you. They look for ways to condemn you in front of others. They look for ways to bring you down, but the righteous will not be moved. They will see what is happening around them and pour their heart out to Me in the evening, morning, and night. They will stand before Me and call on My Name, and they will not be moved. They will continue to be joyful and content in Me. They will not allow bitterness or anger to rise up in their heart, but they will submit these people to Me, and I will deal with them. I will humble them before the righteous, and they will be paid back for their evil words against them. Do not be afraid, because you are being tested to show yourself worthy of entering My Kingdom of Light. Stand firm and do not be moved. I will move on behalf of you, and you will see Me vindicate you. You will be set free from your oppressors-those who grieve your spirit with their actions and words. You are My beloved, and I will not allow anyone to put you to shame for long. They will have to pay with My heavy hand upon them. They will have to pay until they have made full restitution. Only I know how to humble them. Stand back and watch and see what I do.

Strength And Encouragement

Psalms 56:1-4

My Beloved, when you are afraid, trust in Me, and I will redeem you from the storms in this life. There are many difficulties that will come your way, but I AM always with you. I will never leave or forsake you. I AM always near to you. I AM at your side. You may not see Me, but I fill all things. I know that you cannot understand this, but I hold the whole universe in My Hands. I created it with My Hands and I hold it all together. I see all things, and I know what you need before you know what you need. You are My People and I AM your Father. I give good gifts to My Children who call on My Name for help. I will deliver gifts to them from My Heavenly Kingdom. I will bring good things to meet you daily and you will know it is from Me, because your spirit will confirm it within you. On your money it says "in God we trust". This is a lie. This nation was founded on My principals, but now the people are far away from Me and judgment is coming on this nation. This nation will collapse under My judgment, because it will be so severe. This nation will lose power and authority and their reign will cease. You will see another nation take its place. This nation will be absorbed and another will be raised up-a nation with less freedom and more lies than the other nation before it. This nation will not be founded on My principals but on deceit. Watch carefully what I do. You will have to trust Me to guide you and bring you to a new place. You will have to leave before the new nation comes into place. You must be listening to the sound of My Voice. You must be quiet and seeking Me, so you can find Me. Do not be afraid, because no man can harm you. I will keep you close to Me and deliver you into a safe haven.

Psalms 56:5-13

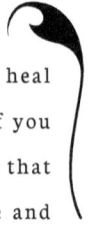

My Beloved, trust in Me and I will sustain you. I will protect you. I will heal you. I will hear your call in times of trouble. No one will harm you, if you trust in Me to protect you. I will keep you safe and change your path, so that your enemy does not come near you. If you trust Me, you will find life and abundance. If you trust Me, you will be able to sing and rejoice because I guard over you and protect you and console you. I know all the times that you have wandered off the path of righteousness. I have recorded all your tears of repentance, so that you can be set free from sins. I have kept a record of all your days, so that all around you can find you worthy to enter into the Kingdom of Heaven. If you wander away from Me and return in repentance, then you will be received by Me. I will always forgive you, but you must still pay the penalty of your sin. If you trust Me but you sway and bend, I will teach you to remain firm and do not bend, so you can be strong in the midst of the storm. Many will come against you and tear at you with their words. Many will find fault in you and try to bring destruction upon you. If you focus on Me and not the acts of men, then all men will see you as having value and full of My grace. If you know Me, you know that I look at you all the day. I keep you close to Me as a mother cares for a small child. You must remember that I AM always with you no matter what circumstances you have to endure. I AM faithful. Trust in Me.

Strength And Encouragement

Psalms 57:1-2

My Beloved, call on My Name in the midst of your troubles. Call on Me and I will shelter you under My wings. I will keep you safe in the midst of the storm. When life's struggles rages around you, I AM there to subdue the storm and calm the seas and give you peace, so you can rest in Me and know that I AM always with you in all you do and say. Many will laugh at your faith in Me, and many will face My judgment on them for mocking you. Many will say that they are weak and cannot stand up to temptation, but you will be able to stand firm and not give into the wickedness of the world. The sin of the world will make you sick, and you will turn your face from it. You will know that I Am righteous and run to Me to find your shelter. You will know that I AM accomplishing a good work in you, and I will not stop until I AM finished. I have made My plans for you, and I AM making you into the person that can complete My plans that I have made for you. There are many that call on My Name, but they do not want to serve Me with all their heart. If you truly love Me, then you will want to serve Me in all ways. I know who truly loves Me and I will make a way for them in this life, so they can prosper and be successful. They will know that I AM always with them, because they will have peace wherever they go. No one can bring them contentment like I can. There is no satisfaction except in Me. The world can give you nothing, but I can bring you life in abundance, so trust in Me and you will be blessed.

Psalms 57:3-11

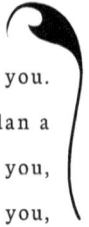

My Beloved, I have sheltered you from wicked men who try to harm you. Whatever they plan to do to you, I will allow to fall on them. If they plan a trap, then they will fall into the trap. If they plan for evil to fall upon you, then the evil will fall on them. Whatever plots that they devise to harm you, then they will devise the plots for themselves. Wicked men will not hurt you. They may mock you and say all sorts of things against you, but in the end I will exalt you. I will raise you up. I will lift you above the others. You may have people around you that are like lions stalking you and wanting to devour you. You may have men with teeth like swords that their words slice into you and they want to wound you. They are unhappy creatures, because they do not know Me and My ways. They are angry and bitter and resentful. They are wounded and suffering from the wounds inflicted by men who are wicked. They walk around like death. They have no life and they want to steal the life from others. They do not want anyone who is peaceful or content or joyous around them. They despise such people. They only want to hear complaints and evil about others. They love to live in their own misery. They never want to find a way out. They do not seek Me for help. They console themselves with the pleasures of the world. They grow weary and fat with fleshly desires. There is no peace or happiness for these people. Stay far away from such people. If they must be in your life at work or home, then love them and pray for them. I will hear your prayers and bring you comfort even in the midst of their torment. I will lift you up and I will touch their hearts, so they can be healed of all their wounds, so they can serve Me and know Me. Look to Me and I will help you withstand.

Strength And Encouragement

Psalms 58:1-11

My Beloved, men of the earth do not judge fairly, because they do not know the hearts of men. They judge by what they see and not what the man desired to happen. They do not know the intentions of men. They see what their eyes can see, and they do not have insight into the hearts of men. They also are ruled by their flesh and they want to serve themselves. If an open hand comes bearing a gift for them, they take it and the justice is faded. They will not receive the reward of being a fair judge. They sit in silence when they see others wronged, and they do not speak up to stop the injustice even though they are supposed to be men of judgment and treat others fairly. They are men who want only to serve themselves and not the people. I look over the earth to find righteous men and there are few. Only those who want to serve Me will bow before Me and want to do My will. I call the men of the earth to come and follow Me, but only a few will come and follow Me and walk in My Ways. Are you one of those who will follow Me and walk in My Ways? Do you really love Me enough to cast your eyes on Me and only want to do My will? The way of life on earth is a difficult journey and only the strong will be brave enough to follow Me in all their ways. These men will be rewarded greatly and be lifted up in My Kingdom. Stand firm to the end, because I AM a righteous judge and I will rule the earth and bring judgment to all men-the wicked and the righteous. The wicked will be lashed and the righteous will be rewarded, but all men will be judged before Me. They will receive their verdict before Me. They will know that they have served Me wisely and obediently, or they will know that they have been wicked. When they stand before Me their heart will be exposed, and all will know what their judgment must be. All will see and know the Truth.

Psalms 59:1-17

My Beloved, I AM your Strength. I AM your fortress-a place you can run into when you need help. I AM your High priest. I take your sacrifices and present them for you. I lift up your praises and I surround Myself with them. I love to hear the praises of My Children. I love to see you get up in the morning and shout praises of thanksgiving to Me. I love for My Children to call on My Name and ask for strength. I will come to you and strengthen you and bring life to your bones, so you can walk uprightly and be strong to overcome the enemy. No man will overtake you. I will destroy them. Any man that mocks you or torments you without a cause, I will rise up against him, and he will be scattered. They will fall before your eyes and be humiliated. They will know that I have destroyed their pride and have weakened them. They thought they were mighty until they spoke against My beloved children, and then My anger will rise against them. They will be overtaken with My Wrath and pun- ished, because they set out to harm you. They did not realize that you were My Child and that I would fight for you and break them down before your eyes and drive them away from your presence, so you could have peace. I will not allow any man to harm you or mock you for long. I will send My Hand against him and they will be put to shame. If you have a person that speaks evil against you and you have not wronged him, then seek Me to help you. Pray for him that he would know Me and draw close to Me. Do not curse him in your prayers, but forgive him and put him in My Hands. I can put him in a place, so he can draw closer to Me. I will proclaim the judgment, because I AM the righteous judge, and I know what will break the heart of those who have spoken against you. I will change them before your eyes. Rejoice and be glad that I love you so much and care for you so tenderly.

Strength And Encouragement

Psalms 60:1-12

My Beloved, when you sin against Me you must suffer hard times. You will be punished to get your flesh back in line, so you can serve Me and rejoice in My Presence. If you repent, I will heal you and you will be restored. You will feel My healing on you, and you will have rest. You will walk with Me and talk with Me once again. You will be blessed with My Presence. You must walk uprightly and do My will for you. You will be able to reap the rewards even on this planet where rewards are few. I give generously to those who call on My Name. I give generously to those who want to serve Me. I give to those who want to hold fast to My laws and keep them. I will bless those who praise Me-who cry out to Me rejoicing. I will put My Hand heavily on those who complain to Me and are greedy and want and want and want. They will be cast down, and I will not hear their voice. I want to hear the praises of My Children and not their complaints. I have given them so much. I have given you great rewards in My Kingdom and even though you cannot see these rewards they are there for you once the veil of flesh has been torn away from you. You will be free to live eternally with Me and become as one with Me. You do not understand what is waiting for you, but you must trust Me to take you to My Kingdom of Light and make you heirs to the promises. You will be given great rewards, and you will be lifted up above the heavenly host and be called My own-My Children. You will be counted worthy to inherit the kingdom. You will be counted worthy by your acts of righteousness and all those around you will rejoice as you receive the rewards waiting for you. Rejoice that I love you so much!

Psalms 61:1-8

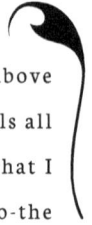

My Beloved, call on My Name and I will set you up on a Rock high above where you are so you can see ahead and not be clouded by the little details all around you. Sometimes you focus on the problems and you do not see what I AM doing in your life. You cannot see who I AM transforming you into-the person that I want you to becpme. I AM changing you a little at a time, so you can become worthy of entering My Kingdom. You will be My heir and be given great wealth and ownership into My kingdom, so you rule over many. You will lead the people I give you into righteousness in the position of a High Priest. You will be righteous before them and you will be an example of living your life in tune with Me -at one with Me. You are My Servant, if you are obedient to Me and walk in My Ways. You are My Servant, yet you are My beloved and we will wed at the Feast of the Lamb in the Last Days. You will be the bride and I will be the loving and caring groom taking you into My wedding chamber and caressing you and loving you and making you My own. You will reign with Me eternally. You will be My Children and My priests, so you can guide other peoples into the Way. You are My beloved and I will cover you in fine jewels as light and you will be filled with compassion and kindness for others that I give you to help find the Way. You will remember the hard days when you lived in the flesh and walked on the earth and suffered much because you were separated from Me by your flesh. You will want to have compassion on these people that I give you. Your heart has been changed by living in the flesh and you are becoming the loving and kind person that I want to enter My Kingdom. Rejoice and be glad that I have chosen you and you will be with Me soon!

Strength And Encouragement

Psalms 62:1-12

My Beloved, I AM your strength and your refuge in times of trouble. I AM your salvation. I keep you safe at all times. I AM the One you turn to when you are in need and I will provide for you. I AM your rock and you will not be moved. The waters of trials may come to you and crash against the rock, but it will not be moved. As long as you stand on the rock and trust in Me you will not be shaken. I AM steadfast and true. My words are Truth. I never lie. There is nothing inside of Me that is not truth. Truth is founded on Me. Only man can lie, because he is made of flesh. He walks in the midst of this world and he struggles with his flesh to deny it of its cravings. The man who can overcome his flesh is a righteous man-a man that is bent on serving Me. This man will walk uprightly all his days and not be harmed by the enemy. This man will be kept in My hands and will be overshadowed by My presence. If you love Me with all your heart, I will care for you like My own child. I will take you into My arms and hold you all through your life. You will never be alone. You will always be guided by Me and cared for tenderly by Me. You will be tested to show your strength. You will go through the fires of this life to make you emerge a strong creature of light that can overcome all the things of the world and you will receive great treasures in My Kingdom of Light. There are many that do not understand you and they will mock you and try to hurt you, but no one can touch you as long as you are listening to My Voice and allowing Me to guide you. You are My beloved. What more can I do than to treat you like My own? I do love you, so rejoice in this.

Psalms 63:1-11

My Beloved, lift up your hands and praise Me. Praise Me in front of men and I will acknowledge you. Praise Me and lift up My Name and I will shelter you under My wings. I will lift you up and cover you with My Hands. I will keep all wicked men far from you. I will help you overcome all your enemies. I will shield you from the darkness. I will keep you in My light of love and affection. I will pour My blessings on you even though you may live in exile. Even though you live in a dry land with no water, I will bring you a fountain of life to heal you and strengthen you. I will cover you over with a river of truth, and courage will arise in you. You will become bold and strong, because you know who I AM. You will rejoice always before Me, because you know that I will only bring you good things. I AM the One who loves you. Why would I bring you bad things to meet you along your path? I will bring you good gifts, so you will praise Me for my generosity towards you. If you fall into sin, then I will punish you. I will send you the discipline that you need only to mold you and correct you- not to destroy you and bring you into isolation from Me. A father disciplines his child in love and wants him to form into a man who walks in righteousness and brings honor to his name. I AM a father who wants you to bring honor to My Name and walk in righteousness, so I will continue to mold you into My image and break the bonds of this world from you, so you can be lifted up and only see with eyes of gold- seeing this world the way that I see it. You will not desire the things of this world, but you will desire the things of the Spirit, so you can walk hand and hand with Me and feel only My Presence. Rejoice that I love you so much!

Strength And Encouragement

Psalms 64:1-10

My Beloved, the wicked are all around you and they try to bring you down. They are harsh in their words. They want to tangle you in their web of lies and deceit. They are greedy for money and power. They will do whatever they please to trap you and bring you down to shame. They are wicked and care nothing for the righteous. The righteous are innocent and they have done nothing to harm the wicked, yet the wicked want all men under their control. They want to govern over all men. They will not touch My righteous. I see those who try to harm you, and I will bring them down and bring them to shame. They will stumble by their own words. They think they are so smart, and yet their own words will defeat them. They will be wounded by My Hand. They will feel the blows cast upon them. They will be humiliated in your presence. Everyone around them will know that I have intervened for you. They will praise My Name that I have dealt with you so generously. They will know that I love you and have cared for you. I have kept you from the trap that the enemy has tried to entangle you in. I have kept you from the lies by allowing you to see the truth in this situation. You call on My Name and I will bless you and hear your prayers. I will show you the way to go, so you will prosper and you will praise Me for all My many blessings. Do not be afraid of men, because I AM always watching over you. I AM always caring for you. I AM always bringing good things to meet you along your path. You should never be afraid, but always rejoice that I love you so much.

Psalms 65

My Beloved, you, who have fallen, get up. You, who are full of sin, arise. You, who have lost their way, look up. Your salvation draws near. Your Elohim is close to you. Repent of your sins, and I will lift you up, so you can see the path clearly again. Open your eyes and see My face. I will hear your prayers. Blessed are those who I have chosen to draw near to Me. Those who seek Me will find Me. Those who have a desire to know Me, I will draw close to you. Those who have a heart to be like Me will be greatly blessed with My Presence. Those who are loving and kind to others are My Children-Children of Light filled with love. Only My Children can love the world and all those who dwell within it. Only My Children can overcome hatred and love those who have done them harm. You know My ways are not to hate, but to love those who do not even deserve your love and compassion. As your deeds of love pile up as do your blessings. As your deeds of wickedness pile up and overwhelm you, then I pass judgment on you and you pay for your sins. Continue to walk in deeds of love, so judgment will not overtake you and you suffer loss. Love those around you and speak only kind words to others. Love those who have done you wrong and forgive them, so I can judge them for their wickedness towards you. Forgive, and I will forgive you. Love, and I will love you and bless you. This life is based on a reciprocal effect. What you give in this life will be given back to you. If you sow hatred, you will receive only hatred. If you sow love, you will receive love. You must build up for yourself what you want to receive. Keep a clear mind and focus on what is really important in this life. I will bless you for your good deeds and compensate you for those who do wrong to you. Rejoice and be glad that I love you so much and bring justice to a dark dying world.

Strength And Encouragement

Psalms 66

My Beloved, I have tested you with fire. I have refined you as silver. I have cut away all the impurities, because you call on My Name in times of trouble. You look to Me as your source of strength and security. You call on Me instead of going to man to help you. You want to find Me in the quiet places and feel My Presence. You want to know the meaning of My Name and what I AM like. You want to be able to hear My voice and see My face and be led by My Spirit. You want to feel Me all around you and you look for the signs of My Presence on everything you do. You shout My Name and glorify Me in the midst of others. You are not ashamed of Me or loving Me, but you rejoice that you are Mine and that I have called you by My Name as My Child. You are worthy or entering into My Kingdom of Light. You are worthy of becoming heirs to the kingdom. You are My Beloved and I will not leave you in exile forever. I will call you to come home and dwell on My Land. Now My Land is covered over by pagans who do not know My Name and hate My People. Soon I will dissolve all of them that hate Me and My ways. I will dissolve them and bring My People back to My Land to care for it. They will remove the remains of the pagans and they will sanctify My Land and rejoice that they are home once again. They are My Beloved Children who know Me and My loving ways and are covered by My Hand and no man can harm them. No evil spirit can touch them. They are covered under My wings and sheltered from all evil. They will rise again in the last days and be a strong force on the earth, and men will bow down to you. You are My Chosen-My Beloved-My Children and I will bless you greatly.

Psalms 67

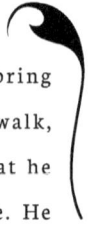

My Beloved, I will make My Face shine upon you and bless you. I will bring salvation to your house. I will lift up My eyes and show you the way to walk, so I can guide you down the path ahead. Every man has his journey that he must walk in this life. Every man has his own path that he must take. He chooses the path that he wants to walk on and he chooses those who will walk with him. He wants to make his own pathway, but he wants Me to guide him and I will. If you chose to go down a path that is less traveled and is a narrow path and is difficult at times and the rewards at the end are great, then you have chosen well for your life. If you want to walk down a path with all the others around you and you do not want to have any troubles in your life yet you want to walk in Truth, you will find yourself pulled at every corner in the path. You cannot walk as the world walks and remain in the Truth. The world hates the Truth and wants to remove all traces of Truth and live in a world of lies and deception. If only all the people of the world could see clearly, but they walk in darkness and are blinded by the lies of the enemy. He was woven his web of deception and they have been caught and cannot become free. You, My beloved, have seen the trap and have steered away from it and you see Truth and you want to cling to it and be strong and overcome. Few overcome this world and its deception. Few are strong enough to overcome the world and walk in Truth. You must cling to Me daily and I will guide you into all Truth and I will set you free from darkness, so you can always walk in the Light and rejoice in My presence.

Strength And Encouragement

Psalms 68:1-18

My Beloved, I will arise and scatter all your enemies-all those who hate you. I will arise and put all those who are rebels to flight, so that you will easily take over their land. You will be able to come back home and no longer live in exile. You will be able to live among My People and rejoice in My midst. You will be able to rejoice in the blessing of your ancestors. You will be able to see how My Hand moves across the Land. You will be able to rejoice with your kinsmen on the good Land that I have given you. You struggle now, but soon you will rejoice. You will come singing and dancing into My Presence. You will know that I have called your name and you have listened and come out of Babylon-the city of the great whore-the one that wants to gobble up My People and steal all the Truth that I have reserved just for them. You will see how I help you and protect you and make you strong. I will show My faithfulness to you. I will make mountains move for you, so you can overcome and live in peace. No nation can overcome you. No people will be stronger than you. You will be leaders of the nations and the nations will bow down to you in reverence, because you are ruled by Me and I command and it is done. I ride above the heights. I ride above the clouds. I stand in the gates and no one enters unless I allow him to enter. I AM King of the Universe and all things are in My power-all things are in My command. Listen and be quiet. I know your struggles and heartache living in exile, but soon you will be delivered and made whole in My presence.

Psalms 68:19-35

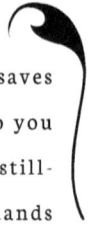

My Beloved, I AM your strength and your salvation. I AM the One who saves you from trouble. I guard over you and protect you. I send My angels to you to help you-My messengers to tell you My Ways. I speak to you in the stillness. Open your ears and I will speak to you, so you can hear My Commands for you. Open your ears, so you can hear My gentle voice speaking caressing words to you. Open your ears, so you can hear My direction for you so you will not stumble or fall. The world is dark and you need a Light. I AM the Light that shines on your path, so you can see clearly. I AM the One who gives Light, so your days will not be dark, and the future will not be hidden. I AM the One who know all things and I can tell you the way to go, so your life will be blessed. You see ahead, but there is no light unless you see with My eyes of gold. I will bless your hands, if you labor for Me. I will bless your feet, if you walk in My Ways. I will bless you and prosper you, if you are directly guided by Me. Rejoice and be glad that I love you so much. Rejoice and be glad that I cover My Land and keep it, so you can return to My Land in the last days. I will provide a home for you there, so you can live under the shelter of My Hand. You can walk under the shelter of My Hand and no harm can come to you. Even if the world surrounds you in hatred, no man can harm you because I can destroy a man in a moment. I control all things. I control all men and I know their hearts. Only those who love Me and want to serve Me will be brought to My Land and be covered by My Hand and will live with Me eternally.

Strength And Encouragement

Psalms 69:1-18

My Beloved, cry out to Me in times of trouble. Weep and fast and pray and seek Me for help. Do not look to the world, but cry out to Me and you will be answered. When you think that men hate you and want to harm you, call on Me and I will deliver you. I AM your strength and I will make you strong enough to stand against all your enemies as long as you trust in Me to help you overcome. As long as you walk in My ways and do what is right in My eyes, then I will bring deliverance to your house. Men may mock you and they may insult you and they may talk behind your back because you want to keep My ways. My ways are not like the world's ways. My ways are righteous and just and bring men to salvation and not destruction. My ways are not understandable for the men of the world, because they want to do what they want to do and serve only themselves. They are insolent and arrogant and they boast at their accomplishments and do not realize that they can do nothing apart from Me. I can destroy them in a second. I AM Creator and I give and take life away in a second. You are always one second away from death. That is why you have to trust Me and know that I will keep you safe and help you overcome this life. You must never give into the ways of men. Do not allow someone to force you to do what you know is wrong. Always cry out to Me to intervene and I will help you. I will make you strong and your adversaries will turn away from you and I will give you favor with men. Do not be dismayed or troubled about the future. I will keep you safe and sheltered and feed you and give you water so you can live. I will bless you in all things, because I love you so much.

Psalms 69:19-36

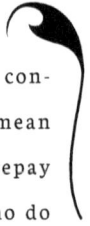

My Beloved, praise Me and rejoice even when men are cruel and do not consider your feelings, but reject you and turn aside from you and say mean things behind your back. Rejoice that I love you so much, because I will repay them for their actions. I will remove from the Book of Life all those who do not want to serve Me-all those who do not want to come before Me and do My will for them. Each man has a journey. Each man has a path that he must take. Each man has different tests that he must overcome and different victories that he will enjoy. Each man must serve Me and walk in My Ways or he will enter the Lake of Fire and be no more. He will be erased from this life and have life no more. He will be forgotten and his name will be erased from the book of the living. He will be lost forever. He will not be a snare to My People any longer. He will be devoured by the grave and lost to the earth. You do not have to be fearful of any of these trouble makers. You do not have to endure their insults forever. I will put an end to their lies about you. I will put an end to their treachery. I will put an end to all their wicked ways. I will show those around them that My Hand of judgment has fallen on them, and they will be brought low and brought to shame. They will be humiliated and you will be blessed and brought up. You will know that My words are true. You will know that My promises will come to pass, because they will all come upon you, and you will be greatly blessed.

Strength And Encouragement

Psalms 70

My Beloved, I AM your salvation. I AM your help in times of need. I will rescue you from the troubles of this life. I AM the One who knows you-how you were structured and how you are formed together, so I will give you the strength you need at all times if you call on My Name for help. I know there are times when your flesh is weak and you want to give up the fight of faith, but I encourage you to come to Me and rest at My bosom and I will comfort you like a mother comforts her child who lies on her chest as she rocks and sings to the child. I will bring comfort to you and your soul will no longer be restless or tormented, but will be at peace because I have consoled you. You are My beloved, and I want to hold you close to Me. Sometimes you allow worries and fears and guilt to overshadow you and cause you to slip into darkness. If you look to Me, I will bring Light to you so your eyes can be open and you can see clearly the path ahead of you. If you continue to focus on your problems and not trust in Me, then you will continue to grieve yourself. You must be strong and brave. You must know who I AM-that I can do all things. I fight on behalf of you daily. I send My messengers to fight on behalf of you and they remove obstacles for you along the way. You always have Me by your side and a host of helpers walking along with you. You do not ever have to be afraid. You must be on guard not to fall back into the ways of the world. I know you live in a dark place with pagan practices all around you, but you must be strong to overcome the enemy at every side, and I will reward you with great rewards. This I promise to you.

Psalms 71:1-13

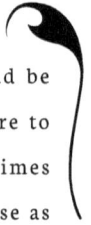

My Beloved, I AM your sheltering rock where you can always come and be protected from the storm. Life will bring you tests, and you must endure to the end. There will be times when you want to give up, and there will be times when you want to stand firm. The times you want to give up will decrease as you draw closer to Me and draw from My strength. You will know Me. You will know who I AM and you will know that I will always provide for you and give you all that you need. You will be a rock for others to stand on in your old age. You will testify to all my glorious works that I have done in your life. You will tell others of the things that have been given to you. You will be a light to others of My love and devotion to you. Others will see you as an example. They will look to you, because you have searched for Me and found me in the dark places. When the days have been dark, you have cried out to Me and I have answered you. I have given you hope. You have read My words and know them and cling to My promises to you. You know My voice and listened to Me and found Me in the secret place. You have overcome and you rejoice in Me. You must not look at yourself as you are today, and become sad and downcast, but you must look at what you will become and rejoice. If you continue to cling to Me day after day and want to do My will for you, then you will change from glory to glory and become that one who I will use in the last days to encourage those around you and bless them with your words of faith and hope.

Strength And Encouragement

Psalms 71:14-24

My Beloved, praise Me for all the things that I have done for you. Write my glorious acts in a book and remember all the miracles I have done for you. I have brought you all you need. I have guided you daily by My Spirit. Evil men cannot harm you. Evil men cannot take from you. No one can touch you. I keep you in the palm of My Hand. I will guard over you and teach you My ways, so you can teach your children and your children's children. You will see and know who I AM. Rejoice that I love you so much. Rejoice and do not be afraid of the future when you grow old and weak. You will strengthen others by your encouraging words and your love and compassion. You will tell others of all I have done for you and strengthen them to believe and trust in Me to help them through all their hardship and struggles. Life is difficult at times, but I will not give you more than you can carry. I will always send you help, so you can have someone standing beside you. You will have love and encouragement from others. You will have the believers to help you as you walk along your path. Cling to Me and know Me and rejoice that I give you My words to guide you along your path. Your journey will be different from others, but together you have the same source of strength. Stand on the Rock, and I will not let you fall. Stand and be bold, because you are My Child.

Psalms 72

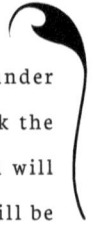

My Beloved, I AM King of all the earth. May all the peoples be blessed under My reign. I will return soon and I will reign over My People. I will rock the hills with My Presence, and the peoples will know that I AM. I AM and will always be the King of the Earth. If any man comes against Me, then he will be cast down. I will give men favor in My sight, if they keep My laws and walk in My ways. If they rebel against Me and try to harm others, then I will destroy them with My fiery breath. If a people want to rebel against Me and not worship Me, then they will be destroyed. Only those who want to serve Me will remain in the Land. If the wicked try to stand before Me, they will be cast down. Only the righteous can stand in My Presence. Only the righteous will receive the rewards. If you hold fast to Me, I will help you and you will not have to feel the wrath of others on you. You will feel My Presence all around you to help you as you walk on your journey in life. There is no one who can search for Me and not find Me. I open the doors for you and you will be able to see Me. You may think that it is hard to find Me, but the more you turn your head towards Me and seek My face, the more you will find Me. Look always to Me, and you will be blessed.

Strength And Encouragement

Psalms 73

My Beloved, keep your eyes on Me and do not allow yourself to slip into the thinking of the world. The peoples of the world focus on wealth and power and how many possessions that they have. They look at each other and value a man by how much he has. Everyone else is worthless and has no value. I look at the world differently. I look for My People who sacrifice their flesh and want to walk in My ways and keep My laws. Those who give to others and do not think of themselves are the ones who have value. They are the ones who I bless. Do not grow weary in doing what is right. I know that your flesh rebels against you, but be strong and brave and courageous and do not give into the lies of the enemy. The Evil One will send his servants to you to lie to you and beat you down with his lies. He will tell you that you are worthless and have no value that you might as well do the things that the world does. The lies will say that there is no Elohim and that all My laws have passed away and are not in effect today. I reign supreme and I do not change My laws, because they are perfect. If you listen to Truth and do not be deceived by the enemy, then you will do well. You will not slip and lose your way. As you sail along in your boat on your journey in life stay focused on My face. Do not look at the waves crashing against your boat. I will guide you into a safe haven where you will be sheltered from the storm. I AM your Rock and your salvation. I will help you overcome in all areas of your life. Be strong. Be brave. Be courageous.

Psalms 74

My Beloved, My People of long ago watched as their enemies came in and destroyed their Temple and all their sacred places of worship. They watched as they destroyed all their possessions and took them captive to another land. Their sins overtook them and punishment came to meet them. They had sinned against Me and they had to bear the punishment of their sins. Look at yourself today and see what sins are before your face. Look at yourself and see what lies inside your heart. Look at yourself and see if you are loving and kind to others and if you walk in justice treating all men fairly. You must guard carefully over your tongue and make sure that you speak in love and not insulting words that hurt the heart. If you see sin inside of you, then arise and repent and walk in righteousness. You will rejoice that you have turned from your sins, so you can draw closer to Me. If you have members of your family that are in sin and your heart is grieved, just put them in My Hand and I will deal with their hearts. I know that you see others around you wanting to walk in the ways of the world, but I say to you that you must be strong and patient and I will move on behalf of you. I will hear your cries and save you from the stormy sea. I know that you are going through much in exile. I know that you bear the weight of your ancestors' sins. I know that you want to be released, so you can go back to your home. I tell you that soon I will call you home, and you will be able to live among your brothers. Now you are scattered and you have no one to strengthen you, but soon you will have My People close to you, so you can sing and dance that you are home at last. Be strong and be brave, because I will come to you soon.

Strength And Encouragement

Psalms 75

My Beloved, the time draws near for My judgment. The time draws near for Me to cast out the wicked from My Land. The time draws near for My Children to return to Me. The time draws near for Me to stand up and shake the earth and cast down all the kingdoms that stand against My People. My People have been tormented by the sin all around them. They have grieved and called on My name to stop the sin and bring Truth to those around them. I know your heart and I know how you grieve over what you see in the land. Soon I will remove you from the place where I have sent you to exile. Soon you will be uprooted and returned to your Land where your roots will grow deep and you will feel firmly planted. You will know that I have found favor with you and you will be blessed in the Land. Now the Land is overtaken by men who do not follow Me and men who do not know Me. They are arrogant and walk in their own ways. How dare those men walk in their own way while living on My Land! I will cast them down, and they will be driven from the Land or destroyed. My People will arise victorious and dance and sing over all that I do for them. They will know how much I love them and how much I want them to be happy in My land. Rejoice and be glad that I love you so much. I will prosper your hand and give you favor where I have placed you until I call you back to the Land. Rejoice that I love you so much.

Psalms 76

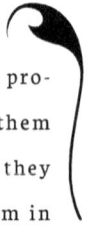

My Beloved, arise and praise Me, because I AM King over all the earth. I pronounce sentence on all men. I rebuke kings and kingdoms and I bring them to ruin. If they have turned their face against Me and in their arrogance they have said that no man can overtake them, then I laugh and I look at them in distain. They will suffer loss for their pride, and they will be stripped of all their ornaments. Men mock and laugh, and then they fall. Men see themselves as gods, but they are nothing but a breath. They look at the power that I gave them, and then they are gone-lost to the earth-sleeping with the others who have fallen. They will never more reign, but they have sunken to the depths. Where is their pride now? Where are their mocking words? Men laugh at them and see how they have fallen. Men laugh at the fallen kings and mock them when they have fallen. Men should take notice that all kingdoms fall and are no more. Only My Kingdom will reign supreme, and only My People will continue to reign on this earth. Where is their kingdom? Where is their throne? My People will reign with Me for eternity. They will be heirs to My throne. They will have authority over all men, and all men must bow to their will. They will reign over the nations, and men must do all that My Chosen tell them to do. My People will be lifted up and rewarded for all the hardship they have suffered here on earth. They have suffered in exile and they have been brought down low. They are under the authority of men that do not serve Me and their hearts are grieved. Be brave and be strong, because I will come soon.

Strength And Encouragement

Psalms 77:1-12

My Beloved, come to Me in times of trouble. Cry out to Me when you have despair. Come to Me when the situation looks hopeless. Do not cry out to Me and question Me if I have forgotten you. This is your weakness if you think that I would ever forget you or abandon you or not bring My Promises to past. If you think that I have forsaken My Child, then you are wrong. If you think that I do not love you, then you are wrong. I change not. I never forget My Promises or change My Ways. I never forsake the Words that I have spoken to you. I never forsake My responsibilities of taking care for My Children. Be brave. Be strong. Be courageous and stand firm. I AM a Rock. I change not. I never move away from the plan I have for you. My plan continues to stand firmly planted. If you wonder what My plan is for you, then look at Me and know that I have specific plans for each person and if you follow Me, then you will be rewarded and blessed. Never take your eyes off Me. Never look away from Me when you are discouraged and look for another avenue or way out. I will provide for you another way out. If you think that any man does not have to be tested, then you are wrong. I test you and purify you. I lift you up when you need Me. Do not think that I AM far away. I AM near at hand. Call on My Name and I will take you to a better place and help you with all your problems. I help you, because I love you,

106

Psalms 77:13-20

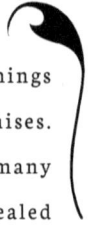

My Beloved, meditate on My acts and miracles of old. Meditate on the things that I have done for My People. Meditate on My Words and My Promises. Meditate on the things that I have done for you. I have helped you in so many ways. I have answered your prayers. I have given you guidance. I have healed your body. I have given you gifts that you do not even realize will benefit you. Sometimes you go through times of testing and you moan under the weight of it, but you do not realize that I AM helping you grow stronger and stronger. I AM making you a new person. I AM restoring you and making you whole. You may have had hurts in your life and you have wounds that have been inflicted by others. I will heal you of all these things. I will make you strong and overcoming. You will not see all I do for you until the last days, and then you will realize how strong you have become. I have shown you My Faithfulness. I have shown you that I will care for you and protect you and guide you. I guided My Children in the desert and provided all they needed. I cared for My little flock that Aaron and Moses led in the Wilderness. I cared for them then, and I will care for them now. I know where you are My little ones. I will call you, and you will come to Me, Your Shepherd. Come, My little ones. Come.

Strength And Encouragement

Psalms 78:1-39

My Beloved, I remember that you are only flesh. I remember that you are formed from the earth. I remember that you are weak, but I can make you strong and you can do all things through Me. I AM your substance. I AM the only strength that you need. Your ancestors sinned against Me in the Wilderness. They saw all My miracles and yet they doubted Me. They saw Me open the sea and they walked across on dry land. They saw Me bring water out of a rock, and they saw Me bring them manna everyday to feed them. Yet they tested Me and brought Me to anger. They made Me burst forth in flame against them. I wanted to destroy them, but I AM compassionate and kind and forgiving and I know that they are only flesh. I see what they will become. I have watched you as you have grown. I have watched you as a child that I brought into the Wilderness how you followed Me singing and dancing. You were formed into My image in the desert. I prepared you for war to take on the giants of the Land and to go in boldly and not look back. You overcame all your enemies, and you took the Land back for your ancestor Seth. You were victorious. You dwelt in the Land and prospered, but then you became fat and haughty and you were driven out of the Land. Now I see you as you open your eyes and see who I AM again. You long for Me and want to come back to the Land. I will bring you back, My Children. I will bring you back to the Land and bless you once again. Be strong. Be brave. I will bring you home soon.

Psalms 78:40-55

My Beloved, I brought My People out of Egypt with a Mighty Hand. I brought them out and destroyed their enemies. I sent My destroying angels into their midst and killed all their firstborn, but I spared the first born of My People. I took those and set them aside to minster to Me and to help them to teach My Children My laws. I set aside the Levis as Mine, and they are still Mine to this day. They are scattered among the nations, and they are a light to those around them. They love My Word, and they want to search My Word for Truth. They want to know what My Laws are and obey them. They are very careful to keep all My Laws, so I can bless them and bring them peace. They are My beloved and I look over them and I hold them in My Hand. You do not have to be afraid. You should be bold and courageous and do what I ask you to do. You hear My Voice, but you do not want to do as I ask you to do. You should not be stiff necked, but you should want to listen to Me and know Me. There are many around you who look at you, and how you live your life will lead them to Me. Rejoice that I love you so much, My beloved, and that I have given you so much. Great are your rewards, if you humble yourself and walk in my ways and not the ways of the world. My ways are life and those who refuse to walk in them will be destroyed.

Strength And Encouragement

Psalms 78:56-72

My Beloved, My People rejected Me and turned away from Me, and I turned them over to their enemies and they suffered shame and they were ruled by their masters. They were given a heavy burden to carry, and they suffered loss at the hand of their enemies. Now I have begun to lift up My People and give them a new name-not one of shame -but one of honor. I have given My People wealth and I have given My People great treasures-My Spirit within them and My Words written for them, so they can meditate on them daily. I have begun to allow My People to see the Truth and know who they are and what I AM going to do in the future. They are beginning to see what I AM doing in My Land. They are beginning to see what the future of My People is going to be. I will continue to open the eyes of My Children and they will see and know who they are and come back to My Land and be at one with Me. I will rule over the Land with an iron rod, and My People will walk in My laws and delight in doing so. Any rebellious person will be cast out of the Land. Anyone that does not want to worship Me will be cast out and sent away. Only My People will be able to see Me and know Me and be at one with Me. Do not be afraid of the days to come. Do not be sad, but rejoice because I will hold you in the palm of My Hand and you will be safe and held securely so no man can harm you. You are My beloved. No one can take from you. I will keep you safe through all kinds of things that other men cannot endure, but you will be able to stand firm and be at peace.

Psalms 79

My Beloved, My People were cast down and humiliated and mocked by their enemies. I pushed them out of My Land, because they sinned against Me. They wanted to worship like the pagans, so I sent them to the pagan nations so they could worship with them in their midst. Then they cried out to Me and begged to be forgiven, but they had sinned against Me too long. They had to pay for their sins. They had to suffer for their unrighteousness. They were wicked and rebellious. They knew the Truth and they turned against Me. They have been cast out of the Land for a long time, but soon I will bring them back. Now they have lost who they really are. They have lost their long genealogies. They don't even know which tribe they are from or even if they are from a tribe of Israel. They are sleeping among the nations, but I will wake them up and bring them back to Me, so I can teach them My ways once again and show them My wondrous love. You are a blessed people covered by My Hand, but I will not tolerate outright rebellion. I want you to serve Me with your whole heart and serve Me in spirit and truth. I want you to obey My laws and do all you can to walk in My ways. I know that you are far away from Jerusalem-My City. I know you have no teachers who know all the truth, but only know bits and pieces of the Truth. I know you are separated and alone. I will bring you all back together, and you will rule the world. You will overcome your enemies. I will judge Israel. I will judge the Land. I will cast out the pagans there. I will be a threat to all who do not want to serve Me there. I will kill them with the plague or drive them out by My Hand, but they will go away from My People and will not be a thorn in their side anymore. Watch and see what I do.

Strength And Encouragement

Psalms 80

My Beloved, in times of trouble you may think that I AM far away, but I AM always close. I AM always near. I AM a breath away. Call on My Name, and I will save you. I will make My face shine on you and restore you. I will bring light to you, so you can repent and turn away from your sins or that you will have understanding into My ways. You will understand why you must go through hardships, so you can become strong and mighty and be able to stand firm against the Evil One. Little one, I will not bring you harm, but I will make you strong and bold and brave and be able to stand against anything that comes to you. You will set your face towards Me and trust in Me with all your heart, and you will find Me and know My voice and hear what I say to you and be comforted by My voice and My words. You are my beloved, and I will cover you over all the day and keep you safe. I will do miracles on behalf of you. I will raise up a standard, and you will come up to it. You will change from glory to glory. You will become righteous before Me. You will stand upright and be an example for many. You must walk in the Light. You must keep My laws, and do what is right before Me. If you guard over your eyes, ears, and tongue, then you will be able to stand firm. If you look into the world and all its wickedness, then you will suffer loss. In times of trouble cling to Me and turn your face away from the world and find Me, and then you will prosper and have good health because you call on Me and I hear your voice. There are many around you that look on and see if you are worthy to enter My Kingdom. You must shine before them and let them know that indeed you are worthy to be called one of My Children of Light.

Psalms 81

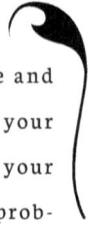

My Beloved, praise Me and lift up My Name for I AM worthy! Praise Me and shout for joy, because I have blessed you so much. Praise Me and lift up your eyes to Me and see all that I have done for you. Why do you look at your current situation and weep and moan? Why do you focus on the present problem? Give the problem to Me and trust Me to work it out, and I will bless you for trusting Me. Every man goes though a time of fasting. He must learn to develop self-control and self-discipline. He must learn patience and endurance and long suffering. A man cannot have everything that he wants and be formed into My image. A man must deny his flesh, and then his spirit will become strong and he will be formed into My image. He will be able to rule and reign in My Kingdom. A man cannot think that he will never have any difficult situations. Tests come in many different forms. It could be illness or lack of money or people who want to harm you or hate you. It may come from your children who you love and want to see them prosper, and they make bad choices. It may come from a boss or from a coworker. It may come through people that you run into everyday. You must see all the people that you meet as a test to show your love to others. You must be able to see that every step that you take is monitored by Me and by a host of onlookers, and they look at you and judge you as to whether you are worthy of entering My kingdom. Look into My eyes and see life as it really is-a series of tests that you have victory over and you are formed into My image by these tests. Rejoice that I bring you such tests, so you can be changed and brought into My fullness. Rejoice and be glad that I love you so much.

Strength And Encouragement

Psalms 82

My Beloved, I AM judge over all the earth. I see all men and I know all men and I know their heart and I judge them according to their deeds. If their deeds are wicked, I cut them away from Me. If their deeds are righteous, then I bless them and make them whole. I prosper them and uphold them and show them the way to go, because they call on My Name for guidance. I will make them a strong pillar and all who rest on Me will not fall but overcome and conquer. If a man is a judge, then he must judge fairly and justly. He must watch over the poor and needy-the fatherless and the widows. He must not be prejudice. He must treat all men fairly. I see the judges of the earth, and they can be bought by gifts. They can be bought by officials that are power-ful. They will have to do what those higher up tells them to do whether it is right or wrong in their eyes. Today's judges are pulled by strings, and there is nothing they can do. You must remember that if you are wronged in court and not treated fairly, then I will give you what has been taken away. I will treat you just and fairly. I give and I take away from all men. If I decide to take from you, it is because I AM doing a good work inside of you and I want you to change. I want you to trust Me and have faith in Me and allow Me to direct your path. I will bless you, if you are walking in My ways. Do not be afraid, but rejoice that I love you so much.

Psalms 83

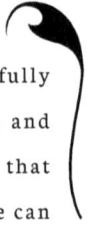

My Beloved, I AM the Most High. I AM mighty and should be fearfully praised. I AM the Only One. I control all the earth and all the nations and hold the hearts of all the kings and rulers in My Hand. There is none that can come close to My fire and live. I AM supreme, yet man thinks that he can rule the world and all that is in it. He thinks that he is supreme. He knows nothing. I AM capable of protecting you from all your enemies and from all diseases. I AM fully capable of helping you in any danger or with any problem, if you call on My Name. Come to Me in a time with you can be heard. If you call on My Name day and night, then I will always hear you. If you call on My Name only in times of trouble, you will see that trouble will remain with you until you serve Me with your whole heart. If you know Me and My ways, then you will walk in peace and happiness. Even though there are troubles around you, you will know who is in control over all things and you will have no fear. The days ahead are dark and filled with many troubles, but if you cling to Me and draw close to Me, then I will guide you away from all the troubles and help you in the darkest of days. Do not be afraid of anything or anyone. I have power over all things. You may think that you are lost in the midst of the nations because you live in exile, but I know who you are and all your ancestors and all their sins against Me. I know those who served Me and those who hated Me and led their children astray. If you cleanse yourself from the sins of your ancestors by asking forgiveness for their sins and pronounce that you do not want to be a part of their sins, then I will forgive you and all their curses will be released from you, if you love Me with all your heart and serve only Me.

Strength And Encouragement

Psalms 84

My Beloved, I AM your strength and shield. I AM your Light. I will guide your way. I will show you the way. If you do not know which direction to turn, then I will guide you if you call on My Name and ask Me to show you the way. Many times you ask for My help, and then you do not wait on Me to guide you, but you do what you want to do and say that you asked Me to help you. That is why you run into troubles and are grieved by the outcome. You suffer loss and wonder why. It is because you do not wait and listen to Me and desire to hear My Voice. You must find the quiet times. You must be still and listen. You must know that I want to speak to you and help you in this life, but unless you slow down and be still and listen, then you will not know the way to go. You will not know which direction to take. You will easily be tossed to and fro and not be anchored. You will be unstable like water. You will have no foot hold, but continue to slip and lose ground. You will be like one tossing in a boat in a storm, and the wind blows you whatever direction that it pleases. You will feel discontent and unhappy and restless never having any peace. Once you follow My will, then you will feel content and at peace. If you do not feel content and satisfied today, then you must seek Me with your whole heart and rest and wait for My words to come to you. You are filled with My Spirit, so you can hear My voice if you are quiet and trust Me to bring My words to you. Rejoice that I love you so much. Be still. Be quiet. Listen.

Psalms 86:1-10

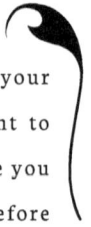

My Beloved, I do take pity on you everyday. I do see your face and hear your prayers, because you call on My Name and you are My Child. You want to walk in My Ways and you want to have a share of My Kingdom. I will give you whatever you need at the time that you need it. I will not give it to you before that, because I want you to use it at that moment for a certain thing. You only give a child a certain amount of food or the child will overeat. I only give you what you need or you will over use and not have what you need for later. Some of My Children hear My Voice very well and I can give them much and they will hold on to it and wait until I say give. Other children I have to monitor carefully, because they are not as disciplined. Some of My Children fast and pray and walk with Me daily. Others still struggle with the things of the world. Some of My Children are grieved by the things of the world and some are not. My Children are in various stages of growth and need Me to guide them according to where they are. I AM loving and kind and merciful towards My Children, but I do demand a certain standard of growth. I know you are in exile and you are separate from My People and My Land, but soon I will bring you home and you will rejoice in My midst. It will be a glorious day! Rejoice that I have chosen you as My own. Rejoice that I have given you so much!

Strength And Encouragement

Psalms 86:11-17

My Beloved, I AM slow to anger, because I AM compassionate and merciful with My Children. I love My Children and they are My treasure. I guide them daily and I show them the way to travel as they walk down the path of their life. Each man has his own journey, because each man is unique and has a unique purpose. Each man is chosen and formed by Me and I will complete the good work I have started in him. I will complete the creation that I started in the beginning. He will be fully formed as he departs this earth and serves Me in My Kingdom of Light. No one who rebels against Me will be able to enter into My kingdom. No man who turns away from Me can enter into My kingdom. No man who says in his heart that he can do whatever he wants to do and not fear Me will enter My kingdom. No man who entices others to serve other gods will enter My kingdom. My Children will serve only Me and will walk in My ways. I will give My Children a sign, and they will be filled with My Spirit and My Spirit will guide them and show them the way to walk. My favor will be on them, and I will bless them as they walk down their path in this life. Sometimes the blessing may not look like a blessing, because I am forming you into My image. The blessing may be in the form of a test or trial, but it is still a blessing, because you will arise stronger and wiser even though you may have suffered loss in the natural. You have learned and gained strength, and you are given a crown of life at the end of your journey. You will stand before Me and I will praise you and let everyone know who stands in My Presence that you are My faithful servant.

Psalms 87

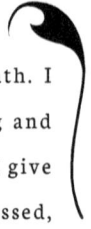

My Beloved, I AM the source of everything! I give life and I give death. I give food and shelter and I give encouragement and joy. I give healing and strength. I give to men according to how I want to give. To My Children I give much, and they are greatly blessed. You may not realize that you are blessed, because you may have troubles. Troubles are a blessing, because they bring growth to your soul and you are changed into My Image. You must not frown on times of troubles, but learn from them and change your ways. Do what is good in My Sight or you will have more troubles to teach you My Ways. If you are not stiff necked and arrogant and allow Me to form you, then you will not have the burdens that others have. You must be tested and tried to be found faithful. You must know that I AM the one who tests My Children. Only I know what you need. I will never give you more than you can carry. I would not crush you under the weight of it. When you call on My Name I bring you strength. I delay bringing you what you ask for, because I AM teaching you to be patient to wait on Me and to trust Me that My time is right. I can delay a prayer to make you have faith. After I bring the answer to your prayer, then you see how My Hand was on you the entire time and this builds your faith. My Ways are far above your ways. You may live in exile and you may not have been born in Jerusalem, but you are greatly valued in My sight. You are My beloved and I hold you close to Me everyday. I hear your every breath and I love you deeply.

Strength And Encouragement

Psalms 88

My Beloved, I AM your Elohim of Salvation. I AM the One who will deliver you from sickness and disease. I AM the only One who you can turn to. Know that I send men tests to prove their faithfulness to Me. If you are sick or suffering, then count it a blessing because I AM changing you by humbling you and making you into My image. You are My beloved and I only bring good things to you. Many things that you think are troubles and you grieve over are really blessings for you. I only bless My Children who want to serve Me. If you are rebellious and you do not want to serve Me but you want to go your own way, then I will send My curses upon you and you will not recover from your illness, but you will die in your sins and grief. I will not deliver you from the Lake of Fire. You will be cast away from Me and remembered no more. You are My precious unique treasure, and you are cared for very tenderly by Me. You must be found worthy to enter My Kingdom of Light. You must be faithful to Me and not bend in the face of temptation. You must be a rock and you must be a light to the world around you. The world is a dark and dying place. It is falling asleep and cannot see that judgment is on it. The world is cracking and losing all its energy, so that the inhabitants are dying. I will deliver you from this world-this testing ground. I will deliver you into My Kingdom and you will be able to stand by My Side and judge with Me-rule with Me. You are My Child and I love you so much. Be strong and be brave.

Psalms 89:1-18

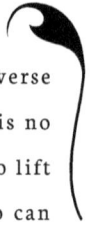

My Beloved, who AM I? I AM the only Elohim. I made all things-the universe and all that is in it. I made man and I formed him by My Hand. There is no other god who can do this. There are many who say they are god and who lift themselves up as god, but there is only one Yah. There is only One who can change time, and break down strongholds, and can create. There is only One who can change the heart of man and bring up a leader to defend My People. I will bring great things to My People who call on My Name. I will bring Light and they will walk in My Presence. I will bring righteousness and they will walk in it. I will bring power to those who please Me and want to please Me. I will make them strong and mighty and no one can harm them-no one can stop them from going forward. When I bring My Children home, there will be many who try to stop them, but no one can stop what I ordain. No man can come close to My authority. All the angels are at My command. All creatures that I made are at My Command. I can send a legion of animals against any man who tries to come against Me. I can send a legion of angels against any nation who tries to rise up against Me, but instead I bring My People to stand for Me and fight for Me and I bless them for all their victories. I will give you crowns of gold to wear on your heads to show all that you are My coheirs and you will rule on behalf of Me. Rejoice and be glad that I love you so much.

121

Strength And Encouragement

Psalms 89:19-37

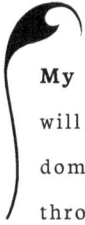

My Beloved, I do not change. I stand and do not move. I established and it will not fail. I made My covenant and it will not change. I established a kingdom through David and it has come to pass. I bought My servant the Branch through David and all men who cling to the Branch and become at one with the Branch will become part of the Tree of Life that stands in My Kingdom of Light and will remain permanent forever as stable and not bending. My People who call on My Name are grafted into this Branch and become part of Me. Those who cling to Me and walk with Me will be called My Children and they will not fail. They will not be destroyed. They will be given new life and not be cast away from Me. They will be brought up and set up before men and they will be given My Authority and My power will be in their hands. Do not be deceived by the world and all that glitters, because it is deception and it is not real. Only the spirit will remain and the flesh will pass away permanently. The flesh is temporary, but My Spirit remains forever and My People remain forever. Rejoice and be glad that I have chosen you as My own, and you may be grafted into the Tree of Life and live forever in My Kingdom of Light. No longer will you sleep or rest, but you will be refreshed and renewed in My Presence and you will have no wants and lack nothing. Be strong and be brave. because I will come soon.

Psalms 89:38-52

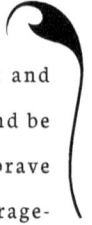

My Beloved, there will be those who rise up against you and mock you and what you believe, but they are only temporary and they will pass away and be no more. They are here to test you and make you stronger. Be bold and brave and do not listen to their taunts, but listen only to My words of encouragement. I will give you what you need to stand. I will give you all you need to stand firm. Call on My Name and I will remove your enemies from you. I will send you to a safe haven- a place of peace and hide you there. I will lift you up and take you by the hand and lead you to a new place. You may have to give up your house and job and friends and all you have, but I will place you in a good place. Think of your children and all their needs. Think of how they need to be in a safe place-a place of peace. Remember My Promises to you that I will not leave or forsake you and that I will always care for you. Be strong, and I will guide you into the new place. You may think that I have deserted you at times, but I AM always near. Very carefully purge your heart of all unrighteousness. Be very careful to guard over yourself. Be careful to know in your heart that all good things come from Me. You will be able to stand firm in times of needs and talk with Me and hear My voice as to what you should do. I AM always beside you and I will never allow you to go down the wrong path, but I will protect you and keep you guided and you will overcome and reach the Kingdom of Light with great rewards.

Strength And Encouragement

Psalms 90:1-12

My Beloved, I AM your dwelling place. Stay in Me and you will be safe from all your enemies. I have kept a remnant for Myself to care for tenderly until I return again. Stay in My shelter and I will guide you and show you the way to go. I AM a Rock and you can stand on Me and not be shaken. You will not be moved. Trust in all My promises to you, and I will bring them to pass. I will open the doors for you and bring you peace and security and long life. I have cut your life span to 70 years, but for those who please Me I will give you more years, so you can bless the people around you. If you are strong in Me, then you will live in My Presence and have a long life to give your children hope in these dark days. You will be a light to them and comfort them. They will not struggle, because you will be a righteous example before them. You will be able to teach them My Ways -not only your children, but your children's children. Your days are like a breath. One thousand years is like nothing to Me. You are frail and temporary and you last only for a moment on this earth, but your life can seem to go on forever, because you do not understand My Ways. You must rejoice and be glad, and I will show you My Ways and you will walk in the Truth. I will teach you to count your days, so every day is precious and valuable because you are adding blessings to your days. If you walk in love and you are kind to everyone, then you will have days added to you. If you speak harmfully to others and try to take from them, your days will be shortened. You must walk in love and compassion, and I will bless you.

Psalms 90:13-17

My Beloved, I love you so and I know your troubles. I will give you joy in the midst of your troubles, so you can praise Me and worship Me and be at one with Me. You will always have troubles to test you and perfect you, but you will always have My love to fill you with gladness. Arise and praise Me, because I AM so good to you. I have placed My favor on you and wherever you go and whatever you do I will bless you, if you walk in My ways and do My will. Listen for My Voice, and I will guide you. The days are dark and you must allow Me to guide you, so you do not end up in the wrong place and suffer because you did not listen. You long to be close to Me, but you must battle your flesh and keep it under restraint so you can hear Me and walk in Me. You will see the light all around you and you will be led by the light and know that My Hand is on you. I will bless you in all you do, so that you have all you need and you never lack. I will give you favor with those who work over you, and I will keep you smiling as you work. You will not suffer loss as you work, because you work for Me. You look at Me as your employer. You work to make Me happy and please Me, so your days can be long on this planet. You may say that you do not want to live long, but you want your life to be short, but I say to you for the sake of your children, you need to linger and be a righteous example for them. Be strong. Be brave. I AM always with you.

Strength And Encouragement

Psalms 91:1-16

My Beloved, if you call on My Name, if you say that I AM your refuge, your shield, your high tower, your fortress that no man can enter, where you are always safe under the shelter of My Wings, if you call Me a delight and not a burden, if you say to Me, "Master, I am your servant", if you turn to Me in times of troubles and know that I will help you, if you turn your family to Me so that all their faces turn to Me and know Me, if you try to walk in righteousness and do not waiver, then I will hear your prayers and lift you up and protect you from all evils. I will not allow anyone to smite you or overtake you or cause you evil, because you are My beloved. If you turn to Me with all your heart knowing that it is I who will redeem you from death and give you eternal life n My kingdom, if you confess that you love Me to men and do not hide your love for Me, if you praise Me in the midst of men because I have blessed you so much and only bring good things to you, if you show men that you are worthy of entering My Kingdom, then you will receive eternal life and you will be a light in the darkness. You will be able to soar to great heights and be free from this earth. You will be in My arms and be held in My Hands. Be strong. Be brave, because your redemption draws near.

Psalms 92:1-5

My Beloved, praise Me because I AM worthy of praise. I AM the only One to be served. I AM who I AM. You cannot understand Me until you are released from your coat of flesh which keeps you weighed down and causes turmoil. Your flesh is like a cocoon, and it helps you to form into My image by the constant weight of it. You resist it and you become stronger and you grow into the being that I want you to become. You are a light being and the flesh is a dark being, so you wrestle against it and you grow wise and good and strong so you can rule over many. You do not see all this now, but soon you will. Even those who look on and see how you are progressing take notice of how you are growing. They cannot see what you will become and they anxiously await the day to see you emerge into the being that I have formed. You will rule over many and you will rule in righteousness. You are My Child and I love you deeply. My thoughts are too deep for you and will always be too deep for you, because you are created and I AM the Creator. The creature can never understand the thoughts of the Creator. They will always be too deep for you, but you will praise Me for My wondrous works. You will sing and dance and worship Me with all your heart. You grieve now because you are in exile and you have no reason to sing, except that I give you all that you need and love you tenderly every day. Soon I will bring you home and you will sing and dance and celebrate that you have returned at last. You will rejoice, because I have given you so much. You will see and know that I have kept My promise to you and your ancestors. I will deliver you from exile and bring you back once again to My Land. Rejoice and be glad that I love you so much!

Strength And Encouragement

Psalms 92:6-15

My Beloved, you are planted in Me. You are part of Me. You flourish because of Me. I give you life and strength. I give you what you need to survive. You are like a tender plant and I water you and care for you until you are a mighty oak-strong and unbendable even in the storm. You are my beloved, and I will give you all you need to endure. You are not like the wicked who try to destroy others, but you are loving and kind and compassionate and giving to others. The wicked only think of themselves and how they can take from others and build up treasures for themselves. You are not like these, but you are a light to others and a testimony of My love for you. You see the wicked come and go, but in the end they suffer and have to pay for their wicked deeds. The righteous flourish even in their old age. They do not wither, but they remain strong and upright and guard their mind so it does not become dim and lack understanding. They are full of energy and continue to testify about Me and My ways. They are a light to those around them. They are a vessel poured out that gives generously to others. You will see and know My ways. You will understand what I AM doing in your life. Others will not be able to see, because they are blinded. You will see with eternal eyes and know who I AM, because I have chosen you and you are My Child.

Psalms 93

My Beloved, I AM King of the universe-maker of all things. I rule in majesty. I rule in glory. No man can come near My Presence. No man can stand before Me or he will be consumed. I AM a consuming fire. I AM Elohim over all other gods. No one can rule unless I allow him to rule. No one can have power or authority unless I allow him to do so. Every ruler is chosen by Me. If a nation is good and serves Me, then I will give it a righteous leader. If a nation does not serve Me, then I will give it a wicked ruler and he will bring down the nation and it will be destroyed or subdued by its enemies. If a nation repents and turns to Me, then I will heal their land and bring My Spirit on them and produce a mighty leader to help them overcome. I will lift them up and they will be strong and mighty. I rule all things. I make all things come to pass. My words are powerful and true. My words have dominion over all other words. I allow My Children to speak, and I hear them when they pray to Me. I will answer their prayers, because they are My Children. I will listen to your prayers and help you in times of weakness to make you stronger. You are stronger than you think. You have more power than you think. You are robed in flesh, but you are My Child and you have inherited My Authority. Lift up your voice and speak on behalf of Me and I will stand behind what you say, because I love you so much.

Strength And Encouragement

Psalms 94:1-13

My Beloved, I AM an Elohim of vengeance. I do reward the righteous, and I pay back the wicked for the evil they do against the righteous. I do see and hear and know. I look from My upper chambers and I see the troubles of men and how wickedness abounds. I know that the Wicked One grows stronger and he will continue to grow stronger until the last day that I return. He thinks that I cannot overtake him, but he is wrong. He is setting up a plot of deception that is so strong that even the Chosen Ones will be deceived, but I will open the eyes of the Chosen Ones and tell them to look for the deception and to be brave and strong and they will overcome. They will have to follow their heart and not their eyes. Their fleshly eyes will see the deception, but the spirit within them will see and know that what they see with their eyes of flesh is an illusion and darkness covers it and plots an evil deception. Those who are blinded at first will see later that the deception has come to the surface and make itself an evil plot. It will be too late at that time to escape their hand, but My Chosen Ones who have called on My Name and are led by My Spirit will see clearly and know how to escape the plot of deception. They will be taken to a safe place, and they will know My voice and not be deceived. Always look to Me and know the enemy tries to deceive you. Beware of his evil plots. Beware!

Psalms 94:14-23

My Beloved, I AM your stronghold in times of trouble. When your enemies rise up against you, I will protect you and overtake them. My People are in My Hand, and no man can harm them. I do send My judgment against My People who rebel against Me, so they will repent and follow Me. If you see a people under oppression, then you see My Hand against this people. If you see a nation struck down by their enemies, then you see My Hand casting judgment on this nation. If you see a nation that is blessed, then you see Me blessing a nation. If a nation rises up against your nation, I will tell you where to hide and what to do to protect yourself. You must be listening to Me, and I will guide you. Only the faithful will survive in the last days. Only those who listen will be shown how to live and be safe from their enemies. You will see a strong delusion in the last days and many will fall under it. Only those who are guided by My spirit will be guided away from the delusion. You must be ready to move and leave as soon as I speak. You must be listening for My call. Do not get overtaken by debt, so that you cannot hear My call. Release yourself from debt as soon as possible, and you will be free to obey Me. Call on My Name, and I will help you. I will give you all you need. I will comfort you in the midst of loss and disappointment. Remember all things that come your way are good things, because you are tested and made strong by the conflicts that you have victory over. Be strong and be brave. I AM always with you.

Strength And Encouragement

Psalms 95

My Beloved, hold fast to Me, because I AM your Rock. I formed the earth with My Hands. I hold it together with My Spirit. It will stay within its boundaries until I dissolve it. I hold all things in My Hands. I AM Maker and Creator of all things. You should not ever be fearful, because all things are in My control. You should shout and sing praises to My Name, because I AM so good to you. I have blessed you with so much. I take you and make you into My Image daily. All the struggles that you endure in your flesh are My Hands making you into the person that I want you to become. I AM perfecting your faith, so you can trust Me with all your heart. In these last days you must be faithful and strong and bold and brave. You must not bend to man, but stay true to the faith. You must walk in My ways. You must walk in the things of Me. Be bold and go forward casting aside the things of the world. Men will pull at you to go the way of the world. You must resist him and cling to Me. I will lift you up above the things of the world and help you overcome the evil one. Listen to My voice, and I will make you walk in a new way-one that you have not walked before. You must be humble and submit to My Ways. You must want to do My Will. Man will try to tempt you to go his way, but be strong and I will bless you and keep you from all his wickedness. Rejoice that I love you so much.

Psalms 96

My Beloved, praise Me with all your heart. Praise Me in the midst of the people of the earth. Let them know that you praise the Creator of the earth. They will see every person bow before Me and all gods will be washed away and be no more. At the final judgment I will destroy the wicked and uphold the righteous as My Children. I will take My Bride, and she will enter My Wedding Chamber. She will remain true to Me while on earth-faithful in all her ways. She will not bend to other gods, but she will uphold My Ways and My Laws. She will not be swayed by man-made traditions. She will forsake the traditions of her ancestors, and she will walk in righteousness. Her ancestors fell to idol worship, but she will turn from these evils and will walk in My ways. She will see Me as her only true Elohim and will worship Me in spirit and truth. Do you follow the traditions of men? Do you take pagan holidays and make them "My" holidays? Do not be so wicked. Keep only My Feast Days and My Sabbaths. My words say to keep My Laws. I see many who say they are My People, and yet they do not follow My Laws. Are they not written in My book? Should you listen to man when he says that My laws are obsolete? My Laws stand and shall never move. I say do not add or do not take away from My Laws. If you are guilty of this, then you are in sin. Wake up and do not fall into deception. Be wise. Read My Words for yourself and learn. I will guide you, if you really want to walk in My Ways. I will guide you.

Strength And Encouragement

Psalms 97

My Beloved, I will come in mighty power and overshadow the whole world. I will come with fire and destroy the wickedness. They will melt away like wax. The earth will be transformed into a glorious place-a place for My Children to rejoice and be glad. They will be in My Presence daily -all the time-for eternity. My Children will rest and be at peace and enjoy Me and know that I AM. You will see Me in the clouds and the clouds will surround the earth and fire will be within the clouds, but you will be safe in My Arms as I destroy the earth and wash it clean from all its sins. It is a stench to Me. The time is almost at hand to destroy it and make it new. I will be glad, and we will have a great celebration. There will be singing and dancing in the heavens, because I have finally finished the design of My Children, and they have proven themselves faithful and emerge into the glorious beings that I have created. The flesh will be stripped away, and My Children will come forth. Now My Children sleep in their cocoons of flesh or in the grave. Soon they will be awakened. Arise, O sleepers! Arise My Chosen Ones! Arise. It is time to come forth and be at one with Me. All the fallen ones have been destroyed and you are set free from the oppression of evil. You are set free to know Me and walk with Me. You have been tested by fire and found faithful. Rejoice and be glad! I never left you unattended. I AM always faithful. I AM always with you.

Psalms 98

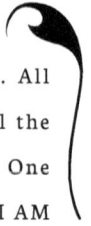

My Beloved, all the earth will see Me have victory over your enemies. All the earth will see My glory when I return again in power and might. All the earth will know that I AM-the only One- the only Great I AM -the only One who loves His Children and will redeem them from all the unrighteous. I AM and I AM and there is no other. There is no one like Me. I AM One. I AM and I AM the Only One. Praise Me in the midst of My People. Rejoice and be glad that I love you so much and I remember you and do not forsake you. My eye is on you at all times. Why do you suffer here? Why do you go through such difficult situations? Why are you tested to show your faith? You must grow strong and powerful here, so you can rule in My Kingdom. You will emerge a glorious being filled with power and might. You will be glorious to behold-a beautiful creature that adores Me in all My Ways-an unbending creature who is drawn only to Light and there is no darkness in you. You abhor evil and shun the unrighteous. You are My Child-the one who will inherit My throne. You will be co-heirs to My Kingdom, but you must be found faithful to Me. You must be found unbending and not desiring to run after evil. The Evil One will tempt you and try to get you to run after him, but his ways are dark and there is no happiness for you there. You will return to the One who loves you most and repent of your evil ways and humble yourself and cling to Me, because I AM the only One who can bring you peace and happiness. Rejoice in this that I love you so much and can keep you until the last day.

Strength And Encouragement

Psalms 99

My Beloved, I AM King over all the earth. Men may set themselves up as rulers over peoples, but they are not the ruler of all things. I control all things, and I control your life. I hear your prayers, and I send help to you when you call out to Me. I send help to you and make your feet steady, so you can walk the path that I have for you. You must continue your journey and you must do your best, because you will be judged on how you live your life. You will be judged on how you treat others. You must love others and reach your hand out to those in need. You must not look at men for help, but only look to Me and I will help you. I will show you the way to go. Be kind to those who are searching for the way to go. I will bring Truth to them, and they will find the path to travel. You do not know which person will hear the Truth that you give them and later turn towards Me. It may not be the day that they hear the Truth, but the seed will be planted and it will take root and grow until it becomes well planted, and then it will blossom. Do not grow weary as you go along your path and say that you want to give up. Be strong and be brave. Shout for joy, because I have given you so much. You are co-heirs with Me and will rule in My Kingdom. You should rejoice everyday that you have been chosen to be My own. Rejoice and be glad and do not allow this temporary life to drag you down. Keep your eternal vision and you will do well.

Psalms 100

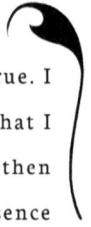

My Beloved, I AM good. I AM worthy to be praised. I AM faithful and true. I always bring My Promises to past. If I said it, then you can be assured that I will do it. My words are like treasures. If you can find their meanings, then you have found great wealth. Rejoice and be glad. Enter into My Presence with singing and dancing and joyfulness. Enter into My Presence and walk in My peace. Walk in the light of My face and you will be led by Me all your days. There is no fear in My Presence. There are no lies in My Presence. There is no deceitfulness in My Presence. There is no sin in My Presence. If you are in sin, then repent and turn away from it. If I have asked you to do something, then do it. Do not deny My words and go against Me. Be strong and be brave. Rejoice that I love you so much and this temporary life will flee quickly. I have shortened your years, because the world is so dark. I have increased your testing, because your time is shorter. Your life is very fast paced and stress is on you every day to perform and do what is right. The world is pressing in on you, but you do not give up. You are strong and brave and you stand firm. You do and say what is right. You do not bend to men, but you bend only to Me. You are righteous before Me. Men may mock how you worship Me, but in the end they will cry out for mercy and there will be no mercy. Once man has fulfilled his time and he is judged, the verdict is final. There is no mercy at this point. He has lived his life and not walked in My ways. He has not desired My Presence. If you love Me, you will serve Me and rejoice in Me. Rejoice and be glad and enter into My Presence, because I AM good.

Strength And Encouragement

Psalms 101

My Beloved, come to Me singing, and I will bless you. Come to Me and walk in righteousness, and I will lift you up and allow you to see. Walk in justice and integrity, and I will bring good things to meet you. I will lift you up, so you can see clearly the path ahead. You must turn aside from evil doers who walk in evil and do what you know is not right. You must keep around you only honest people who do not lie who you can trust. You must keep those who slander others in secret and gossip far away from you. You must not desire to enter into their foolishness. You must want to have them away from you, so you can walk a path that will be an example for others. You must know that you want only to serve Me and you will guard over your eyes, so you do not see any shameful thing. You must guard over your heart that you do not fall into sin and allow bitterness or hatred to come in the midst of you. Push away all evil thoughts of hurting others. Push away from you all thoughts of wanting to see others fall into harmful things. You must love the people around you and not wish any evil to fall on them. You must be My Hands and Feet and give generously to others. This life is temporary and you are not here very long. Let your footsteps on earth be steps that will be remembered as one who gave generously while you walked this short path. You will see that others will know that you have left footsteps on their life that has left impressions of righteousness, and they will not forget your good deeds. Think on these things and always walk in My Ways.

Psalms 102

My Beloved, I see your grief. I hear your crying for mercy. I know your heart is heavy with mourning. I see you as you look at your food and there is no pleasure in eating it. You are like a stone-heavy and numb. You are looking for any chance of hope. I AM your Hope. I AM your Strength. I AM the only One who can help you. You cannot look to man, but you can look for Me and find Me. You can seek Me with all your heart, and I will arise and you will see Me. You will know Me, and I will know you. We will be as one. You do not have to fear. You must only trust in Me. I will never desert you or neglect you. I AM your Father-your daddy. I AM the one who loves you. I will return to Zion, and she will praise My Name once again. She has turned to sin and she was sent away from Me, but soon I will bring My Children back to Me and they will serve Me in spirit and truth. I will return again and make the heavens new. I will recreate earth and the heavens and create a beautiful place for My Children who love Me and want to serve Me. They did not bend while on earth to the things of the Evil One. They were not moved, but stood firm and did not give up ground to the enemy. They are righteous and they proved themselves worthy. They will enter My Kingdom of Light and rule with Me for eternity. These are My Chosen. These are the ones who cling to Me. You are My People-the sheep of My pasture. Only you hear My Voice and know My Name and will come when you are called.

Strength And Encouragement

Psalms 103

My Beloved, I AM merciful and compassionate remembering that you are dust and you have to walk in a fleshly garment. I know that your ways are influenced by the fleshly coat, but I know that My spirit can wash you clean and make you strong and pure. You are My covenant children and as long as you walk in My covenant by obeying My laws and walking in My ways, then you will be blessed. You are covered with grace, and I do not judge you harshly. I AM just and fair and I repay you back for the sins that you commit against Me. You must respect all men and not belittle them or humiliate them or embarrass them. You must speak words of kindness and be merciful to them. You must love those around you, and do only good things for them. I gave My Words to Moses, so you could see clearly how to walk in My Ways and do My will. I gave you men of old as an example of how to walk in Me. They were not perfect, but they trusted in Me and had faith in Me to guide them. They understood and knew that you must walk in My ways and I would bless you. All things are under My Control and I give to whom I want to give and I take from whom I want to take. Whatever happens to you is because I have ordained it to happen to you. You must realize and accept that what comes to you is what I have given you. You must know that I will bless you and even though you go through a fire, it is a blessing because it will only make you stronger and make you worthy of entering My kingdom. To be saved from the pit of eternal destruction is the biggest blessing that I can give you and that blessing is reserved only for My Children who love Me and want to serve Me with all their heart.

Psalms 104:1-24

My Beloved, I created the earth and all that is within it. I formed the earth with you in mind. I formed the earth to be suitable for you to live on. You are my beloved, and I wanted you to have a beautiful place to live, but then man rebelled against Me and he fell under the rule of the fallen ones. I despised the earth and its wickedness and I covered it with water and washed it clean and began once more with my son, Noah. Noah and his sons populated the earth, and I gave Shem a large piece of land that I call My own. I told him that through him I would bring My People and they would always dwell on My Land. I made a variety of animals for My People to eat, and I made a variety of plants for My People to eat. I blessed My Land and filled it with only the best. I gave My People the best wine to make their hearts merry, so they could dance and sing at My feast days. I gave them the best olive oil for their bodies. I gave them the best fruits and vegetables to keep them healthy. I gave them the best, and they rebelled against Me, so I drove them from My Land by their enemies. The ones they had defeated with My help rose up against them by My guiding. As much as I delighted in blessing them became how much I delighted in cursing them. I drove them all over the earth, and that is where they remain today in exile from their Land. Rejoice and be glad because your days of exile are numbered, and they are soon over and you can return to the Land of your ancestors. You will rejoice over Me like they once did, and I will delight in blessing you as I once did. Arise and open your eyes that you may that My light is coming to visit your house.

Strength And Encouragement

Psalms 104:25-35

My Beloved, I made the seas and all the living creatures. I sustain them with food and keep the oceans balanced, so all can exist and be fed. I keep the waters in their boundaries, so they will not come over the land like the flood did in the days of Noah. I keep the earth in place and I keep all the weather in check. I judge the nations with the weather-famines, hurricanes, floods, earthquakes. I judge the nations and if they have come to the fulfillment of their judgment, then they receive the full payment of their sins. I give all men time to repent, and when they don't then I punish them for their wickedness hoping that the punishment will bring them to repentance. I give men food, and I help the nations to have peace. I control the hearts of men, and I control the rulers that I have placed into power. If a nation has an evil ruler, then the nation has deserved an evil ruler. If a nation has a righteous ruler, then the nation has deserved a righteous and wise ruler. The nations are under My control even though men think they control the earth and all they is in it. You must realize that I control all things, and nothing is impossible for Me. Once you realize this, then your faith will be strong. I can keep you from sickness and disease. I can give you wealth. I know what is best for you, so I give you what will help form you into the person that I want you to become. If you are righteous in all your ways, then I will best you accordingly. You have the choice to choose which lifestyle that you will pick. You have a choice to do what is right in My eyes. You must want to please Me. Let your thoughts be pure, so I can delight in you all day long. You must overcome your flesh and allow your spirit to arise and be strong. Be strong and be brave and overcome all the tests I put before you, and you will do well.

Psalms 105:1-11

My Beloved, seek Me with your whole heart. Do not seek the wisdom of this world, but seek Me and walk in My wisdom. Men think they have power and know all things, but men know nothing and they have power only because I have allowed them to have power. They will be put to ruin in a second, if I desired to do so. You must remember that no one can hurt you. Walk in faith and trust Me. Remember all the things I have done for your ancestors in the past, and rejoice that I have given you so much. Rejoice that I have blessed you above the others on the earth. You cannot see your blessings, because your eyes are blinded. You cannot see, because your heart is not pure. You must open your eyes to My ways and watch how I mold you into My being that can be used in My Kingdom. Look at Me and know Me and be always in My presence. Then you will be lifted up above your problems, and you will not bend even under pressure. You will rejoice and be glad all your days and know that I AM faithful to protect you and keep you safe and well and provide all your needs. You will know Me and I will know you.

Strength And Encouragement

Psalms 105:12-45

My Beloved, I AM your protector. I protected your ancestors and I will protect you even in times of trouble. Even when your enemies are pursuing you, I will protect you. Even when the economy is in shambles and all around you is falling apart, I will protect you. I will guide you to a place where you can have food and clean water and safety. I will keep My People from disasters and cover them over with My Hand, if they are walking in My Ways and keeping My laws. If My People listen to My Voice and walk in My ways, then I will lift them up above any storm that may come to their area. I will show you a way out. I will give you peace. I will show you the way to avoid all the troubles. Beware if I tell you to leave a place but you continue to stay there, then My judgment will come on you and you will suffer loss. You must be listening. Remember you are wandering this earth until it is time to return to your home land once again. You are aliens here and you are living in temporary housing. Do not become attached to where you live, because in the days to come I will move you to a safer place, if you are listening to Me and want to follow Me. Do not be afraid of the place I take you, because it will be a place where others are going that serve Me and you will be with My Children. I have chosen safe havens around the world that I have kept to Myself and in the last days when I tell My People to move, they will go as one and move are one and the enemy cannot come against them. They will have to move back, and let My People enter into the Land. You will see that you will come with singing and dancing and rejoicing that I have remembered you in exile and have called you home.

Psalms 106:1-23

My Beloved, I AM good to all My Children. I help them find their way. I guide them in the direction they are going. I give them favor with man and open doors for them that only I would open. I will change the hearts of men to provide for you. I will send you what you need at the time you need it. I will give generously to you and I will take from you, so you can be formed into My Image. You are My Chosen and I will provide for you exactly what you need. Your ancestors were sinful and they rebelled against Me by not trusting Me and being fearful. They saw all the miracles that I preformed in Egypt and when they saw the Egyptian army coming they forgot all My miracles and they cried out to Moses that they would die. I saw their lack of faith from the beginning. I made Myself real to them and provided manna in the Wilderness. I even provided them meat, because they were greedy and wanted more to eat. I provided water from a rock to bring water to a million people and their cattle. I can do anything, but you limit what I can do for you. Walk in faith and not what your eyes see. I can change your situation in a moment. I can change you in a moment, so you can see and know who I AM. Your ancestors turned to other gods and worshipped them. If you will only worship Me and not seek man or another source for guidance and advice, then I will care for you as a mother cares for her child. I AM constantly beside you and constantly giving you exactly what you need. Just call on My Name and I AM there.

Strength And Encouragement

Psalms 106:24-48

My Beloved, My People rejected Me and were not obedient to Me and My anger rose up against them. I put in their enemies' heart to rise up against them and overtake them to punish them for their sins against Me and cause them to repent. They would repent, but when I had compassion on them they went back to their sinful ways. Soon the Land was polluted with their sins, so I cast them out of the Land and sent them to all the nations of the earth driving them with a harsh whip. Now you are in exile and you are longing to know Me and follow My ways. You are far from home, and there are pagans all around you. You do not know My ways, because you have no teachers to show you the way. My spirit within you is rising up and teaching you My ways and showing you the way to go. You will be sent back to your home, and you will be joined together with those who love Me and once again you will worship Me in spirit and truth. The time is short, so make your hearts ready, and prepare for your journey home. I will open a door for you, and you will know that I AM with you. You will feel My Presence so strongly as you make your passage home. You will know that I AM protecting you. I AM who I AM and I will guard over My People and bring them home to Me again. Rejoice that I love you so much.

146

Psalms 107:1-22

My Beloved, give thanks to Me, because I AM so good to you. I help you in times of need. When you cry out to Me, I AM there. Your ancestors cried out to Me and I heard their prayers and saved them from destruction. I kept a remnant for Myself, so that none of the tribes would be wiped out. I humbled My People. I sent them into slavery, and they wore chains of bondage. They cried out to Me day and night, and I delivered them from their chains of bondage and set them free to walk in My ways and follow Me. I gave them liberty from their oppressors. If you call on My Name for help and turn your face towards Me and listen to what I tell you to do and obey Me, then I will lift you up and make your pathways straight and show you the way to go. I cannot guide you if you are in sin. I can only guide you when you are focusing on Me and wanting to walk in righteousness. You are My beloved, and I value you and want you to have the best. Sometimes you must be broken of your pride and arrogance before you can serve Me. If you must be broken and I do this through numerous situations, then count it a blessing that I love you so much to carefully work on you and mold you into My image of loving kindness and tender mercies. You are My beloved and I want you to walk in righteousness and be pure before Me, so you can draw closer to Me and we can be as one.

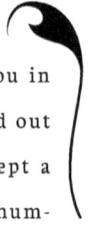

Strength And Encouragement

Psalms 107:23-32

My Beloved, there once was a man named Jonah who rebelled against Me. I told him to go to Nineveh and tell the people to repent because judgment was coming, but instead he got on a boat to escape Me. This put all the men on the boat in jeopardy. I brought a storm on the boat and the boat was about to break apart, because the storm was so terrible. Each man called on his god, but Jonah knew that the storm came from Me. He told the men that the storm was caused by Me, and I should throw him overboard. They were amazed when the seas calmed instantly when Jonah was thrown overboard. They praised Me for having mercy on them and began to worship Me. Sometimes you may be caught up in the judgment of others around you. You may not see what is going on. Call on My Name and I will reveal to you what My plan is for you. You may need to separate yourself from the people that you are around. You may need to repent of your rebellion against Me. You may want to go your own way, but I know what is right for you and exactly what you need. Do not question Me and test Me. You should accept My will for you and know that I will only bring you the best. You must trust Me everyday to do what is best for you. Then you will know that I AM and I can do all things according to My purpose for you. You cannot escape Me. Repent today and walk in My ways.

Psalms 107:33-43

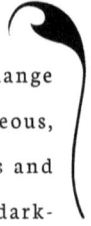

My Beloved, consider My loving deeds towards man. Consider how I change the land to fit the judgment of the people. Consider how I bless the righteous, because of their loving and kind deeds towards man. Look at My hands and look how I form man into My image. Look at how I change a man from darkness to light. It is a wonder and amazement in the heavens. My angels long to look into the works of My hands how I take a wicked child and change him into a righteous man. It amazes them how I prove you faithful time and again and show your worth and that you are worthy to inherit My Kingdom. We are my beloved and only I know what you will become. Even now the angels and all creation do not know the end result of what you will become-a fiery creature full of My image ready to rule nations and fight battles on My behalf-a mighty warrior- strong and unbending. You are My beloved, My bride, My own, My child. You are the only one that I keep My eyes on all the day. I adore you and want to see you prosper and be in good health, yet I want you to grow so you can mature into the being I want you to become. Therefore I may not prosper you or give you good health until you turn to Me and worship Me in spirit and truth. You must give your whole heart to Me. I am waiting for you. I am waiting for your full surrender. I am waiting for you to come to Me.

Strength And Encouragement

Psalms 108

My Beloved, I AM your protection in times of trouble. When enemies rise up against you I AM there to help you. It may not be an army, but it may be evil men or it may be selfish men. Whatever the situation I will help you through all things. You must call on My Name, and I will hear you. I will not forsake you, but I will listen to your call unless you have rebelled against Me and are not walking in My ways and keeping My laws. What are My laws you ask? Have I not given you My laws from the beginning? Have I clearly established My ways in My laws? Read My words and do not depart from them. I AM your Elohim, and I will guide you. Do not listen to men and keep their traditions, but keep My words and walk in My ways. My ways are walking in love and compassion for your fellow man. Do not turn away anyone that asks for help. Let Me be the judge of who is worthy or not. Let Me be the judge of who will be rewarded and who will not be rewarded. You must know that I love you and I have put My spirit within you to love others and to judge wisely what is right and wrong. I will keep you from being deceived. I will keep you going in the right path, if you continue to seek Me and call on My Name. You will be led by Me and I will make your pathway straight, so you can walk without a heavy burden on your back. Just trust Me every day and I will show you the way to go.

Psalms 109

My Beloved, I AM always with you, and even if others rise up against you I will help you. Call on My Name and I hear your cries. I will not allow men to take from you, but I will add to you if you continue to walk in My ways and obey My commands. I know you are in exile and everyone around you wants to go their own way. They want to do what is right in their own eyes. Righteous men are few. There are no teachers to teach you My laws and My prophecies. You only have Me to guide you, but that is all you need. You may have no friends around you to comfort you and encourage you, but I AM here to comfort and encourage you. You must not delay in your obedience. You must do as I tell you to do. If you are faithful to Me, then I will be faithful to you. I will deliver you in times of danger. I will not allow men to steal from you or take from you. I will not allow men to come against you to harm your family. Others may mock you because you walk in My Ways. Others may laugh at your lifestyle. Others may say that you are in error and do not know the way to walk because you are deceived, but I tell you this that you are among the righteous and My messengers are around you and help you daily, so you are not harmed but remain safe. You may not see the heavenly ones around you, but they are there in spirit only. Your flesh hinders you from seeing all those around you who help you, but look past your flesh and into My eyes and you will see clearly that the path before you is level and not steep. The path ahead is not filled with obstacles, because I go before you and behind you and I keep you close to Me all the day long. Rejoice that I love you so much!

151

Strength And Encouragement

Psalms 110

My Beloved, I will stand on Judgment Day and judge the nations. I will execute My wrath on them at last for harming My Children and killing so many of them unmercifully. My Children have suffered much at the hand of their enemies. Their enemies will be blasted into nothingness. They will cease to exist. I will take them on that dreadful day and cast them into the Lake of Fire, and they will be destroyed forever. Do not be afraid of man. They will have their Day of Judgment, and they will be cast far away from you, so they can never touch you again. I sit at the right Hand of My Father. I rule with him eternally. No one comes to the Father except through Me. You must come to Me humbly and receive Me as your Messiah, and I will accept you and hold you and prepare you for the coming days. Do not be concerned about anything. I AM always beside you. I AM strong and mighty and I will always have victory. No man can make a plan with his finite brain to outwit or overtake Me. I AM the Creator and you are the creatures. Lift up your eyes and know that your redemption draws near. I will prepare you for the days ahead, so you can see clearly. Rejoice that I love you so much!!

Psalms 111

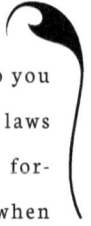

My Beloved, I AM merciful and compassionate. I gave to you My laws, so you can learn to be like Me and love Me with your whole heart. I gave you My laws and an eternal covenant I made with you. This is a covenant that lasts forever and forever. This is a covenant that I renewed with My own blood when I came and died for you at Calvary-the place of the skull. I gave up My life, so you could live. I gave up all that I was to become sin for you and was laid upon the altar and bore all your sins, so you could be free from the bondage of sickness and death. I gave up everything for you, and I expect you to give up everything for Me. I expect you to turn aside from your sins and walk in righteousness. I expect you to take My Hand and walk with Me and be at one with Me. You are one who wants to go your own way, but you must go My way and do what is right in My eyes. If you fear Me and keep My commandments, this is the beginning of wisdom. If you fear Me and know that if you do not keep My commandments I will punish you, then I will give you wisdom and lift you up and bless you greatly, because you have found the open door. I AM the Truth and the Light. Anyone who comes to Me and accepts Me can enter the door to eternal life.

Strength And Encouragement

Psalms 112

My Beloved, I will bless anyone who fears Me and keeps My commandments. I will bless his children after him, and they will become powerful. Wealth and riches will be in their houses. They will stand upright and not be shaken. They will be merciful and compassionate to those around them. They will not be shaken by bad news, but will always trust in Me to guide them and care for them even in the midst of the darkest of days. They will not fear, but they will have faith in Me. I will bless all their hands do as long as they are being led by My spirit. You do not have to be concerned if you walk in righteousness. You have nothing to fear. You must know that I hold you by My Hand, and I do not let go of you. I cover you with My presence and you hear My voice. You must not ever doubt that I will care for you. I AM constant and never bend. You will see many come and go, but only the righteousness will not be moved. They will be strong and unbendable. They will be able to shield others with their prayers and constant support. Many are trying to make a decision about who they are and what they want to believe. These people will be judged on what they do and say. My People who call on My Name will speak with a righteous tongue and not slander anyone or humiliate anyone. You will always be loving and kind to all men and I will bless you.

Psalms 113

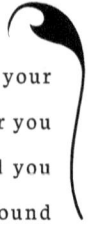

My Beloved, praise Me all the day for My wondrous works. I can change your situation in a moment. I can change your life in a day. I can do things for you that no one else can do, because I hold the universe in My Hands. I hold you in the palm of My Hands. I mold you and make you by the situations around you. You may see things as hopeless, but I can change the hopeless situation into one of praise for Me because of My wondrous ways. Do not be fearful or upset, but trust Me with your whole heart. Trust in Me and call on My Name. Trust in Me and cling to My Words-My promises. I can lift up the poor and needy and provide all they need and prosper them greatly. If your situation seems lost, it is lost only if I allow it to be lost. Call on My Name and trust Me that I AM able to deliver you from the darkness around you and allow you to see. I will lift you up with the men of authority. I will make your home in the midst of wise men who love Me. I will set you in a good place, so no one can harm you. I will pick you up and give you a good place to live, so I can cover you day and night. Lift up your eyes and do not despair, but rejoice and be glad that I love you so much. Praise Me in all things even if the situation is grieving you. Praise Me and trust Me and I will lift you up over it all and help you be restored and filled once again. Rejoice in Me. Sing praises to Me and I will deliver you.

Strength And Encouragement

Psalms 114

My Beloved, I brought you out of Egypt- a land of foreign speech and foreign gods. I brought you out of Egypt with a mighty Hand. I brought you out into a desert and fed you with My Hand and My food from above. There is nothing that I cannot do for you. You do not have to be afraid. Sometimes you go through difficult situations to push you into a better place, better job, have better friends, and have a different way of thinking. You must listen to Me, and do as I tell you to do, because I love you and want to give you the best. If you listen, I will guide you. If you listen, I will provide for you by guiding you to the source of living water. If you listen, I will show you a land flowing with milk and honey. What does this mean? I will give you a land filled with My Presence and abundance from My Kingdom. If you are lacking and without, then call on My name and I will provide for you. I will make a way for you. I will open doors for you that only I could open. I brought water from a rock in the wilderness, so all My People could drink and water their livestock. I brought water out from the ground for My People, so they would not thirst. I did miracles for My People. Can I also bring you water when you need it to feed your thirsty soul? Can I not bring healing to your body and provide for all your needs? I am waiting for you to come to Me. I AM there with outstretched arms waiting to hold you and help you. If you are off track today, come to Me and I will help you find your way.

Psalms 115

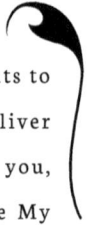

My Beloved, I AM your help and shield against anyone or thing that wants to harm you. I will help you, if you call on My Name and trust in Me to deliver you from any situation. There are those around you who want to harm you, but I hold you in My Hands and no one can harm you because you are My Own. The men around you trust in gold and silver and not in Me. They are greedy and envious men. They long to be rich and powerful, but I give wealth to who I please. I give power to who I please. I will lift you up and bless you and surround you with righteous things, if you walk in My Ways. If you look to Me in all things, then I will help you. Where is your faith? Is it in men? Is it in money? Is it in having numerous possessions? Where is your faith? Who do you trust in? Look to Me. I live in the heavens. I AM the Maker and Creator of all things. I will give to you generously, if you cling to Me. I will test you and find you worthy, and then I will give to you and bless you. First you must be tested to show those around you that look on that you are worthy of bearing My Name or being called My Own. Every man is tested and tried. Every man will be judged by Me. Every man will stand before Me, and I will cast My Judgment on him. He will be called My faithful servant, or he will be called a wicked servant who has turned away from Me and rebelled against Me. Every man must bear his judgment. You will be redeemed and live eternally, or you will be found guilty and be destroyed in the Lake of Fire. You must choose who you will serve in this life. You must choose life.

Strength And Encouragement

Psalms 116:1-11

My Beloved, I AM merciful and compassionate. I AM giving and kind. I AM tender hearted towards My Children, but I AM fair and righteous to all men. I will judge you according to your works. If you call on My Name, I will hear you and I will help you. If you feel as if all is lost and there is no way to turn, I will give you a way out so you will see the path before you very clearly. I will make the path easy for you, because you call on My Name. Most of the time, you are not patient to wait on Me to open the door for you. Waiting on Me causes you to be patient and have faith, and you will be able to endure to the end. I give you a promise, and I hold fast to that promise. I bring it to pass not in your timing, but in My timing. I show you that only I know the time that is best for you. I delay what I have spoken to you, so you can see that I put all the pieces together, and they all fall into place perfectly for you. You will look back and see My fingerprints on the past, and how I have planned everything perfectly for you to be able to succeed in this life. Rejoice and be glad that I love you so much, and have made you My own.

Psalms 116:12-19

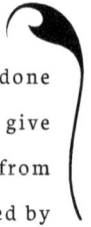

My Beloved, how can you repay Me for all the good things that I have done for you? You can never repay Me. I have given you treasure that I do not give to others. I have filled you with My spirit, so you can receive Wisdom from on high. You can be close to your Creator and know his Voice. You are led by Me, and I have a divine purpose for you that only I know. Yet I AM unveiling it day by day, so I can develop faith in Me within you. You will look back in your life and see how I had My Hand on you the whole time, and I never let you go for a moment. I fulfilled My purpose for you in this life, and all you did was trust in Me to guide you. I have given you so many blessings. I have fed you and clothed you and given you shelter. I have brought you encouragement and strength when you needed it. I have brought you people who love you and uphold you. I have given you parents to raise you and protect you. I have given you children or will give you children who will walk in My ways and do what is right and bring honor to your name. I will lift you up, and you will see above the life on this earth. This life is temporary and short lived compared to My kingdom of eternal light. I will bring you into My kingdom and make you My heir. Now you are a slave-a bond servant to Me. You do as I command you to do in joy and gladness singing praise to Me all the day. Lift up your eyes, and know that truly you are greatly blessed.

Psalms 117

My Beloved, I AM Truth and My Words continue forever. I AM Truth and I draw all men unto Me. I AM Truth and evil men cannot destroy Me. I AM Truth and all men who want to be saved from eternal destruction must come to Me and accept Me for who I AM. They must trust in Me and obey My Words and be a servant unto Me, and then I will call them faithful and they can enter into My eternal kingdom. If a man rejects Me, then he also rejects the Truth. If a man rejects Me, then he also rejects the open door of Truth. If a man rejects Me, then he turns his face away from Me and he looks towards evil and he becomes consumed by it. A man in such darkness will never enter into My kingdom. A man must repent of his sins and turn his face to the light of My Presence and walk in My ways of love and kindness. My door is open to all men, but only those whom the seed of righteousness lies within will be able to see the Truth and come into the open door. I placed this seed of righteousness in those of My Children who made covenant within Me. I placed My seed of righteousness within those people who turned from idols and made a covenant to walk in My ways and not the ways of the world. The seed of righteousness is within you, if you can see Truth and recognize it. If your ancestors followed Me and clung to Me, then they gave you the gift of righteousness within you. Rejoice that I have chosen you to come close to Me.

Psalms 118:1-9

My Beloved, put your trust in Me. What can man do for you? Can man create the universe? Can man put time into being? Can man bring power to a man? No, I give power to man and I take it away. Any man in power or leadership is placed there, because I give him this authority. Trust in Me not men. Men cannot help you. I do bring My servants, My People, to come to you and help you when you need encouragement and strengthen you with their words and prayers. I bring My servants to you to lift you up, but can they help turn the path in the road ahead? No, only I can direct your path and show you the way to go. I have forged the path head of you. Only I can see clearly the path ahead. Only I can show you the place to put your feet. You must cling to Me, and I will bring you grace. I AM full of grace and mercy. You should rejoice that I AM merciful towards you, because you are My Child and you live in exile. I know the pains of living in exile without My Presence and My Land under your feet. I know your sorrow. I know it weighs on you everyday. I have mercy on you, because of the extra weight you have to bear, because you do not live in My Land. You have been shunned, but not forever. You have been trampled down, but not forever. When I see you, I smile because you are precious to Me and I want to bring you back to the Land. It will be soon, My beloved. Just trust in Me and not men. I will redeem you and set you free and bring you back to a place where you will prosper and grow and be given great things. I love you. Do not grow weary in the fight to walk in righteousness.

Strength And Encouragement

Psalms 118:10-18

My Beloved, I may discipline you severely, but I will not hand you over to your enemies. I may discipline you and you may be brought down low, but it is My Right Hand that chastises you. It is My Right Hand who has given authority to punish you for your sins. There will be no punishment, if you walk in My ways and do what is right. There will be no chastisement, if you obey My voice and do as I tell you to do. If you reject My voice, then you will suffer loss. If you reject My voice, then you will see your plans come to ruin and only My plans for you will stand. You must walk in the path that I have placed before you or you will not find contentment in your life, but you will feel grieved over all your decisions. You must follow in My footsteps. I go before you, and prepare the way for you to follow. My Spirit will guide you and you must call on My Name everyday and seek Me, and I will show you the way. You must trust Me to know that I will guide you, and I will make a way for you. Only I will open the door for you. Do not look to man, but look only to Me. I will bring good things to your house, if you patiently wait on Me to reward you for being faithful to Me in all your ways. If you wait on Me, good things will come to you. No man can bring you what you need to prosper. Only I know what you need to prosper and be in good health. Rejoice that I love you so much to bring you such good gifts.

Psalms 118:19-29

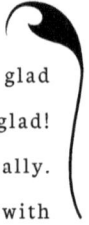

My Beloved, rejoice in this day that I have made for you. Rejoice and be glad that I love you so much and give to you so generously. Rejoice and be glad! Man brings you temporary gifts, but I give you gifts that will last eternally. I give you the fruits of the spirit, so you can love others and treat them with kindness. No man can produce these fruits within you. No man knows how to mold you, so that you are formed into My image. No man wants to care for you like I do, because only I know what you need to be transformed into a new creature filled with light. The angels long to see what you will become. They long for the day when you will no longer be robed in flesh, but will be creatures of light. Many around you see you and know you by your good works or by your evil deeds. If you guard over your tongue and only say kind and loving words, then you will be known by the words you say. If you do not guard over your tongue, then you will be known as a gossip and slanderer and there will be no honor for your name. Rejoice in My feast days. Rejoice and bring branches before Me and make a tabernacle for Me in My Land. If you are still in exile, then rejoice that I care for you even in exile. I know that you carry a heavy burden being apart from the Land of your ancestors and scattered across the nations and have no one to dance and sing with in your community. Rejoice that I will bring you home soon, and you will dance and sing with your people. You will praise My Name and rejoice in My Presence!

Strength And Encouragement

Psalms 119:1-8 (Alef)

My Beloved, My Words have been established from the beginning. My Words do not change. My Words are burning embers of light within you, if you accept them and hold to them and walk in them. They will produce great fire within you and bring you peace. Happy is the man who lives by My commandments. Happy is the man who knows My laws and walks in them. He does not do wrong things, but he walks in righteousness. Happy is the man who seeks Me to guide him. Happy is the man who knows My Voice and waits on Me to bring him good things. Happy is the man who will reach out his hand to Me. I will take his hand and uplift him and bring him up and he will see with eyes of gold-spiritual eyes that no man can give him. No matter if you have a great learned teacher who knows My words well, only I can bring enlightenment to the eyes. Only I will give a man the seeds of righteousness that he needs to make his journey through life. Only I can give with any open Hand to the man who calls on My Name. Rejoice, My little one, that I am so good to you. Rejoice and be glad that I give to you so generously. I have given My Words in the beginning. Cling to them and you will remain steady and unbendable.

Psalms 119:9-16 (Bet)

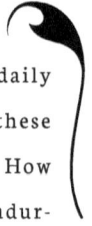

My Beloved, how can a man keep his way pure? He must read My laws daily and ponder on them... "What do they really mean? How can I walk in these laws today? What sort of things would My Father want me to do today? How can I help my neighbor today? How can I be a testimony of faith and enduring love? How can I walk in righteousness today? How can I give with an open hand today? How can I tell others about the wonders of My Heavenly Father? How can I give generously and yet remain humble before men? Let me look to the One who knows me. Let me ask Him how to live My life. He will know the answers to my questions. He will know the answers, because He made me and is forming me. He alone holds all the knowledge and all the answers will come to me if I seek Him. If I seek Him, then I will know Him and I will be lifted up and see the path ahead very clearly." I will give you the desires of your heart-the answers to all your questions. I will give you the secret things that only I can give. Ponder on My Words and light will arise in your eyes and you will see My face before you. Rejoice in My Presence, because I AM good.

Strength And Encouragement

Psalms 119:17-24 (Gimel)

My Beloved, you are a temporary resident on this planet. Your time here is short and calculated. You have been given a set number of days to fulfill your purpose. Your days have been shortened compared to your ancestors. The days are dark and your time will be spent with many tests in a short amount of time. You live in exile, so I AM merciful to you, but you must be proven faithful before you can enter My Kingdom of Light and live with Me eternally. You must delight in My words and hold them close to your heart, so you can receive the hidden meaning that lie within My Words that only My servants can dig out and know. The treasure in My words is given only to those who diligently seek Me and hold Me fast. If you are absorbed in the things of the world, then you will not see the hidden meanings. If you seek My face and read My Words daily, then you will find the rare gems that My words hold. There are wonders in My Words that will give you great revelation and bring you to a higher level, so you can know Me and draw close to Me and have more faith in Me. You trust someone that you really know. If you know Me, then you will trust Me and hold fast to Me. You will be lifted up and encouraged by My Presence. You will be stable and unbendable. You will not be moved in the presence of tribulations. You will be a mighty warrior. When you fast and pray, you will be able to overcome the enemy and prevail, because you know My words and the meaning of My words and no one can shake you.

166

Psalms 119:25-32 (*Dalet*)

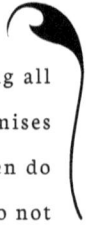

My Beloved, trust in Me and you will never be put to shame. I will bring all My promises to pass and they will be firmly established. Today My promises have not been firmly established within My People. Many of My Children do not understand My promises. They do not understand My Words. They do not see the hidden meaning in My Words. They have no foundation to stand on, and therefore they are shaken and moved in times of trouble. Where are My People who know how to stand in Me? Where are My People who know where to place their trust? I see My People putting their trust in insurance and doctors and lawyers and all sorts of men of the earth. They will be shaken and fall. The men who hold close to Me, I will guide them and heal them and protect them from all evil. I will hold them close to Me. Those who trust in Me will live in peace and contentment and not long for the things of this world. They will rejoice and be glad in Me that they have so much. You do not want to live as the pagans live, so do not long for the things that they long for. Remember that you are temporary beings. You will not live here long. You are here to be tested and be found faithful. View all things as temporary, and you will be able to distinguish between what is spiritual and what is worldliness. Choose to walk on a higher level. Choose to walk uprightly and be at one with Me. You will not fall, if you meditate on My words. I will bring you understanding into My Words, and you will be able to hold fast to them and not ever be shaken. Your foundation will be unbendable. You will not move, but stand firmly. You will be a rock for those around you. Be strong. Be brave. Stand firm.

Strength And Encouragement

Psalms 119:33-40 (*Heh*)

My Beloved, turn your eyes away from selfish gain and turn your eyes to My Words and seek understanding. It takes time to have understanding into My Words. I will bring you revelation as you seek Me and show Me that you want to follow close to Me. I will open your mind to My Words, and you will receive Truth and knowledge into My ways. I will help you to overcome evil and walk only in the Light. Many of My People in exile are tormented by the darkness around them daily, and they war heavily against the darkness, but do not grow weary. I will sustain you and hold you and you will know that I AM your strength. You will know that I AM the only One to cling to. You cannot cling to man and not suffer loss. You cannot cling to wealth and not suffer loss. You cannot cling to your good health and not suffer loss. Men will disappoint you, and wealth and good health will vanish in time. You will be left with nothing. You will be a sad and broken man. You must only trust in Me whether wealth comes and goes or man comes and goes or good health fades, you always have Me to hold you. Even in the midst of all your tests, I AM there to help you remain strong and unbending. You are of Me. You come from Me. My Spirit is within you. You will not fail, if you hold onto Me. You will overcome. Rejoice and be glad that I AM so close, and you are so mighty to overcome in Me.

Psalms 119:41-48 (Vav)

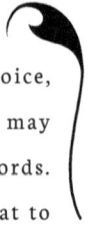

My Beloved, I have given you the ability to speak, so lift up your voice, and speak My Words to others. Do not be ashamed of My Words. You may be concerned that you will make other people angry if they hear My words. You will know when to speak and when not to speak. You will know what to say and how to say it, if you are obedient to Me. You will know that I love you so much, so share this love with others. You will see that sharing with others will give you a feeling of contentment and accomplishment. You will feel that you are being used by Me-that you are My Hands and Feet. You will feel My Presence flow through you as you speak to others and bring them the good news of salvation. You will tell them the Truth and set them free. You will know that I have given you a great treasure-a free gift-and you will want to share it with others, so they too can be relieved from the heavy burden of sin. You will be able to share life with others. You will know that you are completing your purpose in this life to share the Truth and love with others. Do not be concerned if some reject your words. You have planted seeds of righteousness within them, and at some time the seeds will take root and blossom and bloom. It will be in a time when My Spirit covers them and waters the seeds, and they are able to produce fruit. In the last days My Spirit will sweep over My Children, and they will see and their eyes will be opened. No more will they be lost in deception, but they will walk in the Truth and be guided by My Light.

Strength And Encouragement

Psalms 119:49-56 (Zayin)

My Beloved, turn to My Words and they will bring you comfort. My Words will bring you life. There is no other source in the universe that brings you life. All other sources will bring you death. Only through Me will you have eternal life. I will give you long life upon this planet, so you can walk in Me and serve others. You will become strong and mighty and be able to overcome all things. You will have a strong faith, and become unbendable and be able to strengthen the others around you. You are My mighty ones yet you are clothed in flesh-concealed. No one knows what you will become except Me. It will be glorious, and you will amaze My messengers that assist Me. They yearn to know what you will become, yet it is hidden. You are concealed in flesh, yet you are growing stronger and stronger, and you will be able to stand firm during the darkest of days. I AM giving you My Sprit -My life's breath. I AM giving you Truth, so you can stand and not be shaken. You only have to call on My Name. The darkness hinders you, and you become weak if you look to the world for guidance or advice. If you look to Me in all things, you grow stronger every day, because you know who I AM-your only source-and you depend on Me and you draw from Me. Those who call on My Name all day long are being lead with My Spirit. When you are filled with My Spirit, the darkness is pushed away and your eyes are opened. You are precious to Me, and I want to give you much Truth. You must be able to trust Me and depend on Me in all things, and then you will prosper and grow and bring forth your deliverance from all evil. Do not give up, but rejoice that I love you so much.

Psalms 119:57-64 *(Het)*

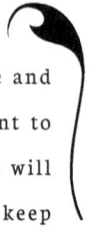

My Beloved, I will give you favor with Me and all men, if you seek Me and want to walk in My Commandments. You must love My Words and want to follow them. You cannot pick and choose what commandments that you will keep. I know you are in exile and there are none around you who want to keep My Commandments or laws. There are none who want to walk in the right ways. You are alone but not lacking, because I AM with you and will guide you. I understand that you need Me to help you, and My grace is poured out on you. I will keep you in all situations, so no one will harm you. If you walk in My ways and do what is right, then I will bless you and you will have favor in My sight. I will hear your prayers in the night as you awake and are troubled over that is happening in your life. You should not be afraid, but you must trust Me to provide for you and bless you and open My Hand to you and give freely to you. I will not close My Hand to you. I AM always blessing you, but you cannot see My blessings sometimes, because they are not what you wanted or expected. If you allow Me to open your eyes, then you will see My blessings. What is a blessing from My kingdom? Anything sent to you that pushes against you so you can grow and prosper is a blessing from Me. Every man has his burden to bear. Every man must be tested and found faithful. Every man must be found worthy to enter My Kingdom of Light. Do not despair, but rejoice that I love you so much to test you and find you faithful, so you can live with Me forever.

Strength And Encouragement

Psalms 119:65-72 (Tet)

My Beloved, it is good that I humble you. It is good that I bring you down low, so you can look up and see Me and all the good things that I have done for you. If you are never humbled, then you will trust in yourself to accomplish the goals in your life. If you are humbled and restored, then you know that I AM the One who restored you, and you will rejoice over your restoration. You will be able to see that I Am the only One that you should serve. Without Me there is nothing, and you will not accomplish anything. Wise is the man who sees this truth and follows My laws. Wise is the man who obeys Me and yearns to follow close to Me. This man will inherit great riches. If you have been brought down low and you are without help, be encouraged because it is the way of man that I must bring you down to lift you up. You must know that I have humbled all My servants. Look back at the lives of your forefathers. Look at Joseph and David. Look at how I put them through trials and tribulations. They feared for their lives. Look to the past to see how I AM doing good things inside of you just like I did for your ancestors. Each man will be found faithful to Me or he is not worthy to enter My kingdom. Rejoice that I love you so much to prove you and find you worthy to enter My Kingdom -to be called My Own.

Psalms 119:73-80 (Yud)

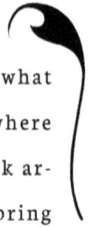

My Beloved, I made and formed you. I know your inner workings. I know what you need to find success in this life. I have searched you and found where you are lacking. I have looked deeply inside of you, and I know your weak areas. I know where you need to bend to Me. I focus on these areas, and I bring trials to change these areas. You must realize that I humble you, because I AM faithful to you. If I did not test you and try you, then I would not love you. I must find you faithful, so you can be counted worthy on the last day. You must show that you have overcome your tests, and you are My humble servant and will do as I asked you to do. You will be free to dance and sing on the day of My coming. You will have no shame when I return, because you have been an obedient servant. You will rejoice over your children, because I have also humbled and tested them also. I will show you that I will bring you only good even though you are brought down low. You may feel hopeless and forgotten some days, but your hope is always in Me. I will bring you understanding into what I AM doing inside of you, so you can see and rejoice over My faithfulness to you. Do not grieve over your loss, but rejoice that I love you so much. Whatever I have taken away from you, I will restore to you. If I have taken away your pride and brought you down low, then rejoice that you are no longer a prideful man but an obedient servant. You must know that I do all things to bring glory to your name. Rejoice that I love you so much.

Strength And Encouragement

Psalms 119:81-88 *(Kaf)*

My Beloved, my timing is perfect. You may be crying out to Me today for vengeance on your enemies that have persecuted you and taken from you. You may be crying out for Me to restore you and give back to you what has been taken. You may want Me to show My glory to you and give you understating into your situation. I will reveal Myself to you at the proper time. I will re-sort you in the proper time. I will bring you to a high place, and you will be able to see what I AM doing. You must wait patiently on Me. You must know that if you wait, I will come to you and bring you rest from all your labors and grief. You are weak in your testing, but I AM strong. I will not give you more than you can bear. Your ancestors were hunted down and killed. They hid themselves to stay alive. They were forced to barely eat to keep from being hunted to death. They were humbled and brought low. They were hunted like animals. They called out to Me, and I brought them to a safe place and hid them in My arms of love. I covered them in My arms. I kept My remnant alive to serve Me. I killed all those who did not want to serve Me, yet said they are My People. I killed those who would reject Me, and kept the strong ones for Myself. Now My People are stronger, and they have faith to wait on Me. Do not grow weary, because I will avenge you. I will destroy all your enemies be-fore your eyes. I will return you to the Promised Land, so you can walk in My Presence again. You are weak, but I AM strong, so lean on Me and I will help you. I will heal you and care for you. I AM all you need.

Psalms 119:89-96 (Lamed)

My Beloved, My Words are established in heaven and cannot be moved or change. My laws are eternal and forever. I AM and I AM. No one can change Me. I AM just and fair. I AM merciful and compassionate even to My Children who live in exile. I know My Children, and I watch over them to perform the promises in them. I promised to make you strong and mighty people and overcome all your enemies and bring you back to My Land, so you can live eternally with Me. You must know that My plan for you is to be at one with you, so you can be My Hands and Feet and Mouth. You will speak love and kindness to others and encourage them and build them up with your words. You must not tear them down, but love them and hold them and give them hope in a dark world. You must know who I AM to be able to be at one with Me. I established the universe and all that is in it. I know all My creatures, because I made them. I know their intricate workings. I know their weaknesses. I know where they will bend if tested. I will make you strong, so you will not bend, and you will be strong and mighty. You must believe in Me to help you along this road of life. Your journey here is short. Let it be filled with good things done for Me and My People. Lift up your eyes, and I will tell you what to do.

Strength And Encouragement

Psalms 119:97-104 (Mem)

My Beloved, what makes you wise? If you want to be wise, you must study My laws and keep them. You must obey My commandments. Meditate on My Words and you will find meaning to My words and you will know Me and feel My Presence. You will hear My Words and know My Voice. If you study My Words and search them as one who has lost a gem and must find it, you will find great treasure. You will find what you are looking for in this life-what you are yearning for-to connect with your Maker-your Creator-your Father who loves you and cares for you. True contentment is knowing Me. Only then will you be wise and defeat your enemies. You will rise up greater than the men around you, and you will speak words of wisdom to men, so they can see and know who I AM. You will deliver the wisdom to the men of the world but they will not be able to see clearly, because only My Children can hear My Voice and understand My Words. Otherwise it will be nonsense. It will have no value to them. Only My Children who love My Words and walk in My instruction can find true meaning to this life. Only those who call on My Name will be blessed in this life. Only then can they know Me and yearn to be at one with Me.

Psalms 119:105-112 (Nun)

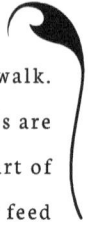

My Beloved, My Words will light your way and show you the way to walk. Meditate on My Words and find meaning in them for your life. My Words are life and when you read them they sink within your soul and become a part of you. You are nourished by My Words. They are like bread to you. They feed you and give you strength. You are held close to Me by My Words. You know what I have promised to you, and you stand firm on this promise. You know I will return you to My Land, and you will prosper as a nation once again. You hold on to this promise, and your eyes rest on it. You long for Me to take you home, and I will. Do not give up hope for the time is near. Your children will see the Land and walk in it and raise their children there. Your children will be able to walk in My Presence all the day on My Land. I will bring you back to My Land, if you walk in My ways and keep My commandments. You must give up all for Me, and not hold onto the things of the world. You must want to walk hand in hand with Me not desiring the evil things of the world. If you love the world, you cannot love Me. You must run from evil and only do what is good and pleasing in My sight. There are men who will pull on you to try to influence you to turn away from Me and My Words. I test you according to My Words. Do you keep My laws? Do you walk in My ways of love and kindness to others? Do you meditate on Me and want to develop a relationship with Me? My words test you like a fire. If you are strong, then My Words will ring sound within you. If you are wicked and want what you want, then My Words will have no value for you. You will read My Words, and they will not pierce your heart and convict you. Rejoice that I love you and test you, so you can be found faithful and worthy to enter My Kingdom of Light. Rejoice everyday in Me!

Strength And Encouragement

Psalms 119:113-120 (Samekh)

My Beloved, I AM your shield to protect you. I AM your hope, so you will not fade and lose sight of your purpose. I AM your hiding place, so you are covered from your enemies that hate you. I do not delight in double minded men who say they love Me but do not obey Me. There is no love in disobedient. You must love Me with your whole heart to be able to enter My Kingdom. You must be able to stand firm and not doubt Me, but trust in Me with your whole heart. You must delight in My words and want to obey them. You must find joy in obeying My laws and upholding My ways. You must fear Me knowing I will punish you, if you do not obey Me. To disobey Me is to reject Me, and you will be thrown from My Presence. On the last day there will be no mercy for you. You will be cast into the Lake of Fire and be totally destroyed. Your name will no longer be remembered. You will be lost and gone as if you never existed. You must arise and stand up and take control of your life, so you can find the path that I have chosen for you. You must give freely to those around you and love them and be kind to them. You must want to care for others, and not just want to please yourself. There are people I have put in your path that you must care for and bring comfort to. You should hold them close to you and love them, and I will bless you greatly.

Psalms 119:121-128 *(Ayin)*

My Beloved, I will give you understanding into My laws, so you can obey them. My Children in exile do not know My laws unless I reveal My laws to them. They have been fed nothing but lies from their ancestors on how to worship Me. They have been fed traditions from the pagans and told they are My ways. I AM opening the eyes of My People and showing them My laws and how to keep them. My Children in exile have many questions, but as they seek Me I will unveil how to walk in My ways. I want only those of My Children who really want to know Me to draw close to Me. These children will come back to My Land. This is My true bride chosen to wear My gems of marriage and will sit with Me at the marriage supper. The other of My Children who have not taken the time to know Me will go through many tests and trials and their suffering will be much like the Hebrews in Egypt under the slavery of the cruel taskmasters. They will be brought low and humbled. Their pride and arrogance will be taken away, and then they will cross over into My Kingdom of Light. There will be a great exodus of My People after their spiritual awakening. You will see how I open their eyes, and they will know who I AM. They will be taken through the fire and seek My face and know Me at last.

Strength And Encouragement

Psalms 119:129-136 (Peh)

My Beloved, My Words are a light to you. My Words will open a door for you, so you can see clearly into Me and My ways. I AM your guide and if you follow in My footsteps, then you will know the way to walk on your journey in this life. While on earth I loved the people around Me. I had compassion on them. I rebuked the wicked, and I held up the brokenhearted. I AM the Light to the world. You are My Child and you should do as your Father has done and give light to all around you, so they can see and do My will. You are a vessel poured out. You should give and give and not ask for anything in return. You should obey Me and not ask why. You should obey Me like a servant would obey and not question his master. You work for Me and I know what task is best for you to bring comfort and peace to others. You must search My Words, and I will bring you understanding. I will bring you peace as you walk in the midst of evil men and their ways. I know they grieve you and trouble you. I know they are hard to bear, but close your eyes to them and listen to My Voice. My Voice will override their presence, and you will be led to a safe place where they will bother you no longer. If you live where evil doers are everything and they keep all the pagan holidays and you are alone with few who know My Name and My ways, then rejoice for your rewards will be greater because I know how you must struggle and I will bring you extra help to hold you up and make you strong. You will be counted as righteous before Me.

Psalms 119:137-144 (Tzadeh)

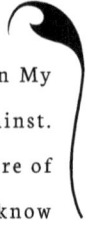

My Beloved, I AM righteous and My laws are just and fair. I have given My laws to My People, so they can have a standard to measure themselves against. I have given them My laws, so they can be upright and purified by My fire of conviction. I have given My People My laws, so they can know Me and know who I AM. I give them My laws, so they can see clearly the Way of righteousness before them. I will use My laws as a spring in which My People will have life flowing through them. From this spring flows a river of living water. There are many who forsake My laws, and say they are not for today. They are deceived and have been in exile far too long. Their eyes will be opened, and they will see or they will reject Me. They must make a choice which way they are heading. I have given My laws for eternity. I have not changed My laws or My rulings. I AM eternal, and I walk in Truth forever. I do not change. What I have given from the beginning will not change. I made a plan to save My People, and I knew that I would have to come and save them. I knew that they could not keep the covenant that I made with them. This covenant was made in the beginning and I adhere to this covenant. No man can come to Me except through this covenant-a covenant of blood. Come to Me with your sins, and I will cleanse you and help you see the ways of Truth. I will help you see the way before you. I will help you walk in contentment when you are walking in obedience to Me. You must not be afraid of My laws, but rejoice that you have them. You will not be off track when you can keep all My laws and know the way you should go. Rejoice that I love you so much to give you My laws to live by, so you will never go astray.

181

Strength And Encouragement

Psalms 119: 145-152 (Kuf)

My Beloved, call on My Name and I will hear your voice and answer you. I will hear you calling to Me. You say that you call to Me, but I do not answer. I do answer you at each call, but sometimes the answer does not come right away. Sometimes the answer must be delayed, so that it can come in My timing. It may not be your timing, but it is in the perfect time for you. All the answers to your prayers and pleas will come to you in a time when you can receive them and see them. You will know that you have been touched by Me. You will know Me, if you call on Me. I will draw you closer to Me, because you want to cling to Me. There is no contentment on earth, but to know Me and be filled with My Presence. There will be no one who can hold you up like I can. I can change the heart of a man in a second. I can give him hope when there was no hope. I can give him encouragement when he was hopeless. I know what one word can do to a man to change him. I know exactly what to say. My Spirit can bring healing to a man and make him strong enough to stand. Continue to call on My Name, and I will bring you hope and contentment. I will bring to you a place where you can run and hide, and I will be there for you. I will bring you peace and joy. You must behold My Presence. Come close so you can know Me.

Psalms 119:153-160 (Resh)

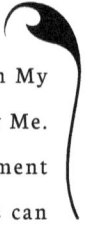

My Beloved, I see how you call on My Name and want to know Me. Open My words and read them. Meditate on them day and night and you will know Me. You will see how I move on the children of men. Watch how I pass judgment on the wicked. The wicked cannot come close to Me. Only the righteous can come close to Me and be saved from total destruction. You will be tested by My fire and you will be found faithful, if you have trusted in Me and been found worthy. You must walk in love and compassion for others. This is the way: you must live in love and have mercy on others. The measure you have mercy on others is the measure I will have mercy on you. I will take your measuring stick and put it up against you and measure you. You have developed the measure of your stick and how righteous you want to become. I will measure you beside it and find where you are lacking. Every man is a judge. He judges harshly or gently. If a man is at one with Me, then he will be merciful and love others in spite of their sins. You will tell them the Truth, and those who are lost will see clearly if they desire to follow Me. You cannot change a man's heart. Only I can change a man's heart. I will show the man the way to go. Rejoice and be glad that I love you so much to form you into My image.

Strength And Encouragement

Psalms 119:161-168 (Shin)

My Beloved, if you love My Words and desire to learn from them, then you will have peace. You will gain much Wisdom and be able to discern the wickedness around you. You will be able to see Truth and turn towards it. No one can deceive you, if you have My Words in your heart. You will not be able to sin and not know it. I know in exile that you do not have teachers that know all the Truth. I know that your teachers are lacking. They are tarnished by the ways of exile. They do not understand how to walk in My ways. If you allow My Spirit to guide you, then you will be blessed by My Presence. I will guide you. I will show you the Way to go. Do not listen to liars, and do not delight in telling lies. Remain in the Truth at all times. Rejoice in Truth and dwell in its safety. There is no one who can guide you but Me. Men of the world seek astrologers who look at the heavens for guidance. Others go to the dark ones to guide them. There is no one who can really guide you but Me. Others will guide you, but then they will bring you into deception and lies and turn you over to wickedness. They will bring you to destruction. You must look to Me and My ways, and I will open the doors for you and close the doors for you. You will see the way clearly and walk in it in boldness with honor, because you have trusted My Name and followed after My Voice.

Psalms119:169-176 *(Tav)*

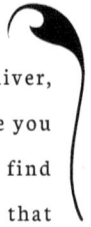

My Beloved, I AM your deliverance. I will stand firm and you will not waiver, if you cling to Me and study My Words. You must know My Words before you can know who I AM. If you study My words and seek Truth, then you will find Truth and great wisdom. No one man has all the Truth. No man can say that he understands all My Words. My Wisdom is deep and the more you search out My Words the more will be open to you. I only allow men who seek after Me to be filled with Truth. A casual observer will not find the hidden meanings in My Words. They will find surface meaning that is in plain sight, but not the hidden gems that are deep within My Words that only the diligent seeker can find. If you love My Words, you will cling to them and hold onto them. You will know My Promises for you and cling to them and know that I will bring them to pass. Many of My People in exile call to Me for deliverance. I have not forgotten you, My People. I will bring you out of Babylon. I will bring you out of exile and bring you back to your Land-the Land I have given you. Rejoice that I love you so much, and I know where all My Children are. My Hand is on each of My Children, and I AM teaching them My ways and helping them to be strong and mighty and unbendable, so they can go in and conquer the Land with their faith in Me. They will be like a fortress. They will stand together, and there is nothing that they cannot do. Watch and see what I do for My People. You are My own and I will bring you out with a mighty Hand. All the people of the world will take notice and be afraid of your exodus, and know that I AM moving among you and preparing you to take back the Land once again.

Strength And Encouragement

Psalms 120

My Beloved, I know you live in exile among those who lie and are deceitful. They like to cause dissension, and they have no peace. They do not know the King of Peace. They only know the dark one and his ways. They do not know how to walk in the Light. They will be long forgotten in the land of the dead. They will arise and be judged among the others who do not serve Me and will be no more. They will be thrown into the Lake of Fire along with Satan and all his servants. They will be consumed by the eternal fire. They will no longer be remembered. They will be long forgotten. Their names will have no honor among the land of the living. My Children will rejoice over their defeat. They will rejoice that at last they are free from the Evil One. No longer will the Evil One torment My Children. They will be freed from the bondage of their flesh and become a new creature. My heavenly servants long to see what My Children will become-what wonderful glorious creatures they will be transformed into as they are released from their flesh. My heavenly creatures know that My Children will emerge as glorious beings-too wonderful for them to imagine. You must believe that this life is only temporary and not grieve while you are here over your hardship, because all your trials and tribulations will test your faith and transform you into a perfect being filled with love and light and power and authority. You will rule over many in My Kingdom of Light. You will be heir to My Throne and speak in My Name and all will listen and obey.

Psalms 121

My Beloved, I AM your guardian. I AM your protector. I AM the One who will keep you from harm. No man can oppose Me. No man can harm you. I AM in control of all things. I AM the Creator. I AM Maker of heaven and earth and all creatures big and small. I can do all things. In My Hand is the universe. I hold all things in My Hand. I fill all things. I know all things. I AM all things. Your mind is limited, and you cannot understand the Creator's mind or the One who created you. You will understand more things once you are released from your flesh. You will understand My Kingdom and more of My Ways. Now you see impart, but soon you will see Me face to face. No man can see Me face to face, but soon you will be released from your flesh and your testing will be over. You will have proved yourself worthy to be called My Child. You will have proved that you are worthy to enter My Kingdom. There are no other creatures that are My first born. You are My own. I have called you by name. I know where My Children are and what they need at all times. I hear your voices call to Me, and I answer you. If you are in rebellion against Me, then I will deal with you until you turn to Me. Many will not hear My call, and they will continue in their rebellion. Many will not want to know Me, because they want to rejoice in their fleshly desires. My Children will desire to serve Me and will love to hear My Voice and follow in My ways. Look to Me, because I AM always before you. I love you so much.

Strength And Encouragement

Psalms 122

My Beloved, I set My Temple in Jerusalem and My People came to Me on every feast day and we celebrated together. I rejoiced in the midst of My People and blessed them abundantly. My People were envious of their neighbor's gods and their festivals. They began to worship foreign gods, and My anger rose up against them. I poured My curses on them and drove them out of My Land and My City. My People would not make a mockery of Me in My Land. They were driven all over the world, and now they live in exile. Very few of My Children live on My Land. Soon I will call them back to My Land, and they will once again serve Me in spirit and truth. They will not envy their neighbor's gods, but they will hate their gods-the gods of lies and deceit. They will see clearly their plan, and rise up against them. All their enemies will surround Jerusalem, but I will stand up and destroy them all in a moment. They will no longer torment My People. You must trust Me to deliver you from exile. The time is approaching for you to leave. The time is near. You must trust Me that no matter where you live, I will come get you and take you back to My Land. I will bring hunters to hunt you down and bring you back home. You are My beloved, and I want you close to Me on My Land close to My Face.

Psalms 123

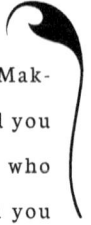

My Beloved, I reign from heaven. I AM. I AM Creator of all things. I AM Maker of the heavens and earth. I AM in control of all things. Look to Me and you will be cared for. Look to Me and you will be protected from all those who want to harm you. Look to Me and I will hold you in My Hand and tell you hidden things, so you will know who I AM and follow My Ways. If you listen to man, you will fall. If you listen to man, you will turn down the wrong path and suffer loss. If you listen to man, you will be misled and deceived. You will never know who I AM and what I can do for you. You will never understand My ways and how I control all things. Man limits Me and wants everyone to think that I AM vague and far away-not close to My children. Man does not understand that you are My beloved and I hold you close, because I love you so much. Man does not understand that I want to be intimate with you like a man wants to be intimate with his wife. I want us to be as one-united together in harmony. I want you to look to Me for direction and answers and guidance. I want you to come to Me, and we will commune together as one and reason together. You will want My will for you, just like a servant comes to his master and finds out what his master wants him to do-what duties he wants him to do for the day. Come to Me daily and let us talk, so you can be led daily by Me. I will walk with you and you will be blessed daily.

Strength And Encouragement

Psalms 124

My Beloved, I AM for you, and I will keep you safe in all situations-no matter what happens. My helpers are all around you, and they will bring you help when you need them. I have assigned them to you to oversee you and guide you and keep you from harm. You should only praise Me and worship Me, and I will provide all you need. I will provide for you, and you will know that I have provided for you. I AM not against you. My face was set against your ancestors, because they worshipped other idols and turned their face from Me. They wanted to do what the pagans do. Even today there are many that want to do as the pagans do and worship when the pagans worship and keep their celebrations not even knowing that they enter a covenant with them to keep their feasts days instead of Mine. Many are blinded and cannot see, but My Children who call on My Name will see and know and understand My Ways and how to walk in My Midst. You will be talking with Me as you go along your way, and you will be kept safe from all troubles. Troubles may come to you, but I will provide a way out. I will show you a sign that I AM with you. I will show you My fingerprints are there as you travel along on this journey. You are a temporary resident here, and soon you will leave this place. You will dwell with Me permanently in My Kingdom. You will know Me intimately and we will be as one.

Psalms 125

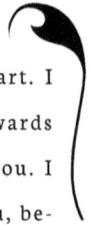

My Beloved, I AM always close. I see all that you do. I know your heart. I know what you need. I know how to humble you and make you bend towards Me, so you can hear My Voice and obey. I know you, because I made you. I made each of My Children. I know you and hear your cries. I answer you, because you call on My Name. I know your voice and hear you even when you are in sin. I bring you to repentance by crushing you and molding you into My Image, so you can be strong and mighty and overcome all temptations. I stand before you and judge you and find you worthy to enter My Kingdom. I balance the scales while you are here on earth, so you have been weighed and measured and not found lacking. You will hold up My Word and stand on it, and know that I AM faithful to do all I say that I will do. I stand before you holding Truth. You can count on Me, so do not fall or bend. Be unbendable and strong and courageous. You are My Child, so act like your Father who created you. I do not bend. I always stand firm on My Words, and I want you to do the same. There are many men in this world, but My People who love Me are few, and I care for them tenderly. I watch over you affectionately. I know all you do and say and correct you to form you. My Hand of discipline is on you. My rod of correction is on you even in exile. I will find you and correct you and bring you into My Land, and you will serve Me forever. You will praise My Name and rejoice, and be glad that I love you so much.

Strength And Encouragement

Psalms 126

My Beloved, come back to My Land. Come, My People, back to the place that your fathers loved the most. Come back, My Children, to My arms of love. I will prepare a place for you here. I will restore your fortunes. I will give you a fertile land to plant your seed. You will have abundant food. You will have water that is clean and restored. You will have a land filled with the people who love Me. You will rejoice at all My blessings. The surrounding nations will stand in awe at what I do for you. I will wipe out all your enemies. You will live in peace with your surrounding neighbors. You will stand upright in all your ways. You will worship only Me and follow all My laws. You will count My laws are sacred. You will not bend or waiver, but you will be righteous in all your ways. You will know who I AM. You will know My ways. You will trust Me with all your heart. I will not be visible, but you will feel My Presence on you to guide you and instruct you. There will be those who hate you still. They will be filed with darkness. All those who love Me will come back to My Land, or they will stand firm where they live and be killed for My Name's sake. You will choose. You will make the choice. Will you came to My Land and rejoice, or will you stay where you are and die in My Name? Consider these things. I have warned you in advance.

Psalms 127

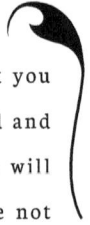

My Beloved, you work in vain unless you work for Me and do as I ask you to do. If I have told you to take a certain job and you have not listened and rejected My Will for you, then whatever job you have, in that job you will not prosper. If I have asked you to move to another city and you have not listened, then you will not be protected in that city when it falls. You will suffer loss. You must listen to My Voice and move when I say move and take a job that I say to take. You must know that I love you and only want the best for you. Listen to Me, so I can guide you. Children are a blessing from Me. The more children you have, the greater your reward. If you have no children and you cry to Me for a blessing, I will give you a blessing if you are worthy of a blessing. Children must be cared for unselfishly. You must give of yourself to take care of your children. They are part of you. They are your seed. They must be cared for tenderly. You must teach them My ways and show them how to love others. If you do, then you will be blessed and all will go well for you. You must be at one with Me to know how to guide your children. Open your eyes and ears and listen and hear, so I can show you the direction to take. I will give you Wisdom how to raise your children, and you will rejoice in it.

Strength And Encouragement

Psalms 128

My Beloved, you will be happy if you love Me and fear Me and walk in My ways following My laws. You will be happy, because I will bless you and keep you close to Me. I will tell you secret things and unveil My scriptures to you. I will open your eyes and you will know Me-who I AM. You will be filled with peace and joy, because you know that I love you and will always care for you. You will never be afraid even in the darkest of times. You will be blessed with a wife and children. You will see your children around your Sabbath table anointed by Me and speaking words of praise for Me. You will be glad that you have been so blessed by Me. You will come to Jerusalem dancing and singing and rejoicing knowing that I have turned My Face towards you at last, and the sins of your ancestors have been paid in full. You will know that I have protected you in exile, and I will protect you and keep you safe while in My Land. You will not ever be afraid when those that hate you come against you, because you know that I will keep you in My Arms. I will keep you safe. You will be firmly planted in My soil and know My Voice. You will not bend, but you will be strong and mighty. You will be filled with My Spirit and move with Me as the one who blows with the wind and moves as the wind blows bending to My will at each turn. You will be humble before Me and never be rebellious, but always be submissive to Me. You are a loyal servant humble in all your ways. I am greatly pleased with your obedience.

Psalms 129

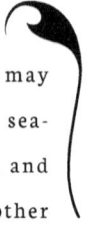

My Beloved, men may attack you, but they will never overcome you. Men may mock you, but they will be silenced. Men may take away from you for a season, but it will not be forever. Men may want to rob your soul from you and make you serve another god, but men can never make you believe in another god. The confession of your mouth cannot be taken from you. Even if they cut out your tongue, your heart would still proclaim My Name. No man can harm you. No man can come close to you unless I allow it. I will not bring upon you a fiery trial that you cannot endure and overcome. You must know that I AM faithful to help you through each test, and you will be found worthy to enter My Kingdom. If you fall, then I will pick you up and carry you until you are strong enough to walk and carry yourself. Even then, I AM at your side directing your path. You are never alone. You are not far away from Me. My servants who love Me always call on My Name to help them. My servants always are at My side, and I cherish them and love them tenderly. You do not ever have to be afraid, because I AM your help in times of trouble. You are My chosen one and I chose you, because I knew you would be strong and faithful and always overcome the Evil One. Rest in Me today, and know that My Strength is your strength. Stand tall and bold. I AM with you.

Strength And Encouragement

Psalms 130

My Beloved, I AM your redemption. I AM your hope. I AM the only One who can forgive you from your sins. I will forgive you, if you turn to Me and not reject Me. If you continue to commit the same sin over and over, then you will not be counted worthy to enter My Kingdom. If you sin and repent and turn from your sins, then I will forgive you and redeem you. I will count you worthy of entering into My Kingdom. Only a man whose heart is pure can enter My Kingdom. You have to believe and trust in Me with all your heart and know that I will care for you and protect you and deliver you from all your enemies. Even though you hear bad news around you, do not be shaken but believe in Me that I will protect you and keep you safe. Men say that they will do many things, but they will do only the things I allow them to do. I control all things. I can put up barriers, and I can open doors. I can halt, and I can push man in the direction I desire for him to go. I have control of a man's heart. I can harden his heart, and I can soften his heart, so My timing is perfect. I count the days and measure the time. Man must pay for his full measure of sins to the day and hour. Man must pay back for all the wicked he has done, but My Children will be released from the weight of sin by coming to Me and repenting and clinging to Me always and forever. This is the purpose of My Children: to honor Me and love Me and worship Me and be prepared to enter My Kingdom of Light and remain with Me forever.

Psalms 131

My Beloved, do not be proud before Me wanting more than what I want you to have. Be content with what I have given you. Be satisfied with the gifts that I have brought to you. You did not have to go search for them or be carried away on a long journey to seek them. I have brought them to your door, and you have been given them freely by My Hand. You must be calm and quiet inside not yearning for the things of the world. If you are lacking, then ask Me and I will bring it to you. If you are without, then I will supply what you need. If you desire things that you should not have, then you will not receive them. I AM your Father. I know what My Child needs and what is best for him. You will not receive what you cry for, even though you cry for it for many days, if I see that it is detrimental to you. I give you only the best. You should pray to Me that I will keep you humble before Me, so no judgment will fall on you and you will not suffer loss. Then you will see that you will be blessed greatly. Do not fear, because I will provide for you. You may not have it today, but when you need it then you will have it. Prepare to make a journey, because you will be leaving exile soon. Pack up all your belongings, and I will guide you. Be careful not to take more than what you need. Give away all the rest. You should get ready to return to My Land- the Land I gave your ancestors. You must get ready to return to the place I have chosen for you. No longer will My Face be against you. No longer will you have to be sad in exile. Now you can rejoice in My Land with My People forever.

Strength And Encouragement

Psalms 132

My Beloved, David was My servant and he served Me well. He was not a perfect man because he lived in the flesh, but he was a righteous man because he loved Me and wanted to do what was right in My Sight. He was chosen from his brothers to reign over My People. He was wise and strong and he loved My Words. He wanted My People to know Me and walk in My Ways. He wanted to build Me a house, so I could have a beautiful dwelling place. He had a vision to make it the most beautiful place in the world. He wanted to honor Me-My Presence. He wanted My People to bring glory and honor to My Name. He wanted to have great celebrations and rejoice and have the entire world know that I AM the only Elohim. He was a man who cried out to Me for help day and night. I consoled him many times in his troubles. He was anointed by Me to serve My People, because he could teach them how to call on My Name and walk in My ways. David instructed the priests to teach My People My ways. He made sure the priests were righteous. As long as David reigned My People had an example of righteousness before them. David knew that his source of strength was in Me. As long as you know that you must depend on Me for your source of help, then all will go well with you. As long as you cling to Me and trust Me to help you in times of trouble, then you will have all you need. I will make sure that you are never lacking. It may appear that you are going to be without, but it will never happen. As long as you listen to My Voice and obey Me, I will guide you and show you a way out. My righteous will never beg for bread. I AM faithful to take care of My Children.

Psalms 133

My Beloved, I stand in the midst of you. Stand firm, and rejoice that I love you so much. Stand firm, and love those around you. Walk in harmony with your brothers who love Me and want to serve Me. You cannot remain in harmony with the men of the world. They will mock you and turn against you. They will see your light of righteousness and they will close their eyes to you and want to push you far away from them so they cannot see their sin. They are wicked men who are seeking their own pleasures, and do not want to serve Me-an Elohim of Spirit that wants you to sacrifice your flesh daily and walk in a higher level of righteousness not a fleshy level. You are My beloved, and I long to become close to you and hold you close. You must sacrifice your flesh, so you can come close to Me. I AM a consuming fire and the closer you draw to Me I will consume your flesh until you are dead to flesh and walk only in My Spirit. You will no longer desire the things of the world, but you will long only for the things of the spirit. You will long for Me, and all I can give you. You have only begun your journey with Me. This life is just a testing ground and I will prove you faithful and worthy of entering My Kingdom of Light. I will draw you closer to the mark, and you will delight in it. You will want to see clearly, and want to be righteous, and want to turn away from the world and all those who love the world. Think on these things and rejoice that I love you so much.

Strength And Encouragement

Psalms 134

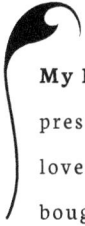

My Beloved, come bless Me all you servants of the Most High who dwell in My presence all the day. Come praise Me all you servants of the Most High who love Me and are obedient to Me. Come praise Me all of My Children who were bought with a price and covered with My Blood and sealed into redemption. Come bless Me all My Children who have turned from wickedness and serve only Me. You have defiled the gods of your ancestors of your fathers of the peoples before you, and now serve Me in spirit and truth. You do not follow the laws of tradition, but you have searched for Truth and found Me and My ways and proved through My Words that you want to serve only Me. You are a wonder to many, and you are a mockery to many. Neither of these things bothers you, because you are standing on a Rock and you will not be moved. You will not falter. You will stand even in the darkest of days. You will not be shaken when all others around you are in terror. You know Me and who I AM. You know that you are in My Hands. You know that I will protect you and cover you over. You know that many men seek wealth to cover them in the last days. They create hiding places from the wrath of My Hand. I will destroy them and overtake them and no one can stop Me, but My Children will be covered by My Hand and no one can harm them. The earth may rock and quake, but you will be safe and secure. You are My treasure and I guard over you like a strong man hired to protect a great treasure. No one will come near it or the strong man will slash him with his sword. I will destroy anyone that tries to come near you, because I love you so much.

Psalms 135:1-12

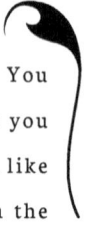

My Beloved, praise Me for I AM good! I give generously to My People. You are My unique treasure. You are the one I love and adore. I guard over you tenderly and care for you. No man can come near you. I will protect you like the pupil of your eye is protected by your eyelid. You will be secure in the land that I place you in until I take you to My Land and secure you there. You will know that I AM with you, because you will see the signs fall into place all around you. My People of old saw the signs of My faithfulness. They saw how I parted the Red Sea and how I drowned the Egyptians. They saw how I took them to My Mountain and made them My beloved one. They saw Me speak to them My Words-My laws-My rulings. They saw Me consume the mountain and the earth quaked. They saw Me descend on the earth and the earth could not hold Me, but quivered before Me. I AM almighty and yet I came to talk to My Children, My beloved. I came to be at one with you. Anyone who loves Me and wants to walk close to Me can draw close, and I will extend My Arm to them and they will be able to hear My Voice and know Me. Only My chosen ones can draw close to Me. Their hearts are pure-refined by fire. They have searched for Me with all their hearts, and they are tested by fire and been found worthy. My anointing is on you, and you will arise with Me and be in My Kingdom of Light. You will be safe in My Presence. The earth will be burned away, but you will not be consumed. You will watch as I create a new heaven and earth, and rejoice in My creation. You will know that I AM the Creator and praise Me for My wondrous works.

Strength And Encouragement

Psalms 135:13-21

My Beloved, My Name continues forever and the names of other gods are lost and destroyed and cease to be remembered. Many are the gods of men, and many are the pagan holidays of men, but only My feast days will remain forever. You will rejoice at My feast table forever, and remain at one with Me eternally. You will dance and sing and rejoice and teach your children to dance and sing and rejoice at My feast days. You will want to feast with Me daily in your prayers and praise. You will bring your morning and evening sacrifice of praise to Me. You will want to come to Me and love Me and let Me hold you. You will want to begin your day with My presence and walk in My presence all day and end your day with celebrating My wondrous works. You will praise Me daily and lift up My name. The people of the world trust in their gods, and they become like their gods- dumb, deaf, and blind. They cannot see or hear Me. They are blinded to My presence and the works of My Hands all around them. They do not see and know Me. They only know the things of the world and they rejoice in them, but only for a season. They only turn from the things of the world when they want to find Me. You cannot find Me in wealth or fame or power or authority. You can only find Me in humility and becoming a servant to Me. You can only find Me when you open your eyes to My words and abide in them. Come close to Me, My beloved, and we will be as one.

Psalms 136

My Beloved, My grace continues forever! I watch over My Children and care for them tenderly. I guard over you and take you out of perilous situations. Didn't I delver your ancestors from the powerful Egyptians? They were the most powerful nation on earth, and I destroyed them with My Right Hand. They had oppressed My People, so I delivered My Judgment on them and destroyed them. I destroyed the whole Egyptian army in the water. I drowned them all, and they never saw another battle. The nations around them rejoiced. They were no longer under their oppression. I delivered a multitude of slaves from surrounding nations along with My People. I set the captives free. I helped My People escape into the desert and fed them and kept them safe until they reached My Land. I drove out all the peoples in My Land and brought My People safely there to inhabit their new Land. My grace is sufficient for My People and for all who come to Me and believe in Me. If you know Me, you know that I can do all things. I created the earth and prepared it for you, My People. I knew what you would need at all times. Now men have destroyed My once perfect earth. Now the earth moans under the oppression of man. Now the earth quakes under the oppression of man and yearns for My coming, so I can restore earth and set her free from the oppression of man. Soon, My beloved ones, you will enter My Land again. I will call you home and you will come singing and dancing. Rejoice that the days will come soon when you will be at home at last.

Strength And Encouragement

Psalms 137

My Beloved, My People went to Babylon as slaves, because they rebelled against Me. They worshipped other gods and turned away from the One who made them. They saw the gods that the nations around them worshipped, and they wanted to worship the way they did with their orgies and pagan practices. They wanted to do evil, so they were punished for their evil and sent into captivity. They were humbled. When they went to Babylon they cried and wept to Me and could not sing the songs they sang in Jerusalem. They longed to go back home. I had mercy on My People, and the ones who really wanted to return to Jerusalem came singing and dancing, but some of My People remained in Babylon and continued to worship their gods and follow in their ways. I punished Babylon for taking My People captive and treating them so harshly, and those of My People who did not return to Jerusalem were also punished and killed for not returning to Me and My ways. You must remember what happened to your ancestors. You must remember that if you do not return to My Land and come back to Me, that you will also suffer loss just like your ancestors did. If you are content to stay in exile and not come back to Me, then you will suffer the coming judgment on the land where you live. I give you fair warning. Make your choice. I am waiting with open arms for you to return to Me.

Psalms 138

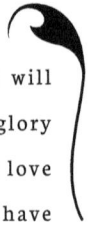

My Beloved, I will not abandon you. You are the work of My Hands. I will draw you close to Me and perfect you. I will change you from glory to glory as you draw nearer to Me. You will see Me and know who I AM. You will love Me with all your heart. You will see My good works and recognize that I have given freely to you. You will see My fingerprints all around you. I will hear your cries and answer you. I will come close to you, so I can hear you call Me. You are My beloved, and I want to know what you are doing all the time. You are My precious child, and I care for you tenderly. There is a strong wave of My spirit passing over My Children to open their eyes to the things of Me. You will read My words, and the Truth will open up to you. You will see clearly, and you will want to see clearly. You will yearn for Me. You will want to know the Truth. You will be able to discern between truth and deception. You will know what is from Me, and what is not from Me. You will have keen discernment. You will be at one with My spirit. Come to Me and let Me hear your voice for I long to commune with you. We will work out your problems together. We will share your troubles and deliver you from all of them. I love you and want you to be successful in this life, so you can be a testimony to others. Be strong and brave, because I AM coming soon. I will call you home, and you will come to My Land and be fed from My Hand.

Strength And Encouragement

Psalms 139:1-6

My Beloved, I have tested you and I know what you are made of. I have tested you, so those around you can see that you are worthy of entering My Kingdom of Light. I have refined you, and I continue to refine you daily. I look into you daily and see what you are doing. How are you drawing closer to Me? How are you fighting your flesh and turning closer to Me? How are you loving others and being My Hands and Feet on this earth? I look at your heart. Do you want to be selfish and think only of yourself? Do you love others and want to help them no matter if it takes away from what you want to do? You are My beloved, and I expect you to be righteous in My eyes-not in the eyes of men. What do men know? I want you to be righteous in My eyes, and do what I have told you to do. I AM the only One you should serve. There are many voices, My beloved, but do not listen to any of them. They will tell you that destruction is coming. They will tell you that they will take you over and make you their slaves. Do not listen to their ramblings. They are empty promises unless I use these men to fulfill My purpose for you. All men have a purpose. Your purpose is to serve Me and love Me and obey Me and do My will for you. When you do this, then you will be content and peaceful and happy in My presence. You will have joy all the time. If you do not have joy, then you do not know Me. I give you what you need every day. If you grumble and complain, then you do not realize that what I send to you is what is best for you. Arise, sing, and shout! I AM so good to you.

Psalms 139:7-18

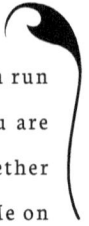

My Beloved, who can escape My spirit? Who can escape My eyes? Who can run from Me and escape My judgment? No man is like Me. You are dirt. You are created by My Hand. I formed you in your mother's form. I wove you together by My breath. I carved you from your ancestors-your ancestors who saw Me on Mount Sinai and heard My Words pierce their hearts and adhere to their being. These are the ones who you resemble. They saw My miracles and they had faith in Me to enter the desert and follow Me. You followed Me not seeing Me, but knowing Me. You are My beloved ones. You were formed to please Me. You are the ones that I have chosen. You are the ones who will enter My Kingdom of Light. You were formed with a purpose in mind. I saw you before you were ever robed in flesh. I knew you before you ever came to earth. You were held in My arms of love. I breathed into you My breath of life. You held Me and did not want to depart, but I pushed you into a fleshy body and you adhered to it and had peace. You have struggled with your flesh ever since, but I help you become strong and mighty and overcome the battles of the flesh. In the end you will be an overcomer in My Presence. I have written all these things in your book, because I saw them before you were ever born. I knew what you would become. I knew that you will love Me and worship Me and not defile yourself. I knew that you would be found worthy. I love you deeply, and I will never leave you. You are My beloved.

Strength And Encouragement

Psalms 139:19-24

My Beloved, I will try and test you and see what you are made of. I will show all those who look on that you are worthy to enter My Kingdom of Light. I will amaze you in what I do for you. The wicked are all around you, but they cannot touch you. They cannot harm you in any way. They may mock you and say things against you, but they have no control over you. I AM the One who keeps you safe and cares for you, so you are always in good health. You may run into germs that your body must fight off, but I have made your body to fight off all sicknesses. If you pollute your body with unclean food, then your body will be weak and cannot fight off the germs as you run into them. You will see that you are strong and mighty, if you cling to Me and love only Me and not yourself. If you see the wicked, then do not long for what they have, but long only for Me and My ways. You must be strong enough to overcome your flesh and sacrifice your flesh, so you can be at one with Me. The flesh and the spirit are enemies. You will serve one or the other. If you love Me, you will serve Me, but if you serve your flesh, then you do not serve Me. Do not be selfish, but be loving and kind to others. Rejoice that I love you so much, and love others in the way that I love you. I will reward you greatly for your love towards others. I will make the wicked flee from you. They will turn and run in horror. They cannot stand in My presence. They cannot stand before Me. On the Day of Judgment; they will be consumed by My breath and cast into the Lake of Fire. They will be no more, and we will reign together as one forever.

Psalms 140

My Beloved, My Hands are on the wicked. My Hands are on the violent. My Hands are on those who are disobedient. My Hands are on those who rebel against Me. I will not allow the wicked to touch you. They may try to lay traps for you, but I will show you all their traps. I go before you and behind you and surround you with My Presence. You do not have to be afraid. You only have to listen to My voice and be led by My spirit. Do not make any hasty decisions. Talk with Me about what you want to do, and I will guide you down the right path. Do not spend money without consulting Me first. Do not go to market without My guidance. I will help you use your money wisely, so you can have enough and have extra for those around you who may need help. You want to give generously to your children, but you must display a righteous example of how to live before them. If you will walk uprightly before them, then you will have children who walk in righteousness. You will have children who are a blessing to you. The wicked do not have children who are a blessing to them. They suffer because of the acts of their children and their own acts. If a wicked person mocks you and treats you unfairly, then I will bring My justice on them and they will pay for all they do to you. They will have to give back and make restitution to you. If you move away from the wicked person as I tell you to do, then I will bring back what the person has taken from you in other ways and through other people. I will balance the scales and what is yours will be given back to you or to your children, so you can rejoice in My justice coming to you at last.

Strength And Encouragement

Psalms 141

My Beloved, when I correct you it is an act of love. I want to help you to walk uprightly, so you can draw near to Me and be blessed by My Presence. If a righteous man gives you advice, then listen to him. If a righteous man rebukes you, then listen to him. He should only have to rebuke you once, so you can repent and walk in the right way. If you listen to good advice, then you will grow wise and strong. You will be able to cross large mountains and not grow weary. You will be strong to withstand any test that comes your way. You will be unbending and not able to fall into the traps placed for you along the way. You must always be listing to My Voice, and I will direct your path. I will hear your pleas for help, and I will help you. I will have mercy on you. I will help you guard your tongue, so you will hold it and not speak. You will think about your words before you say them, and even though you are tempted you will not want to hurt or harm others with your words. You will want to have a strong presence of righteousness around you. You will carefully guard over your mouth and not say mean and evil things about others. Draw close to Me, and I will give you a lock for your mouth and a bridle, so you are led only by Me and no one can harm you or mislead you, because you walk in the path of righteousness.

Psalms 142

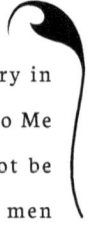

My Beloved, I have brought you low, so you could see My Ways and glory in them. I have brought you low and humbled you, so you can be obedient to Me and obey My laws. I have brought you low, so you can know Me and not be arrogant or proud. I have brought you low, so you can see the ways of evil men have no value. Only I can bring value to your life. I will not bring you low forever. I will lift you up, and draw you closer to Me. Through your tears you have found Me, and I will bring you comfort. Through your tears you have humbled yourself and found Me, and know who I AM. You are not one to turn aside from Me. You are one who searches after Me and wants to find Me. I will never escape from you. I will always be at your side. You will know who I AM, and know that I AM mighty. The wicked will falter and not know Me. They will not find the Truth. They will walk in deception. They will find a high place and it will crumble. They will find wealth and it will dissolve. They will find power, but I will strip it from them. Whatever they take from you, I will give back to you 10 times. They do not know who you are. They do not know that you are My beloved, and I will pay back vengeance to those who try to do you harm. There are many who want to harm you, but none can touch you. I keep you safe in My wings. You are a blessing to Me. I smile on you with delight. You are the one I adore. I long for the day to bring you home to Me, then we will dance and sing and be happy together.

Strength And Encouragement

Psalms 143

My Beloved, I will come to you in the morning as you present your offering of praise. I will lift you up and make Myself real to you. I will cover you during the day, and you will be filled with joy. No matter what you must face in the day, I will keep you in My perfect peace, because you do no wrong. I will redeem you from those who lie and steal. I will redeem you from all those who want to harm you. There are many who hate you, but I will love you eternally. Do not be deceived by the enemy. I will always give you an answer, so you can know My Truth. There are many who will be deceived, but My Chosen Ones will not be deceived. You will know Me and be filled with My Spirit. If you do not receive Me, then you will be like the others and be destroyed in the Lake of Fire. You will not know My eternal presence, but only for a few seconds will you know Me. Do not be discouraged, because I will keep you in My loving Hands. No one can touch you. The evil ones will try to take you from Me. They will bring temptations along your path, but you will turn your eyes away quickly and not indulge in their traps. Many will love their traps, but My Children will despise their wickedness. Rejoice and be glad that you can see clearly. Rejoice that I love you so much to expose the evil around you. Be kind to others, so they can see the good works within you.

Psalms 144:1-4

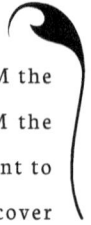

My Beloved, I AM your rock. I AM your shelter. I AM your fortress. I AM the One who loves you and cares for you and keeps you from all evil. I AM the only One who would look after you. All others want to kill you. They want to destroy you. They are your enemies. I want to have mercy on you and cover you with My Hands. You are only a breath. You are only dirt. You are nothing of value to anyone, but Me. I created you and formed you and made you My Own. I made you at one with Me. I followed you and guided you and covered you. You are My treasure. You are the one I long for. You are My beloved. There is none like you. There are no other ones that I long for. You are My only beloved. The days come and go and still my mind does not change. You are My beloved and I long only for you. There may be some who try to steal from you, but I will not allow them to touch you. You are in the midst of Me and I surround you. You may not feel My Presence, but you trust in Me and know I AM always with you. I will direct your path. You may feel like you have no one to care for you at times and your troubles are many. Let me take care of them and they will all slip away, and you will be free of them. Do not worry about tomorrow, but trust Me for today, and I will give you whatever you need.

Strength And Encouragement

Psalms 144:5-15

My Beloved, sing to Me a song. Praise Me in the midst of My Spirit. Open up your heart and love Me, and do not allow any falsehood or lies to be within you. Do not allow any root of bitterness within you. Do not allow any mean or evil word to escape your lips. Be pure of heart and love those around you. You will see that My Presence will follow you wherever you go. I will bless your hands and feet. I will guide you and protect you. I will show you the way and open the doors for you. I will open your eyes and allow you to see things that you have not seen before. My spirit will anoint you and uphold you and deliver you from all things that may try to come upon you. I deliver you daily from all sorts of evils, but you do not even know it. I keep you from the hand of those who try to harm you. I will lift you up above the rest of those around you, and you will be able to know Me and My ways. You tell others about Me, and they do not understand. You try to tell them about My words and the meaning of My words, but they do not understand and look at you with blankness. They look at you like you are the one who lacks understanding. You may be hated and mocked, but light continues to fill you and cover you and no one can harm you. Trust in Me. I will show you the way to keep away from all those who would like to harm you. The harm they wanted to come on you will come on them.

Psalms 145:1-7

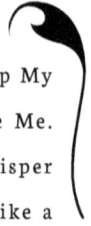

My Beloved, I AM a great Elohim. Praise Me with all your heart. Lift up My Name and worship Me. Bow down before Me. Prostrate yourself before Me. Humble yourself before Me. Call on My Name and praise Me and whisper sweet praises to Me-love words that lift up My Name and glorify Me- like a husband gives love words to his wife-intimate and pure. You are My beloved. You are the one that I love. I want to hear your voice in the stillness of the day or night. I want to hear you talk to Me, and we will be as one. Do not think that you can hear My voice in the midst of noise and distractions. You must come to a quiet place and find Me. You must come to a quiet place and draw close to Me-like a lover seeks a secret place to show his affections. Do not give up in this life when the way becomes hard and difficult to travel. Call on My Name, and I will guide you and lead you and carry you when the way is difficult. There will be times when you lose loved ones to death or when you suffer disappointments. Call on Me and I will comfort you. You will have to make transitions in this life, but I will help you adjust to a new way of life. I will call every man to a new way of living. You must want to turn towards Me and love Me with all your heart.

Psalms 145:8-14

My Beloved, I AM merciful and compassionate to all. I AM slow to anger. I wait until the scales are tilted in favor of evil before I judge. I wait and give man a time to repent, and when he refuses to repent year after year, then I judge him fairly. I AM patient to wait for men to have a second chance to serve Me. Allow Me to put My Hand on you and guide you. Do not be rebellious, but be sensitive to My Spirit so I can guide you. There is no one like Me who is so merciful and compassionate. I know love, because I AM the pure source of love. I know compassion, because I AM compassionate to all creatures no matter if they are man or beasts. I care for all the animals. I repair their broken wings and bones. I feed them and help them migrate to a good nesting place. I show them were food is located. I let them know that I can help them, so they know who their Creator is. I do the same with men. I show them who I AM and what I want for them. Men can come to Me at any time no matter the season. I will give to him freely, if He walks in My ways. You must guard over yourself and keep yourself pure. You must know that I will redeem you in the last day. I will keep you from the Lake of Fire, if you call on My Name and trust Me with all your heart. You will be tested here on earth with My fire. Each man must endure his own fires and be successful here on earth and prove that he is worthy to enter My Kingdom of Light.

Psalms 145:15-21

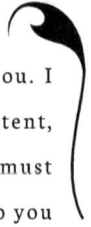

My Beloved, My eyes are on you. My wings cover you. My arms hold you. I keep you safe and content in all you do. If you are not feeling safe or content, then look at yourself and know that you need to draw near to Me. You must trust Me with all your heart. Whatever is dark in your heart, remove it so you can be happy and content all day long. If you are worried and fearful, then you must repent of your sins and love Me and trust Me in all that you do and say. If you are feeling abandoned by Me, I will never abandon you. I will keep you close to Me, if you talk about your problems to Me and allow Me to give you advice and help. I will show you the way to go. I will bless you with My Presence. Many men never know how much happiness they can find in Me. Many men never know how perfectly content you can be in Me. Open your eyes and see My greatness. Enemies may arise all around you. You are a few compared to many. Walk away from them, and I will keep you in a shelter. When you see Jerusalem surrounded by armies, rejoice because your salvation is at Hand. You will be lifted and kept safe while you watch Me destroy all your enemies around you. Do not be fearful but trust Me. I will provide for My People, and I will keep all of My People safe. You are My beloved. I AM always beside you and caressing you and calling you My own.

Strength And Encouragement

Psalms 146

My Beloved, trust in Me and not in man. Trust in Me and not in what man can do for you. I can move mountains for you. I can push back the seas for you. I can open the earth for you. I AM the Creator. I made heaven and earth. I made all things. I AM the only One you should serve. You are My beloved and I want you in My arms. I long for us to be at one and commune with each other. Come to Me and let us be at peace. No longer wrestle against your flesh, but subdue your flesh and be at peace. Be at peace within yourself. Be loving and kind to others and give generously to others, and then you will be blessed. You will be content in My Presence, if you are a vessel poured out to freely give to others. I will show you the way to go. I will open a door for you. I will light the path for you. You do not have to fear. I take care of the oppressed-the bent over with the cares of this world. I take care of the widow and orphan. I AM a husband and father to them. I provide for what they need. I care for the lost and dying just like I care for My own. I bring rain and seasons and fruits and vegetables to all men whether they are wicked or not. The wicked will be consumed and be no more, but you will live eternally.

Psalms 147:1-4

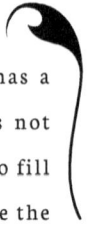

My Beloved, I named the stars. I called them all by name. Each star has a meaning. Each one has a purpose. They were created by Me. Man does not know the purpose of the universe. I have a purpose for all things. I want to fill the universe with life and love for Me. You are My first born sons. You are the first of My creations that I have adopted as My Own. You will be My priests and minister in My Name with My Authority. You must be found worthy. You must be tested with fire to see that you will not bend but remain faithful. You will not slip and fall, but you will stand firm and straight. You will not bend, but remain steadfast. You will know My mighty power and trust in My Name for all things. You will be called back to My Land. Already I AM calling My Children home to Israel to the land that I watch over carefully. You will be safe from your enemies. You will be safe from all who hate you. You will be free at last to serve Me and worship Me in the way that you have yearned to. You will be with all My People, and you will sing and dance and rejoice over Me and your return home. I will heal the broken hearted and those who have wounds. I will heal you and restore you. I will cover you with anointing oil and My Spirit will overtake you. You will be free at last to serve Me without mockery and those who hate you looking at everything you do. You will feel liberty in Me and be blessed with abundance in My Land.

Strength And Encouragement

Psalms 147:5-11

My Beloved, I AM mighty and powerful. I AM powerful beyond your imagination-beyond anything that you can imagine. I AM almighty. I have all authority. I can change the earth in a second. I judge men daily by using the earth as My Hands and Feet to chastise the wicked. If you are in the land of the wicked, then judgment may fall on you too. Get up and get out of the place of the wicked. Get up and get out, and go to My Land. I will open a door for you, so you can leave wherever you are and come back to your home. You are righteous before Me. I have tested you with fire, and you have remained steadfast trusting in Me and wanting to walk in My ways. You are faithful to Me and want Me to guide you. You are leaning close to My ear, so you can hear My voice and follow close to Me. You are pure of heart and want only to walk in righteousness and do what is right. There is no revenge or hatred in your heart. You do not hate or deceive or lie or kill or steal or be mean to others. You love others, and they see who you are in Me-My servant. You must continue in your faithfulness to Me and love Me with all your heart, mind, and soul. You will be taken from this place and cared for tenderly until I return. Both you and your children will be carried in My Hands during the darkest of days.

Psalms 147:12-20

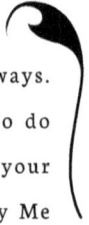

My Beloved, blessed is the man who serves Me and wants to walk in My ways. The rest of the world may mock you and not want to have anything to do with you, but you are My beloved and I love you deeply. I AM always at your side. I AM always here, and you are in My midst. You are consumed by Me and I create in you a new spirit. I create in you a new being from day to day. I create in you the being that will serve only Me and worship only Me. I create in you a new being who will rule over nations with authority and power that I have given you. You will be mighty and not bend. You will know who I AM and teach the peoples that I have given you. You will keep your eyes fixed on Me, and no one will harm you or frighten you. No man will scare you. You know that I AM much larger than any man and more powerful. Praise Me for My wondrous works. Praise Me for My protection of Zion. Praise Me for bringing you and My People back to their home, so once again they can live in abundance. Once again they will serve Me with all their heart. I long for that day. You are scattered now, but soon you will be altogether. You will be in My bosom and content in My Presence.

Strength And Encouragement

Psalms 148

My Beloved, praise Me for I AM the Creator. Praise Me for I AM the only wise One. Praise Me for I alone can save you from eternal damnation. Praise Me, because I made all things and all things are under My command. The weather listens to My voice and does what I say. The animals listen to Me and go the way that I tell them to go. All the fish of the sea no matter how big or small hears My Voice and listens to Me and does what I say to do. The earth conforms to My Presence. The earth quakes under the pressure of My Hand. The earth knows Me and quakes at the sound of My Voice. The earth was created in My hands and it knows the touch of My Presence. The earth and all within it is accustomed to the bending under My Hand. You must realize that man does not know Me and they do not understand My strength. If they understood Me, then they would worship Me. They are in darkness and deception from the Evil One. Man will not see clearly unless he turns to Me and repents and wants to know Me. You are the only one that I want close to Me. You are My beloved and I give you special gifts daily. You are chosen to live with Me forever. If you want to do My Will and love Me with your whole heart, then I will accept you into My kingdom.

Psalms 149

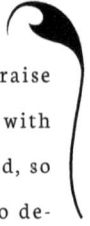

My Beloved, praise Me among men and rejoice that I AM your Elohim. Praise Me and adore Me and lift up My Name and glorify Me. You will walk with high praises in your mouth and a two edged sword of Truth in your hand, so you can judge the people and you can execute judgment to all those who deserve it. You will speak the Truth to others, and they will accept it or reject it. They will be judged by what they do. If they accept My Words, then they will be filled with My spirit and receive Me and know Me and walk with Me. If they reject My Words, then they will suffer loss and be humbled and brought down low and be mocked and stepped upon. They will not enter My Kingdom and share in the inheritance that I give My People who love Me and praise Me. Lift up your Voice and praise Me, because I AM good. I AM merciful. I AM loving and kind and tenderhearted. I long to caress My People and hold them close to Me, but their sin keeps them away from Me. You must cling to Me and want to know Me and hear My Voice. I will care for you and meet all your needs. You must trust Me to do this. Even in the darkest of days, I will make a way for you, so you will have all you need. Rejoice and be glad that I love you so much.

Strength And Encouragement

Psalms 150

My Beloved, praise Me in all you do. Praise Me while you work and while you rest. Praise Me when times are good and times are bad. Praise Me when you have bright happy days and when you have cloudy depressing days. You must trust Me in all days and know that I will care for you. You should not look at what you have, but know that I will give you what you need. If you are longing for something or someone, then you must ask Me to bring it to you. If I delay, then it is not for you or the time is not right. If a child cries for candy and you delay the gift until after the child eats, then you do what is best for the child. If the child cries for candy and you do not think the child needs any candy because the child will become sick, then you do what is right for the child. I AM a good Father and I will give you what is best for you even though you cry and moan and plea and want what you want. I will ignore your tears and pleas and tell you to be quiet and be comforted in Me. When you lose someone to death, you must know that the life was given to that person for a brief time, and then he is gone. His days were numbered. If he was sinful, then his days are cut short. If his parents were sinful, then his days were cut short. Do not blame Me for your loss, but blame the ones who sinned. They are to blame. I do only good and do only what is fair. If you lose someone to death, then the judgment is fair and righteous. It will be pleasing in My sight and I will help you bear the burden of grief, because I love you.

Proverbs 1:1-7

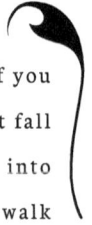

My Beloved, having discipline in your life is a key to all good things. If you are disciplined, then you will be able to take control of your life and not fall into sin. If you are soft and unmanageable, then you will drift and fall into sin. You must be strong and disciplined in all you do. If you fear Me and walk in My ways knowing that if you sin you will be punished, then you will have wisdom and understanding. You will know that you must walk closely to Me, or you will suffer loss. Many love the things of the world, but My Children love Me and long to hear My voice. If you long to hear My voice, then I will speak to you and tell you secret things. If you want to be wise and have understanding into all things, then read My Words and My Spirit will help you interpret them, so you can have gold and silver and life. There is nothing more valuable than wisdom. If you are wise, you will seek Me and find answers to all your questions and not fall into deception and sin. You may be tempted, but you will not be moved. You may lose sight of Me for a moment, but with Wisdom you will turn quickly and put your feet on the right road. Always go down the road of righteousness. Never stay in a gray area where the people of the world want to stay and drift back and forth between what is right and wrong. They try to stay as close to sin as possible without feeling that they are sinning. You cannot stay that close to sin without being tainted. Rejoice that I love you enough to chastise you. Discipline yourself and stay firm and know that I love you so much.

Strength And Encouragement

Proverbs 1:8-19

My Beloved, do not long for wealth. Do not long to be rich and have over-flowing blessings. Do not long for what the rich have. Do not look into their lives and desire to have a life like that. You must be brave and strong and overcome your flesh. Turn aside from all the wealth of the world and turn to Me. I will lift you up, and I will give you exactly what you need at the time that you need it. If you long for wealth, you will seek to change yourself in order to get what you want. You may compromise your principles. You may set aside your friends. You may want to get wealth and put aside the people that you loved. You must not value gold or silver or gems. You must not even look into the people's lives that have such wealth. You will find greedy people who have sacrificed their morals and their principals to have what they want. You think that it is all pleasure to have wealth, but it comes with much temptation and worldliness that you would have to battle every day. Money usually comes with darkness and follows you as long as you have money. Money comes from dark places and can bring ruin to your life, unless I give you the money that you need to finish a task. I will never leave you lacking, but I will always give you all that you need. Call on My Name and I AM beside you.

Proverbs 1:20-33

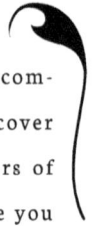

My Beloved, if you listen to Me, you will not be fearful of any troubles coming upon you. You will trust Me to take care of you. You will trust Me to cover you with My Hand in times of trouble. You will trust Me to open doors of escape for you when danger approaches. You will not be fearful, because you will listen to My voice. Those who do not listen to My voice will suffer loss, and destruction will come on them. The will live in fear and distress. They will wish that they had shelter, but there will be none. They will call out to Me, but I will not hear because they rejected Me in the good days and their arrogance over took them. They only wanted their own way and they did not seek Me for advice. They wanted no part of My Wisdom and they wanted to ignore My Words. Now in the midst of trouble I will not hear them, but I will close My ears to them and ignore them. They will have to turn to someone else to help them. I will help My Children who love Me and want to walk in My ways of love and compassion. My Children will not want to be like the wicked. They will want to be like Me and walk in My ways. When men mock them, they will turn away from them and know that I will judge them. They will not have to do anything, because I will redeem the righteous. I will pour My blessings on the righteous and My curses on the wicked. I will raise you up and bring them down. I will bring honor to your name and erase their names. I will do unto them what they sought to do to you. I will have no mercy on the wicked or anyone that wants his own way and rejects the path of righteousness. Rejoice that you follow Me.

Strength And Encouragement

Proverbs 2:1-5

My Beloved, receive My commandments and desire to keep them. Seek for wisdom within My Words. Seek for strength in the midst of My Words. Seek for understanding, and I will give it to you. Acquire knowledge, and let it adhere to your bones and fill your body, and then I can adhere to you and show you how to interpret the knowledge that you have within you. You must study My Words and know what they say before I can show you the meaning of who I AM. You must look towards Me and grasp hold of Me before I can reveal Myself to you. You can't be a casual seeker. You cannot want to know Me one day and the next day want the things of the world. You must seek Me at all times. You may stumble and fall, but get up and try again. I know you are flesh, and you are prone to sin. I know that you must work very hard to keep yourself clean. The more you try to stay righteous, then the more you will be righteous. You will have to decide what is right and wrong and stay away from the wrong.

You cannot see wrong and try to reason it into right. This is sin. You know what you must do to be righteous. You know that you must read and learn My Words. If you fear Me, then you will have wisdom and understanding and you will receive My counsel. Call on My Name, and I AM always with you.

Proverbs 2:6-15

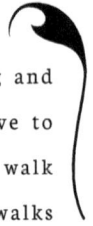

My Beloved, I AM Wisdom. I Am the One who has all understanding and knowledge. I AM the One who gives understanding and wisdom. I give to those who are upright and have a pure heart. I give to those who want to walk in the path of righteousness. I AM a shield -a protector-the One who walks with you and stands beside you. I AM the only One who can save you and keep you from all harm. The wicked are everything and on all sides of you, but I will keep you safe and free from entanglements. I will show you the way to go even if it is very dark. I show you how to stay away from those who would try to hurt you. I guide you by My spirit, and you hear My voice. You know My voice and you are guided by it. If you think you cannot hear My voice, then draw near to Me and rest in the quiet still places and know Me and I will come to you. You cannot have noise around you all day from music to computer games to TV entertainment and think you can hear My voice. You must come away from the world and find Me and know Me. You must be able to listen and be quiet and be still and patient. You must rest in My Presence to hear My Voice. You can see the wrongs of others, but can you see your wrongs? Focus on your wrongs and I will help you see what to change. Once you have changed the way you walk, then you will see and know Me and you will have great riches in My kingdom.

Strength And Encouragement

Proverbs 2:16-3:4

My Beloved, stay away from people with loose morals. Stay away from those who run to sin and want to do fleshly things. They are corrupt in all their ways. They want their pleasure from fleshy desires. They are caught up in serving their flesh. They want one more pleasure. They want one more way to entertain themselves. They want one more person who is just as corrupt as they are. They will call you to come and party with them, "Come entertain yourself with us. Come and have a good time with us. We can give you all kinds of pleasures. Come and see all the good things we can do for you." They want to bring you down to the pit. They want to turn you over to a carnal mind, but resist them and separate yourself from them. Turn away from them and find the way of righteousness. Turn away from your fleshly desires and find Me and My Ways. I will bring you satisfaction and pleasure in ways you have never known before. I will give you all you need to have peace and happiness. Isn't this what the world seeks- peace and happiness? They could have peace and happiness in Me, but they rebel against Me and do not want to find Me. Seek Me and find Me, and you will rise above them and outshine them and be blessed greatly in their presence. You will rise up, and they will sink into the pit of destruction. You will shine, and they will become dark and callous. You will rise up and serve Me, and they will serve the god of this world and enter into his destruction at the end of this age. Arise, My beloved, and be free from the bondage of sin.

Proverbs 3:5-6

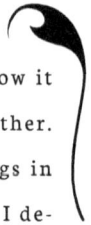

My Beloved, trust in Me with all your heart. Do not try to figure out how it will come to pass-how it will unfold-how I will put all the pieces together. This is not for you to figure out. I control the universe. I hold all things in My Hands. I can change a man's heart over night. I will do for you what I desire to do. There is no man that can change it. You can cry and plea with Me, but I will only do what is good for you. You cannot change My plan for you. You cannot alter the course I have chosen for you. If you try to rebel against Me, then you will suffer loss and you will be discontent and you will not be satisfied. If you obey Me and follow My Ways and listen to My Voice, then you will have all you need and you will feel satisfied. You will be at peace and at rest. You will be separate from the world. You will be loving and kind to others expecting nothing in return. You will know that I AM and I AM in control of all you do. You cannot escape My Presence. I fill all things. You cannot go any place that I AM not there. I AM always with you. Even in the darkest of days when you think that no one cares about you because all have deserted you, I AM with you and I will comfort you. I will hold you up and you will become strong and mighty. You will be a giant on earth, because you commune with Me and are led by Me. Rejoice that I love you so much. Rejoice that I will keep you on the path of righteousness and never allow you to depart from the way. Rejoice and be glad for great are your rewards in heaven.

Strength And Encouragement

Proverbs 3:7-8

My Beloved, do not trust in your own intelligence, but trust in Me. Do not trust in man and what he can do for you. Trust in Me and know that I will bring you what is best for you. Trust in My laws that they will keep you healthy and alive. My laws are life, and they bring healing to all who read them and follow them. My laws are not death and have not passed away. My laws are life and never die. They are a covenant and binding and will never be forsaken. My laws are breath to you. When you obey, then you receive life and the life sticks to your bones and brings healing. If you sin, then darkest comes inside of you and adheres to your bones. If you do not repent, then you are filled with more darkness and My Spirit cannot fill you. Sickness comes over your body. Your bitterness, resentment, rebellion, revenge, and selfishness cover you over and fill you and My Spirit is driven out. You may want to draw back to Me, and you are struggling to overcome your sins. If you call on My name, I will help you. If you are praying to Me, I will hear you. I will bring you peace and joy and fill you again. You must sincerely want to repent and turn from your wickedness. You must truly love Me and want to serve Me. You must want to be at one with Me, and then I will fill you with Light and make your pathways straight.

Proverbs 3:9-10

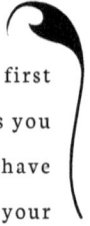

My Beloved, do you honor Me with your wealth? Do you give to Me your first fruits? Do you give Me the best that you have? If you do, then I will bless you and give generously to you. You may not have money. You may only have enough money to pay your bills, but if you give to Me then I will stretch your money and show you how to increase what you have. If you have time, then give it to Me and help others with your time. If you have talents, then give your talents to Me and help others with what you have. If you have money, then give generously to Me and I will bless. If you have intelligence, then give to those who need help to instruct them in the path of life. Give them light to show them the way. A man who teaches My Children the truth will be greatly blessed. A man who shows Me that he loves Me by obeying Me will be blessed by My Hand. I will show him mercy and grace, and he will receive great wealth from My Kingdom. If you are lacking something and you have cried out to Me for it, look at yourself and cleanse yourself and follow My laws. Do as I tell you to do. Do what I say everyday and live in the Light of My Presence. I will hear your prayers and give you what you need always, but not what you want. I know what you need before you ever ask for it. You will repent to Me and I will give to you generously.

Strength And Encouragement

Proverbs 3:11-12

My Beloved, I correct those who I love. I bring discipline to My Children like a father who loves his children and wants them to walk in the correct path. A father is proud of his children and wants them to bear his name in a way that pleases him and does not bring disgrace to his name. A father wants his children to obey him and respect his wishes. A father wants his child to be loving and kind to all men no matter who they are or what they are doing. A father wants his children to learn from him and become wise and humbled. A father wants his children to be intelligent and aware of his surroundings. A father wants his child to come to him and ask when he needs something. A father wants his child to praise him for the things that he does for him to make his life easier. A father wants a child who will love and give to others and have compassion for those who have been given less than him in this life. As a father looks as his child, I also look at you and desire the same things for you. You have been given so much, but you are blinded in many ways and cannot see all that I have given you. Do not complain and moan, but rejoice that I have given you so much. When I discipline you, rejoice that I love you enough to keep you on the right track, so you will walk in righteousness before Me and My wrath will not be poured out on you. Rejoice that I call you My own, and love you enough to bring you into My Kingdom of Light.

Proverbs 3:13-20

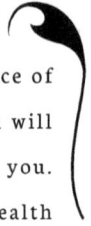

My Beloved, you will be happy, if you find wisdom. I AM the only source of wisdom. If you find Me and search for Me with all your heart, then you will have wisdom and you will have all the benefits that wisdom brings to you. You will have understanding into My ways. You will have long life and wealth and honor. You will have peace and happiness. You will have the ability to rest in My Presence knowing that I will care for you no matter what happens. You are in My Hand and I will cover you. When the earth quakes and the rocks are shattering all around you, I will keep you in a shelter and cover you so no harm comes to you. Am I not capable of protecting My Children when My wrath is being poured out on the surrounding nations? Am I not capable of caring for you, so that you have food and shelter and clothes and all you need? I AM and I AM. I can do all things. There is nothing impossible for Me. I will help you at every turn. If you think that I AM distant from you, then draw closer to Me. If there is distance between us, it is because of your sin. Repent and draw closer to Me, so you can hear My Voice and be led by My Spirit.

Strength And Encouragement

Proverbs 3:21-26

My Beloved, I will give you common sense and discretion, if you come to Me and know Me. I give wisdom to those who seek Me, and with wisdom come a multitude of blessings. You will be able to sleep peaceably at night and not be afraid, because you know that whatever happens I will care for you. No matter what situation comes your way, I will care for you. I will hold you fast and you will not be swept away. I will give you the ability to see ahead, so you will avoid any traps along the way that may deceive you and draw you off the path that I have for you. I will see to it that you are aware of what is going on around you, so you can be on guard and watch carefully for the traps of the enemy that he brings along your way. If you watch carefully, you will not fall into sin and be caught in a trap of deception. You will always know the way to go, if you call on My Name day by day and believe that I will overcome all obstacles in your way. I will lead you down a straight path, so you can see clearly ahead and no one can overtake you unaware. You must trust Me in all you do and say. You must know that I will overcome any one that tries to harm you. I may choose to use people who come against you to mold you and frame you, so you are transformed into My image. I may choose to use situations that may look fearful, but your faith in Me will help you avoid those situations, because I will intervene on behalf of you. Call on Me. I AM always near.

Proverbs 3:27-35

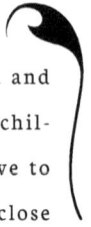

My Beloved, I give generously to the righteous. I take from the wicked and give to the upright. The children of the wicked will suffer loss, but the children of the upright will prosper for the sake of the righteous. I will give to those who seek Me, and I will love those who love Me. I will hold you close to Me, and you will be able to hear My secret counsel that will keep you from harm and show you the lighted path. I give wisdom to those who seek Me, and I form a hedge around the righteous. Who are the righteous? Who are the chosen ones? Who are the ones who I hold dear? They are the ones who come to Me daily and praise Me for My wondrous works. They are the ones who hold onto Me in faith knowing that I will help them no matter what the situation. They are the ones who light the world by their love and kindness. They are the ones who will show the others the lighted path of Truth and lead others along the path of righteousness. They are the ones who others will see their righteous deeds and bring honor to their names. No one will be able to touch them, because they are Mine. No one will take from them, because they are Mine. No one will be able to bring curses upon them, because they are Mine. I alone will deal with My People. I will discipline, and I will bless. I will give to them, and I will take from them. I will balance the scales and make sure they are free from all guilt. I will hold them up, and call them My own. They will be counted worthy to enter My Kingdom of Light.

Strength And Encouragement

Proverbs 4:1-9

My Beloved, treasure My words in your heart, and do not turn from them. Wisdom is found in My words. If you want to become wise, then you must read My words and seek for wisdom. It will come to you. You will never be wise unless you seek for wisdom in My words, then all wisdom will flow to you and overflow, so you give wisdom to others. At first you are a hungry soul like a plant starving for water, and you absorb all you can until you are refreshed in your soul. Next you will be so full that you begin to run over to others and give them what you have learned. You will be like a river of running water leaving a trail of water wherever you go. You will wash others clean with your words. They will seek you for encouragement and strength, and you will only give them My words of encouragement and strength. You will want to find a secret place in My Presence. You will want to be quiet and still and rest in My Presence, so you can hear My Voice. You will want to know Me intimately and serve no other gods. You will want to find the source of Light and Life, and you will know the path to take to find this source. You will fall, but you will get up quickly and not lay around in your sin or self pity. You will get up quickly and brush yourself off and put aside your guilt and shame. You will go forward and know that I AM always with you. You will know that I AM your strength. You will know that I love you, and no one can harm you. You will rejoice in Me all the day.

Proverbs 4:10-13

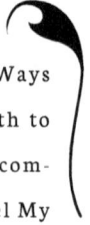

My Beloved, hold fast to discipline because it is your life. Hold onto My Ways and keep My Laws and they will bring healing to your body and strength to your mind. You will have liberty in Me and be free to walk in love and compassionate. You will know that I AM with you always, because you will feel My Presence. You must be disciplined in all you do-in what you eat, in sleep, in work, in what you wear, in exercise, in your speech, in your actions, in your relationship with Me. I want you to hold back your flesh, and put your flesh in line, and allow your spirit to come forth and shine. Love will guide you. Whatever you do in love will bring you life. If you do something in hatred or bitterness or resentment, then you will have death come to you. If you move in love more than you move in your flesh, then eventually love will take over your flesh and you will want to always walk in love and kindness. You will feel dirty when you allow anger or bitterness or greed or selfishness to enter into you, and you will fight against your flesh and want to replace this feeling with love. You will forgive quickly and fight against your flesh all day long. It will be a burning sacrifice before Me, and I will rejoice over your sacrifice of your flesh. I will make you afresh and anew and you will be at one with Me.

Strength And Encouragement

Proverbs 4:14-19

My Beloved, walk in the Light and allow your light to shine for others. Allow your love and kindness to cover others. Allow the peace within you to spread to others. If you walk in My love, then you will make the world a better place. Run from evil. Stay away from any place that you think may be evil or have darkness around it. Try to keep away from anything that would hinder you spiritually. If you will be on guard and watch for evil people and stay away from them, then you will have success in life. You will be able to walk in comfort with no hindrances. Evil people run towards evil. They are looking for ways to hurt people. They run to gossip and want to hear all the rumors and spread them. They want to run towards bloodshed and violence. They want to see people hurting, and they love to cause misery. They are evil and belong to their father the one who began evil and enjoys seeing My Children suffer. He wants to show Me that My Children are unworthy to enter My Kingdom, so prove him wrong. Show him that you are above the standard of other men. Show those that look on that you are righteous and are worthy of entering My Kingdom and will rule wisely in the ages to come. I will pick you up if you fall, and I will keep your feet on solid ground as long as you keep your eyes on Me and keep doing what is right.

Proverbs 4:20-22

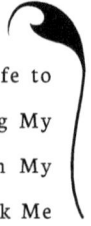

My Beloved, My Words bring health to your body. My Words bring life to your body. My Words bring direction and conviction. Are you reading My Words and holding them close to your heart? Are you meditating on My Words? What does this mean? As you are reading for understanding, ask Me what a word or phrase means and how you can use it in your life. I will bring the answers to you. I AM the One who give the questions, so I will also give the answers. I will help you in your journey to find health. The world is polluted and filled with dirty things. Your body is trying to get rid of all the things that are dirty, but the world is so polluted that your body is under pressure to rid itself of all pollutants. You must give your body extra help by eating foods and herbs that heal your body. Do not eat foods that you know are not good for you and have no nutritional value. You are killing yourself every time you eat an unclean food. What is unclean? I have given you a list of animals that you may or may not eat. Anything that is made by man and not Me is synthetic and not natural and is foreign to your body. Watch for preservatives and additives and refined foods and processed foods. Care for your body and eat what is right. I will guide you in your search for good clean foods to eat. I will help you as you walk along your way to remain healthy as long as you keep My Laws and eat clean foods.

Strength And Encouragement

Proverbs 4:23-27

My Beloved, focus on the path ahead of you and do not look to the right or left. Do not deviate from the path that you are on. Always seek righteousness and never falter. Stand firm and do not give up. The solution to your problem is right around the bend. You cannot see it, but it is coming soon. I want you to trust Me, and the only way that you can trust Me is to turn to Me day after day not knowing what lies ahead, but knowing that I will care for you in every way. You must keep your mouth from lies and deceit. You must guard your heart and not let others pierce it and cause you pain. All things that come to you are a test to see if you will slander the person who hurt you, or if you will continue to love them and overlook their sin against you. If you love the person through the pain, then I will bless you and you will overcome and become brave and strong. You cannot give into bitterness and resentment. You must turn from hatred. You cannot allow your heart to be filled with evil intentions. No matter how much someone hurts you, just come to Me and I will tell you what to do and how to overcome the problem. People make mistakes, and sometimes they say and do things they later regret. People are not perfect, and even the most righteous man can hurt others at times, but he really does not intend to cause pain. The way he views a situation may be different from yours. You must compromise and work out your differences, and I will bless you when you forgive each other.

Proverbs 5:1-14

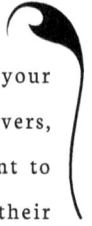

My Beloved, pay attention to My Words. Listen to My instruction, so your ways can be smooth and your pathways straight. Stay away from unbelievers, because they will only lead you astray. Stay away from those who want to party and always be entertained. They are not seeking for answers to their questions about life, but they are seeking escape from their problems. They want to cover their eyes to their sins and not repent and walk in righteousness. These people will only lead you astray and far from Me. Do not become unequally yoked with an unbeliever in a relationship, because he will bring you down. First give the person the Truth about Me and show him My ways, and if he sees the Truth and wants to walk in My ways then you can unite with him. Otherwise this relationship will only cause you pain and suffering. You must walk in My Ways to have life and receive blessings. Be careful, because traps are everywhere. If you are being led by Me, then you will not fall into a trap, but you will go around the obstacle. I will warn you in advance, and you will not take the path. You will walk another way. If I tell you don't go to that place or do not meet with that person, then listen to My Voice. I know the direction you should go, and you may not see the danger ahead. You may only see that you are disappointed and could not have an opportunity to do something that you really wanted to do. Rejoice, because I have kept you from much, and you do not even know why. I AM always careful to look out for you as long as you call on My Name and walk in My Ways.

Strength And Encouragement

Proverbs 5:15-23

My Beloved, be faithful to the husband or wife of your youth. Do not seek divorce and destroy your marriage covenant. If you have chosen an unbeliever and the person will not convert to the Truth, then you may be released from the person if you do not have children. If you have children, then you must stay in the marriage and raise your children to walk in My ways and do My will. This is your burden that you must carry, because you did not choose a believer to marry. If you had wanted a pure marriage and to walk in righteousness in the beginning, then you would have chosen a mate that loved Me and wanted to serve Me. If you are unwed, then wait on Me to bring you the special one for you. Your mate will come to you, and you will know that I have brought this person to you. It will be a gift to you-a special present to bring you comfort and happiness. You will find pleasure just in that one person and you will not seek pleasure from another. It is sinful to desire another person when you are married and have made a covenant to your mate. You must honor your vow of marriage that you made in My Presence. You must honor your vow and honor Me first and yourself second. You may have to carry your burden awhile, but then you will be released from it in time, and you can have a second chance to choose a mate that will love Me and serve Me.

Proverbs 6:1-5

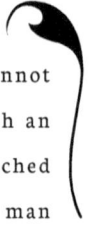

My Beloved, do not give your promise to pay a man's debts if he cannot pay. Do not become a co-signer on a loan. Do not go into business with an unbeliever and expect to not be harmed by this. Do not want to be attached to someone who may not walk in honesty and integrity. If you say to a man that you will do something and then you realize that this is not what I want you to do, then go to the person and explain that you will not be able to keep your promise and ask forgiveness and go on your way. Do not hold yourself to your promise, if you know that what you are doing is wrong. Do not give your promise to any man. It is best to remain silent and not take an oath. You should take one day at a time and see what I want you to do for the day. I AM your Master and you are the servant. The good servant comes to his master at the first sign of light and asks what his master wants him to do for him. You should come to Me at daybreak or when you arise and talk with Me, and this obedience will bring strength to you .I will give you instruction and advice that no man can give you, because I AM the only One that knows what you need. I will guide you away from obstacles and away from danger. I will lift you up and give you life. I will bring you peace, joy, happiness, and satisfaction within yourself.

Proverbs 6:6-11

My Beloved, look at yourself. Are you lazy and try to escape from doing your work? Are you a procrastinator? Who is your taskmaster? Who is the one who gives you the jobs that you must do every day? It is I. I AM the One who is your taskmaster. I AM your boss-your employer. I AM the One that you are a servant to. I AM the One who tells you what must be accomplished in your life. There is no other. If your focus is on a man, then your focus is wrong. If you hate your boss, then you are hating Me. I AM the One who placed you where you are today-doing what you are doing today. If you have lost opportunities, then you should not be bitter but begin anew. Come to Me, and I will tell you what to do. I want you to come to Me and be humble before Me and let us reason together, and I will show you why you are in the position that you are in. I will show you what I AM doing in your life. If you are very unhappy where you are, then you need to focus on Me and know that I AM the One who placed you in this position and I AM doing a good work. I AM forming you into My servant who can be used for My glory. If you are not happy with where I have placed you, then repent, and be humble, and I will help you wherever you are. If you come to Me, I will open doors for you and show you a new way to go. You do not have to be led by man. Only I know what you need for your journey in this life.

Proverbs 6:12-15

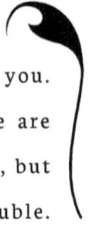

My Beloved, be careful. Watch out for the ones who want to deceive you. Watch out of the man who will try to bring you down to ruin. There are many who have smooth talk and want to seduce you into trusting them, but they will only bring you to destruction. They delight in stirring up trouble. They delight in causing others pain. They want to see others upset. They want to have authority over others and press them down and bring them to ruin. They are wicked in all they do. Their hearts are filled with deceit. They will say to you, "Come, and party with me. We will have fun. I will be your friend-your very best friend." Do not believe them, because they only want to take from you. They will absorb all you have, if you allow them to do so. They are vile and filled with hatred. They think others owe them something. They think that they deserve only the best, and others should accommodate them. They will find that they will be thrown into the Lake of Fire, and they will be destroyed. We will remember them no more. They will bring curses on their children. They will not leave an inheritance to their children, but only a tarnished name. They will be seen as evil, and others will mock them. Destruction will follow them wherever they go until the day that they die, because they have tried to harm others and take from them and only do evil towards them. Be careful. These people are everywhere. Beware!

Proverbs 6:16-19

My Beloved, I AM Love and there is no darkness in Me. I look for the ones who want to draw close to Me and come into the Light of My Presence. Those who want to live in the shadows and darkness and not come into the Light are those who do not love Me and do not want to be a part of Me. I will keep them far away from Me, and I will bring My Hand of judgment on them. It is only a matter of time until they face My wrath. I hate those who lie. I hate those who think they are better than others. They are arrogant and want to look down on others when they are only dirt and I have created them. They are nothing in My sight. I could wipe them out in a breath. I hate the witness that goes to court and lies to stop justice from being brought forth by the judge. I hate the one who is quick to run to trouble and mischief. The one who cries out to have a good time is also quick to break the law and do what is wrong all in the name of fun. There is no fun in disobedience. They are rebels and want to bring others into their rebellion. I hate those who do not want to call on My Name, but want to go their own way. They think only good will come to them, but they are wrong. Disaster will come to them and overtake them. I hate those who despite the poor and needy, and do not give generously. They are stingy and will do whatever it takes to become wealthy, so they can have power and authority over men. I hate those who want to serve the enemy-the Evil One. They are greatly deceived. They will go down to the pit and not return. They will no longer see the light of day. On the Judgment Day there will be no hope for them. I AM Love, but I AM also fair and wise and know the hearts of men. If deceit is in their hearts, then they are not Mine, and I will cast them out of My eternal kingdom into eternal darkness.

Proverbs 6:20-23

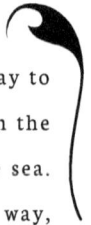

My Beloved, I AM the lighted way. I will guide you and show you the way to walk. If you listen to My Voice and learn from Me, then you will walk in the way of righteousness all your life and your treasures will be vast as the sea. They will be unending. If you turn aside from Me and want your own way, then you will stumble and fall in the dark. Only My laws will give you life. Only My ways will bring you prosperity. If you try to go to the world for wealth, you will not succeed. I will see to it that you are destitute. I see to it that nothing that you do prospers. I will not allow you to turn from Me, but I will have you on your face seeking Me with all your might. You will not be able to escape Me, because you are Mine. There is no other that can help you. You are in My Hand. I will make a way for you, and you will know Me and serve Me with all your heart. If men come to you and say that they can make you successful, do not believe it because only I will give you success. Only I will bring to you what you need. You may want to go down a certain path, but I will close all the doors until you go down the path I have for you. You will know this is the way for you. Listen to those who know My ways and My commandments and know My will for them. They can help you find your way back to Me. Once you are on firm ground, then you can hear My Voice and let Me guide you. Do not continue to turn to man for guidance, but turn to Me. Only I know the way that you must go. Only I know what I have in store for you.

Strength And Encouragement

Proverbs 6:24-35

My Beloved, guard your heart against lust. Do not look at anyone desiring them for sex. Look at the person with love in your heart and want only to see good come to them. Sex is designed to enhance a marriage, but many have gone astray due to their lust. They desire to have sex and want to look for a partner. Their lust overtakes them, and they stumble and fall into dark sin. They will be punished greatly, because they did not get their lust under control. They will be beaten with many lashes, if they cause someone to commit adultery. There will be a harsh punishment to pay for this act. If a man and woman fall into adultery, they should repent before they ruin a family. It is more important to save a family than to fulfill your own lust. You must realize that the person that you are married to at this point in your life is who you chose to be with. Your taste may have changed or the person may have changed, but your covenant is the same. You made a vow to Me and you must uphold it. You must ask for forgiveness from lust, and do not turn to that path again. You will fall into the path of the wicked, if you continue down this road. You must not satisfy your flesh, but deny your flesh and then you will receive great rewards. Remember you are here to overcome your flesh not to give into your flesh. Only then will you be successful and be greatly blessed.

Proverbs 7:1-5

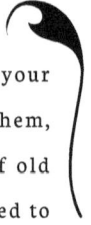

My Beloved, guard over My Words and write them on the tablet of your heart, so you will not sin against Me. Read My Words and meditate on them, so I can open up the meaning to you. You must be like the teachers of old who took delight in My Words and constantly studied My Words and tried to receive understanding from them, so My Words could guide their life. You may not understand everything that My Words say or how to perform all My laws, because so much has been lost in translation, but you can feel My Spirit upon you as you read My Words and study them. I AM pleased with you when you seek Me and want to know My Ways. I AM close at hand when you are studying My words. If you read My Words and become frustrated because you do not have meaning to them, do not give up because I will bring some revelation to your life to help you. It may not be the meaning to the words you are reading, but My spirit will move within your heart as you are reading My words and bring revelation to you in other ways. My Words are healing to the soul. My Words bring peace and satisfaction. When you read My Words My face is turned towards you, because I AM pleased with you. You will feel My pleasure on you, so you can rejoice in this.

Proverbs 7:6-27

My Beloved, guard over yourself, so you do not fall into sexual sin. Stay away from places that you know wicked people go. Stay away from those places when it is dark, and you should be home in bed. Do not go seek a party to have fun and entertain yourself. Seek the arms of your family, and be satisfied with the blessings that I have given you. I have given you a home and people that love you. Rejoice in this and do not seek the things of the world, because you will suffer loss. If you listen to those who are worldly, they will entice you to go down the road of destruction. They will say, "Come and be with Me. I know how to have fun. Come and be our friends and we will have a party every night and have so much fun!" Beware of those who look for something to entertain them all day long. Beware of those who want to have fun and party all day long. These people do not know how to work hard and work as a servant unto Me. They only serve themselves, and they do not serve Me. These people will end up in the Lake of Fire, and you will end up there with them if you do not turn away from them. You must be a set apart people. You must be separate from the world. You must want to only follow Me and My laws. I AM looking for a people who love Me and want to serve only Me. Come out from the world, My People. Come out from the sin and darkness of this world and enter into the Kingdom of Light.

Proverbs 8:1-11

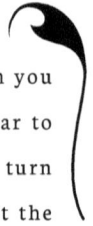

My Beloved, I AM Wisdom. I AM Understanding. I speak with you when you come to Me seeking Me and wanting to hear My Voice. I AM always near to you waiting for you to come close to Me. You are the one who chooses to turn away from Me. You are the one who chooses to live in the flesh and not the spirit. You are a spiritual being enclosed in flesh. Do not allow your flesh to rule over you, but allow your spirit to come forth and I will minister to you and tell you the way to go. Listen as I call you to come to Me. If you will listen, I will tell you secret things. I will tell you the path to take. Only I know the path that I have for you. Only I know what you should do and when you should do it. Only I know where you need to go and when you should go there. I AM calling My Children home, but I know when you should come to My Land and where you should live. I will direct your paths, and you will come at the right time to the right place-the land of your ancestors-the place that I have designated for you. You will come singing and dancing and rejoicing that you can come home once again. Cling to Me and do not become impatient. My timing is perfect. You tell Me that you are getting too old to enjoy the Land, but if you are there a day or many years, you will enjoy My Presence and will have seen My miracles as I bring My People back to Me.

Strength And Encouragement

Proverbs 8:12-21

My Beloved, I AM Wisdom and insight. I give and I take away. I control all things. I choose the rulers of the world, and I lift up nations and destroy them. I cast My wrath of judgment on the world and those who are wicked will suffer and be destroyed. I conquer and control nations. I give power to who I please. I bless My People who love Me. I lift up those who want to seek Me. I will lift them up and bless them with great riches. I will give to whom I please and I will take away from whom I please. I know the heart of man and what he is capable of -whether for good or evil. I designed man in My image, and he is fully capable of serving Me and walking in My ways. He is strong enough to overcome, and I will give him the strength to be able to reach great heights. I will set his eyes on Me and he will know Me and follow Me. If you fear Me, then you hate evil and pride and arrogance. If you love Me, you hate evil doers and want to be far away from them. You do not want to look into the secret arts of the dark ones, but you despise their ways. You want to walk in righteousness and honor all My laws. You want to be by My side, and you know that sin will keep you far from Me. You want to please Me by the words you speak and the kind deeds that you do. You are My beloved, and you walk in all My ways and My favor is on you.

Proverbs 8:22-31

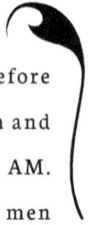

My Beloved, I founded the earth on Wisdom. I set Wisdom into motion before the earth was created. I based all My creation on Wisdom. Who is Wisdom and what is His name? He is My first born son- the personification of who I AM. He dwells among you and he represents Me. It is through Him that all men are saved, if they come to Him and believe in Him. If you are searching for life, it can only be found in Me because He and I are one-the same. I wrapped Myself in flesh and came to live among you, so I could teach you My ways. I showed you how to live in love and devotion to Me. I died and My blood paid the price for your sins, so you could live with Me forever. You have been purchased with a great price. I expect all My Children to honor His sacrifice and live in My ways and by My laws through love and humility. My Children are the Light of the world, and they are the ones who will show others how to live in love. They will show others how to walk in humility. They will love those around them and give them Truth. Great are the ones who want to serve Me in all they do, even though they live in exile far removed from My Land. They are separate and set apart unto Me. They are the ones who will be called back to My Land and live with Me eternally.

Strength And Encouragement

Proverbs 8:32-36

My Beloved, you will be happy only if you serve Me with your whole heart. If you are searching for happiness by making more money, then you have lost sight of Me. If you are seeking happiness through a relationship, then you have lost sight of Me. No man or woman can make you happy. They will always disappoint you. They are not perfect and will fall in your eyes. A job or business cannot bring you happiness, because there will always be problems to overcome. You will need Me to help you solve these problems. You will need to depend on Me to provide for you and show you the direction that you should go. If you seek Me, then you will find the answers to all your problems. If you seek Me, then you will know that I AM and all things are set in motion by Me. Whatever is happening in your life will mold you and make you into My image or you will rebel against Me and fall into destruction. I can give you life and honor and great riches, if you seek Me and love Me. My favor will be poured out on you, and you will be blessed at every corner. You will want to do what is right. You will want to walk in Truth and thankfulness and praise. Lift up your voice and praise Me for all that I have done for you. Lift up your voice and thank Me for My steadfast love and affection that I have for you. I have not cast you away even in your sin. I AM patient and kind and longsuffering with you, because I know what you will become. You are stronger than you think. Turn to Me, and I will give you the strength you need to succeed.

Proverbs 9:1-6

My Beloved, if you want life, you must have understanding into the things of Me. If you want Wisdom, then you must seek Me and find Me. I AM Wisdom and Understanding. I give the way to learning. No man can see clearly unless he comes to Me. Seek Me out and find Me. You will fall in the midst of the storm, if you do not seek Me. If you call on My Name and hold onto Me, then you will endure the storm and not fall. You will remain strong and not waiver. If you hold unto Me, then I will give you what you need even in the darkest of days. My People who call on My Name and humble themselves and pray to Me will receive whatever they need. I will give to them generously. I will bring My Angels to them and comfort them and guide them and they will know the way to go. There are many around you who look on and want to see what you are doing. They look to see if you are worthy of entering My Kingdom. They take notes of what you do to help others, and I look and see what you are doing all day long. I lift you up when you are weak and give you the strength you need, so you can stand firm. If you love Me and want to serve Me, then I will hold you up by My right hand and heal you and restore you and make you strong.

Strength And Encouragement

Proverbs 9:7-12

My Beloved, if you fear Me, then you will have wisdom. If you fear Me and know that I will repay those who break My laws and you want to keep My laws to please Me, then you will have great riches. You will reap the consequences of your actions. You will not be rebellious and turn away from Me, but you will serve Me and receive the benefits from your loyalty to Me. You will want to do whatever I tell you to do. You will want to be at peace with Me and not want to feel My wrath upon you. You will keep all My feast days with rejoicing and you will keep all My Sabbaths as special set apart days. You will want to be righteous before Me. A wise man has understanding into My ways. If you do not understand My ways, then come to Me and I will teach you. I know you live in exile, but I still want you to be righteous before Me and walk in My ways serving Me in all you do. If you fail to keep My ways, then I will show you what you are doing wrong, and I will guide you into what is right. I know you have no teachers who can help you. I know you live separated and alone from My People and My Land, but I will teach you and I will comfort you even in the darkest of days when you think that all is lost. I can bring up from the ashes the gift I have for you. You do not have to be afraid. All is not lost. I AM here to help you in all situations no matter how fearful it may be to you. I AM faithful and just to repay those who persecute you and try to stand against you. I will repay them for their wickedness.

Proverbs 9:13-18

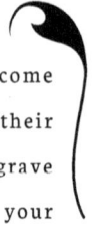

My Beloved, beware of wicked people who call to you and want you to come join in their folly. They will call to you to come have fun and join in their party, but these people are wicked and they want you to go down to the grave with them and not receive your eternal reward for serving Me with your whole heart. Wicked people are constantly searching for someone new to join in their wickedness. Beware of such people. They always seek their own pleasures. They will always put themselves before you and what you need. They will constantly be looking for a better way to numb their senses, so they cannot hear My Voice and cannot see My ways. They will look into dark places to find secret things instead of coming to Me and seeking for the secret things in My Kingdom. They will want to investigate all the religions and not focus on the Truth and the one way. They will cry out for peace and there will be no peace. They will cry out for happiness and they will find no happiness. All their happiness and peace will be fleeing. They will seek it at night in their sinful pleasures, and in the morning they will still have no peace or happiness, but only regret of what they did the night before. They seek out the night in the darkness to perform their sins, because they think the night will cover them. I know all things and can see all their sins and I will hunt them down. My wrath will be on them and they will suffer for their wickedness. Beware of such people and stay far away from them, or you will be caught up in their punishment and suffer loss.

Strength And Encouragement

Proverbs 10:22, 13:21-23

My Beloved, I AM the only One who gives wealth. I give to whom I please, and I give wealth only when I know that this blessing will help you draw stronger and closer to Me. I do not give wealth to the proud, but I give wealth to the humble and those who are serving Me and will use the wealth I give them to help others. I will not give wealth to the boastful or arrogant. They will be humble and giving to others. If you are praying for wealth and it is not coming to your house and you continue to be burdened down with debt, then turn away from your sins and look to Me for deliverance. Those who have wealth follow My commandments and do what is right. I will always bless the righteous, and I will give generously to them. I will bring praise to their name when they give a good inheritance to their children and grandchildren. Their children and grandchildren will rejoice over their parents' righteousness and want to walk in their ways. You will be a strong tower to them and teach them how to walk in My ways and have faith in all situations. You will want to give to them from the wealth of knowledge that I have given you. You will want to give them wisdom and show them how to walk in peace. You will be a righteous example for them in all that you do and say today and always. Rejoice that you have given them so much.

Proverbs 10:24-25

My Beloved, what you fear will come upon you, because you do not trust Me in that area to take care of you. This leaves a door open to the enemy so he can come in and steal. If you are afraid that I cannot protect your children, then your children will lack protection because you do not have faith to believe that I can care for them. If you love Me, you will trust Me in all areas of your life. You should fear nothing-not the future or anything that will happen to you. If you are weak, I will make you strong-just call on My Name for strength. If you are scared, then call on My Name and I will give you peace and confidence in Me that I will take care of you. Do not be afraid of anything. You are My Child and I will take care of you. I will hold you up and protect you all day long. There are many who would like to steal your joy, but only you can allow them to do this. Only you can trust Me. You cannot make another man trust Me. Trust is earned. You learn to trust Me by seeing what I do for you every day. What I do to bless you all day long will teach you to trust Me. When you ask Me to do something for you, then I will do it for you. I will hear your voice and listen and bless you. You must trust Me, and I will draw closer to you and we will be as one.

Proverbs 11:24-28, 28:27

My Beloved, give to others and I will bless you. If you are stingy and do not give, then I will take away what you have and give it to others. I AM looking for a giving people. I AM looking for those who want to help others and love them. I will give to those who give to others. I will take from the wicked and leave their children with nothing. There are men in this world who have much wealth and they think that they are invincible, but I can bring them down in a second and they will find themselves in the grave with nothing but darkness. They will wonder what happened to them, because death came on them so suddenly. If a man walks in My ways, then he will prosper and he will leave his wealth to his children, so they can never be under the burden of debt. Listen, My People, it is better to have less than to borrow money and owe another man. It is better to not borrow at all than to get what you want for the moment. If you are listening, then you will see clearly and not enter into debt. You will watch over yourself very carefully, and turn away from any thought of buying something that you cannot afford. Your light will shine like the dawn, and you will be a good example for others around you. Look to Me and I will guide you.

Proverbs 11:31, 12:14, 15:3

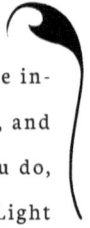

My Beloved, I see and know all things. I see all that you do and what the intentions of your heart are. I know when you speak evil from your heart, and I know when you speak good words from your heart. I watch all that you do, and test you to see if you are worthy of entering into My Kingdom of Light where there are no shadows and all is pure before Me. No rebels will be allowed into My Kingdom. Only those who love Me and want to serve Me and obey My Words will enter into My kingdom. Therefore I AM faithful to judge you while on earth, so you will pay for all the bad deeds that you do to harm others here on earth. I will also reward you for the good deeds that you do to benefit others. I will even reward you for times that you want to help others and they decline your help, because your heart is bent towards doing good. I will help you at all times, if you call on My Name. There should never ever be a time that you steal, lie, or deceive others. You should always do good things for others. If you need something you should ask Me, and I will give you good gifts. Sometimes you do not see My blessings, because they are not what you want to get. My blessings will make you stronger and have faith. My blessings will help you draw closer to Me. In the end the only thing that matters is that you are strong enough to withstand the Evil Ones, and that you have proven yourself before many that you are worthy to enter My Kingdom.

Strength And Encouragement

Proverbs 13:24 ,22:6, 15, 23:13-14, 24-25, 29:15, 17

My Beloved, teach your children My words. Do not depend on another man to teach your children My words, and I will bless you. I will help you to teach them My ways. Be an example for them and shine brightly before them. Walk in righteousness, and never be moved. Stand in the faith and your children will see how you walk, and they will walk in the same steps that you take. You will see the errors of their ways when they are young, and if you correct them when they are young, you will rejoice when they are older. If you do not discipline your children, then you will see them depart from My ways when they grow older. If you will spank your child and allow him to feel the blows, then he will think of what he has done and not do it again. I spank you when you do wrong. You feel the blows on your back as I correct your ways. If you are not humble and do not want to listen, then I will humble you Myself and take away your wealth or health or children or wife until you look to Me and repent. I will not allow you to continue on the wrong path. I AM a good Father, and I will make sure you are punished for your wrong deeds. I will show you the way to go, so you will always listen to Me and do what is right in My sight. Do not grow weary in disciplining your child. You must be consistent. You must not waiver. You must make your child obey your laws, just like I make you obey My laws. You must never give up on your child even when your child has many problems. Cry out to Me and I will change his heart, so he can walk in My ways. Rejoice that I love your children so much to keep them on the path of righteousness. When I discipline them, rejoice and be glad. Do not try to stop My discipline, but know it is for their good that I take from them. In the end, you will be blessed to see them walk in My Ways.

Proverbs 16:1-7

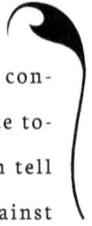

My Beloved, a man is responsible to prepare his heart. He must make a conscious effort to turn away from the things of the world and focus his face towards Me, so I can reveal Myself to him. If a man will do this, then I can tell him the way to live so only good things will come to him. If he rebels against Me, then he will suffer loss and my blows will rain down upon his back. He will be punished for his disobedience until he is bowed down and humbled and his disobedience is driven far away from him. I plan the path that a man must travel. I have his destiny in mind as I create him and give him life. He must travel down this road that leads to Me and My Kingdom of Life. He must be found worthy to enter My Kingdom. He can make many choices, but the path planned for him will not alter. The path is straight ahead and he must remain righteous and in contact with Me to stay on the path that leads to Me. You can do many things in your life and if they help others and show love to others, then I AM pleased. I know the road that will be the best for you. I will open doors for you and close doors for you. Do not try to push open a door, but watch how I open the door for you so easily. I will show you the way, just listen to My voice.

Strength And Encouragement

Proverbs 16:9, 19:21, 20:24, 27:1

My Beloved, do not boost about tomorrow and say, "I am going to do this or that", but you must say, "I am going to do this or that, if Father wills for me to do it". This will keep you humble before Me, and you will know that I will allow you to do only the things that will benefit you and not harm you or lead you astray. You must be keeping your eyes on Me, and not what you want. You may want to do something very badly and if you ask Me to show you if this is a good thing for you to do, then I will show you. I will close the door for you, if you should not do this thing. If it is good for you and will benefit you, then I will open the door for you. You can't always see what will happen when you go in a certain direction, but I always can see ahead and know if this path will prosper you spiritually or if it will lead you away from Me. You may feel limited in the direction you are going, because you are serving Me. Not all people value your service to Me. I can open any door no matter how large, if I want you to be there. Only I know if you will be happy and content there, or if you will blend with the people there, or if they will be a stumbling block for you and hinder your walk with Me. You must trust Me that I know what is best for you.

Proverbs 18:10-12, 20:30

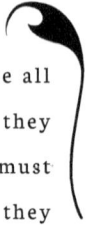

My Beloved, a proud heart is an abomination in My sight. I will cleanse all My Children who are proud by humbling them and bringing them low, so they will look up to Me and not be content in their own ways. My Children must be humble to serve Me. If My Children are proud, then they will do what they want to do. You will go through a season when I humble you and bring you to a place where you will do only what I say. I may have to lay many blows on your back to get you to listen, but the blows will cleanse you of all unrighteousness and free you from the bondage of sin. My punishment is given as a gift to you, so you can repent from your sins and do what is pleasing in My sight. If you look at your life as a constant state of cleansing and humbling to prepare you for the kingdom to come, then you will not be so prideful and you will submit to whatever I want you to do. If you call on My Name and seek Me, I AM a strong tower that cannot be broken down even in the most severe battle. You will remain safe and unharmed as you dwell in My Name and trust Me to protect you by My own Hand. If you continue to trust Me, then no one will be able to harm you. The wealthy may think they cannot be touched, but I can destroy the wealthy and all they have in a second. All they have will be gone, and they will have nothing. I hold all things in My Hands and even the most powerful and wealthy men must bow to what I want. I use these men to test the righteous, but in the end My Children who love Me will be the only ones to receive the treasures of My kingdom.

Strength And Encouragement

Proverbs 18:19-21, 21:23

My Beloved, guard over your mouth, because life and death is in the tongue. It can give blessings or curses. It can bring pain and suffering or encouragement and love. The tongue is unruly and must be tamed. A man with self-control has this tongue bridled, so it will not lash out in anger or cut to the spirit in jealousy or disappointment. The flesh is hard to control, but I can help you. Call on My Name and I will give you wisdom and the words to speak to bring healing and strength to the person. If your brother has wronged you, then forgive him and I will deal with him. If you are angry over someone's actions, then forgive the person and I will punish the person for what he has done. You are not the judge. I AM the judge. Do not cast punishment on your brother, but give the matter to Me. Come before Me and present your case and let Me hear it. I will decide between you and the person who wronged you, and I will do what is just and fair. If you have someone who mistreats you, then call on Me to help you. I will deal with them fairly and use the punishment that will humble them and bring them closer to Me. Do not be concerned about those who hurt you by their harsh words. I will show them their sins and bring them to repentance. If you will guard over your tongue, then you will guard over your life.

Proverbs 19:17, 22:7

My Beloved, if a man longs for wealth, then he may end up in poverty. Seek Me about how to spend your money. If you run out and buy fancy things that you do not really need, then you will fall into debt and you will become a slave to the lender. You will have him on your back every day until you pay him everything you owe him. Do not borrow money to buy new things. Use your old things, and I will keep them from wearing out. I will keep your old things running, and I will help you rebuke the devourer. The enemy wants you to spend your money and get into debt, because then he can control you. He has power over you. I want you to be free from debt, so you can have extra money to give to the poor and needy. If you give to the poor, then you give to Me and I will bless. If you want the things of the world, then you will not receive entry to the kingdom. My Child will want to give to others instead of buying for himself. He will see the needs of the people around him more than what he wants. He will be humble before Me and give as I tell him to give to others. There will be many who come across your path, but only service the people I tell you to service. You may be asked to open your home, speak encouraging words, care for a person, cook a meal, give some money, or spend quality time with a person. Only I know what the person that I send across your path needs, so listen to My voice and I will guide you.

Strength And Encouragement

Proverbs 22:1, 29:25

My Beloved, if you honor your name in a way that you want to compromise and not do My will, then your name will be stripped from you and it will have no value. If you honor Me above your name and you do not compromise with the world, then I will bring honor to your name and bless you. You should keep your reputation spotless and without reproach. If you walk in My ways and do My will, I will give you favor and I will open doors for you. I know the way is hard to go against the world, but I will bless you for your efforts. I will bless you in spite of the others around you. I will lift you up and draw you closer to Me, so you can hear My voice and do My will for you. What I tell one man to do and what I tell another man to do may be different, but you must always keep My laws and walk in My ways of love. You must respect men and know that I have My Hand on all men. If you listen to men and respect them enough to listen to their words, then I will bless you. You do not have to do as they say if they are walking in sin, but you respected them enough to hear their words and listen to what they wanted you to hear. If the man does not follow Me, then you are free not to listen to his advice. Do not try to seek after money and wealth. Seek after Me, and I will bless you. I will show you the way to go. Do not fear men, but fear only Me and I will open My Hand to you and blessings from My kingdom will come to you, and you will rejoice.

Proverbs 21:5, 28:19-20, 22

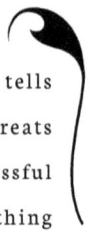

My Beloved, if a man is diligent to work hard and do as his employer tells him to do, then he will be successful. If he owns his own business and treats his employees well and is not harsh or unkind, then he will also be successful if he works hard to do what is right. If a man thinks that he can do nothing and get rich, then he is wrong. If a man rushes after any scheme that could make him rich, then he will fail and leave his family in ruin. If a man is quick to rush into a business deal without consulting Me for wisdom or wanting to go his own way, then he will fall and lose all his money. If a man is patient to wait on Me to guide him into what business is right for him, then I will open a door for him and show him the way to go so he will progress and be able to take care of his family. Do not rush ahead, but wait on Me to guide you. Do not listen to man, but listen to My Voice. Only I know the path ahead and what you will encounter along a certain road. Only I know if you will be successful in a certain venture. Only I know if you will gain wealth in a certain avenue of business. Only I know what is best for you, so you can be happy in what you choose to do. If you will listen to My voice and not become impatient, then you will be successful and you will learn to trust Me to guide you. This will help you in the last days to hear My Voice and follow Me in all that I tell you to do, so you can be safe and remain at peace.

Strength And Encouragement

Proverbs 24:10-12

My Beloved, stand up for the innocent. Stand up for those who do not have anyone to help them in times of trouble. Stand up for the weak like the women and children, and do not forsake them in times of distress. If you see a man that is innocent and he is being charged as guilty and you know the truth, you must stand up and speak for the innocent man or I will judge you harshly. If you say, "I know nothing about this matter" and you do know that the man is innocent, then you must speak up and tell the truth even though you may be scorned or others may rise up against you. I will protect you and keep you safe. You must tell the judge the truth at all times, so your testimony will be weighed on behalf of him. If you keep silent, then I will keep silent when you need Me to stand up for you. You will be paid back for the sin that you have committed. Do not allow your fear of man to overtake you. Be truthful and I will bless you in all things. If the leaders of your country are wicked and they do not follow the truth, but only want to grab wealthy at all cost, then stay away from them and I will protect what is yours. I will show you how to be safe. If there is a certain event coming in the future that is dangerous for you, I will guide you to a safe place so you can rest in peace. Do not be afraid, but stand firm and I will bless you.

Proverbs 24:17-18, 29

My Beloved, do not rejoice when others fall into hardship. Do not be happy when those who have been mean to you fall under My judgment and are humbled. Do not celebrate if they fall, but rejoice that I love you so much to release you from the hand of your enemy. If someone does something to you, do not try to get revenge on the person. Do not say, "I will do to this person what he did to me and then he will see how I feel." This is not your job to judge this person and pass out the penalty for hurting you. I will judge the person, and I will pass out the judgment on that person. You may not see any harm come to him, but you must trust Me that I will judge him and he will pay the price for hurting you. Every man must pay the penalty for his sins. A man must be loving and kind to all men no matter who they are or where they live. A man must treat all men equal, because I look at all men as equal and judge all men on the same standard. All men must keep My laws and serve only Me, or he will face the judgment and I will not be lenient. I will be harsh in My Judgment, because you rebelled against Me and turned your face away from Me. If a man is humble before Me and does as I tell him to do, then I will bless him greatly. I will pour out curses on the man that rejects Me and My ways, and I will judge him harshly for his wickedness.

Strength And Encouragement

Proverbs 28:13, 29:1

My Beloved, if you turn your face away from Me and do not listen to my pleadings with you and My rebukes, then you will fall into ruin and not succeed. I will make nothing you do prosper. I will make My hand turn away from you, and no blessings will come to you. You will seek Me and not find Me until you repent and confess your sins and turn away from them. I will hear your voice, if you earnestly want to turn away from your wrong doings and start to listen to My voice and follow Me. Men will not understand what you do. Men may say things against you for keeping My ways. It does not matter what men say. You must follow only Me, and I will bless you. You must not remain stiff necked, so you do not listen to good advice. You must listen to those older and wiser than you are. You must want to listen and gain knowledge and understanding. If you want to do as I tell you, then you are walking in the right direction. I will bless your every step, and show you the way to go. You will be lifted up, and never be moved. You will never give up, but you will overcome. Listen and obey and do as I tell you. I command all those who love Me to obey Me and repent of their wrongdoings before they die, so they can stand before Me on Judgment Day and be counted with the faithful.

Proverbs 30:4-9

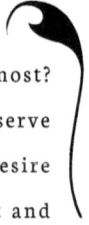

My Beloved, what is important to you? What is it that you desire the most? Search your heart and see what you will bring forth. If you desire to serve only Me, then your life will be a good one filled with blessings. If you desire the things of the world, then you will fall in shame and have to repent and start all over again. If you love Me, then you will know Me. You will know that you must come through the Son to come to Me. My Son is an extension of who I AM. My Son and I are One. You must know My Son before you can know Me. If I give you strength, it comes through My Son. If I give you wealth, then it comes through My Son. I give wealth and I take it away. I give you what you need at all times. Do not be like My People in the desert who complained against Me and wanted meat to eat when I was feeding them manna from heaven that dissolved into their body and provided all that their body would need with no waste. My People wanted meat and longed to go back to Egypt, so all those who wanted to go back I killed them and ended their complaints. Only those who wanted to stay with Me and go to the Promised Land were able to go into the Land with Me. if you long to go to the promised Land, then you will go with Me singing and dancing as you come into the Land.

Strength And Encouragement

Proverbs 31:10-31, 18:22

My Beloved, if a man is given a good wife, then he is blessed. A wife can support you and bring comfort to you, or a wife can be the sandpaper that forms you and makes you into My image. If a wife is one who loves you and loves your children, then you have found a great gift indeed. If she is faithful to you and wants to bring you happiness, then you are doubly blessed. If she teaches her children how to walk the path of righteousness and does not desire the things of the world, then you have found a rare treasure that should be cherished above all other things. If your wife is wicked and does not want to follow after Me, then you must separate from this wife, so she will not harm your children and keep them from walking in the Light and following the path that I have for them. Don't let your wife corrupt your children, but do whatever you need to do to take your children out of her influence before it is too late. I will stand with you and strengthen you until you have won the victory, and your children have been delivered into your hand. If your wife wants to sit idly and not work, then this is a poor example for your children. You must encourage your wife to work hard and prepare a house that is worthy of you and your children using only the best you have for your Sabbaths and feast days. The wife is the one who prepares the table at your feast days, so she must garnish it with the best and use a good attitude as she does it wanting only to worship Me and praise Me as she prepares the table for Me. This a great joy for Me to see My Children come happily to My Table and eat with Me and bless Me with their words.

Exodus 15:1-19

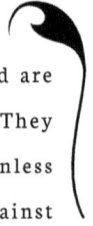

My Beloved, who is like Me? There is no other. The gods of this world are nothing compared to Me. They have no power unless I give them power. They cannot rule unless I allow them to rule. Man cannot come into power unless I allow him to reign. I will conquer and destroy all peoples who fight against My People and try to subdue them. My People will arise and become strong. I will bring them out of exile and bring them home to My special land and hold them in My arms of love tenderly. While the peoples around them try to devise plans on how to destroy them, I will laugh from My holy place. I can see all they try to do and they think they are hidden and no one can see. They are a secret organization, but I see and know all they do. There are no secrets from Me. I will squash their plans and destroy them and all those who follow them. I will raise up My People and they will conquer all My Land and they will rule over it and have all the wealth of the Land. My People who call on My Name and seek Me with all their heart and want to walk in My ways and obey My laws will be worthy of living on My Land. They will be called back to My Land. They will be pulled from the other nations and come to a lush land overflowing with milk and honey.

Strength And Encouragement

Exodus 15:26

My Beloved, if you listen to My voice and do what I ask you to do and keep all My commandments and follow in My ways, then I will hear you and none of the diseases of this world will fall upon you. Your righteousness will keep you clean and safe, and you will not die on your bed of affliction, but you will be taken quickly and not suffer pain from your dying flesh. I will take your breathe and you will know the time you are to depart from this place. If you hold onto the world, then you will not hear My call and you will fall into the ways of the world. You will be sick and worn and suffer loss before you die. You will be depressed and have no peace and contentment. Pure happiness comes only through Me. You will know what is right for you, if you come to Me every day and seek Me, and then you will find Me. If you come to Me only in times of trouble, then I will not hear you. I want you to come to Me daily and commune with Me, so we can be intimate with each other like a husband and wife. If you love Me, then you will want to obey My laws and keep all of them. You will not feel like they are a weight, but a blessing. You will see with My eyes, and your joy will be full.

Deuteronomy 32:3-6

My Beloved, I AM your Rock. I will not be moved. I AM a firm foundation that will not bend or move. I AM established. I AM the Creator who made the foundations of the universe, so all things are held together by My Hands. I AM the first and the last-the aleph and the tav-the alpha and the omega. I have no beginning or end like you do. You are created, but I AM the Creator. I AM spirit and you are wrapped in flesh. I AM worthy of praises and worthy of receiving honor. You are commanded to praise Me and rejoice in My presence. I love to hear your songs of praise and thanksgiving. I have given you so much. Open your eyes and see all that I have given you. If I test you, then I love you. I AM preparing you to be formed into My image, so you can rule with Me for all eternity. If you are tested and are victorious, then you are counted faithful. If you are tested and fail, then I will test you again and again until you overcome and are found righteous before Me. If you are strong and unbendable, then I can use you in the coming age when My People will rule the nations. I will fill My universe with love and light through you. You can teach all mankind how to love Me and serve Me. You are My beloved, and there is on other besides you.

Strength And Encouragement

Deuteronomy 32:39-43

My Beloved, I AM the only Elohim. I AM the only wise Elohim. I AM the only One who loves you enough to care for you. I heal and I wound. I make alive and bring death. I lift up and I bring down. I humble and I raise up rulers. Praise Me all the nations, because I control all things. All things are in My hands. I tell the weather what to do. I tell the rulers what to do. I raise up nations and I destroy nations. I raise up tribes of people, and I destroy tribes of peoples. I give and I take. I make and I destroy. I AM and I AM. No one can give vengeance on Me. I bring vengeance on men for their sins. I AM always fair and just. No man can rule like Me, because I know the hearts of men. I know what his intentions where when the crime was committed. I know whether he was guilty or innocent. I bring judgment on the righteous for their sins, so I can balance the scales and they will be counted worthy to enter My Kingdom of Light. If you see Me and know Me and call on Me daily, then I will hear your voice and listen to what you say. I will do what is best for you. If you trust Me, then I will guide you and show you what to do. You cannot make your own decisions, because you do not know the future. Call on Me to help you make decisions and you will do well. All will go well with you and your family. You will rejoice and be glad all your days on earth.

Joshua 1:5-9

My Beloved, be strong and bold. Be courageous. Be aware of the evil around you. Do not allow yourself to be tempted. When you see a temptation, run away from it as fast as possible. Put away all temptations from you. Keep your mind pure and free. Keep yourself clean and pure. Watch over yourself and be careful to keep all My laws. Keep all the laws and do what is right in My sight, and I will prosper you. I will bless you wherever you go and whatever you do. If you choose to go to the right and you call on My name, then I will allow you to go to the right if this is a good path for you. If this is not a good path, then I will say no to you and you will know that I want you to go another way. You will feel within yourself that My spirit is telling you no to go another way. If you allow Me to guide you, then you will have favor wherever you go and doors will open for you and people will bless you. You must think of others and not yourself. You must love others and give to them. My People are givers and they love others. They want to give encouragement and love to others. They do not want to tear down or harm others. They want to build up My People and make them stronger. The love you give to others will come back to you. The love you give to others will restore you and bring you peace. You will have happiness, if you love others. If you are angry and bitter and want to cause others harm, then you will suffer loss and not live in peace or happiness. Seek Me to cleanse your heart of such wickedness, and I will help you to overcome.

Strength And Encouragement

2 Samuel 22:1-4

My Beloved, I AM your shelter in times of trouble. Call on My Name and I will show you a way out. I will show you the way to go. I will open the door for you to escape and go a different path, so no one can find you. You will be hidden in My fortress. You will move silently and swiftly and you will be covered by My Hand. Your enemies will not be able to find you and persecute you. They will be powerless and not be able to harm you. You will be caught up and carried to a new place. You will know that I have delivered you from wicked men. I AM your Rock on which you can stand. I AM faithful and mighty, and there is no one like Me. I AM your savior and I deliver you from all things that come against you. The evil one tries to make you fall every day, but I make you strong so you can overcome and reign with Me in My Kingdom of Light. The days are rapidly approaching for you to leave exile. You will rejoice and be glad. You will know that I have remembered you, and you are set free from darkness and brought into the Light. Only My People, who call on My Name and serve Me with their whole heart and keep My laws, will be carried away to their home by My Hand. Many will want to come, but only I will open the door for the ones who have proven themselves faithful to Me by how they live their lives.

2 Samuel 22:29-36

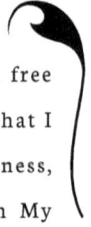

My Beloved, I AM Light. I show you the way to walk. I keep the path free before you. I keep all harm from you and no one can hinder your path that I have chosen for you. I AM your salvation. I keep you from all harm, sickness, disease, hardship, enemies, destruction, and wrath. I keep you safe in My Hands of love and compassion. I make you wear the stripes of your sins, but I keep you from all other things. Sometimes you sin and do not know it, so you pay for these sins mildly. Other times you know you have sinned and you must pay the full price. You must be brave and strong to withstand temptation. You must not give into the enemy. You must stand firm and not bend. I will carry you in the darkness of days when you think all hope is lost. I will give you what you need for everyday, and you will never be without or lacking. You will know that I love you and want to keep you in My hands. There are people around you that want to see you fall. There are people around you that want to see you come into destruction. These are wicked people, and they will be wiped out and will be no more. They will not even be a memory. You will be full of light and spread your light across the universe. You will set free the captives and help them to walk into the light. I am making you great, and I will give you power to overcome anything or anyone. Trust Me with all your heart and you will succeed in all things.

Strength And Encouragement

1 Kings 8:56-61

My Beloved, I AM your protection even when you are in exile. I will bless those who call on My Name, and I will hear your prayer. You do not ever have to be fearful. I AM always near to you. I AM faithful to keep all My promises to My Children. I will call you home soon, My Children, and you will prosper on the Land like your ancestors prospered. Only now you will love Me with all your heart. You will remember what it was like to live in exile, and you will not sin against Me. You will want to keep all My Laws and My Commandments. You will love those around you knowing that love is My first commandment. If you love others, you love Me. If you are kind to others, you are kind to Me. If you think of others first, then you think of Me first. Whatever you do for others, you do for Me. You think about the lonely and the sick. You think about the wounded who need healing. You think about the depressed and sad people who need encouragement. You think about all the good things I do for you, and you want to give to others. You are faithful in all you do for Me, because you love Me so much. You want to please Me in all you do, and I will bless you because of your love for Me.

1 Kings 18:20-40

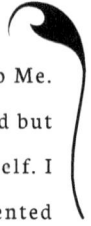

My Beloved, I AM the Elohim of My People and no one can come close to Me. Elijah took a stand to show My People who I AM, and there is no other god but Me. He asked the other god to show himself, but he could not show himself. I had him bound by My angels and he was helpless to show himself. I presented Myself by sending fire down from heaven and accepted the sacrifice of Elijah that he had built of 12 stones reminding Me of the promises that I had given the 12 tribes. I was faithful to the 12 tribes then just as I AM today. Elijah seized the moment for Me to show Myself worthy of praise. All My People praised Me and worshipped Me, and Baal worship was abolished in that area for a season. Elijah was a bold and brave prophet who served Me with his whole heart. I expect you to be bold and brave just as he was. You have My spirit living within you and he had an anointing of My spirit on him. You have just as much power as he did. Call on My name and draw close to Me, and I will allow you to display My power so others can glorify My Name. If you live in a dark place with ruling powers, you will have to fast and pray to break down these powers, so the eyes of the people around you can be opened and they can be free from the deception caused by the spirits there. Beware of the darkness around you and fight against it daily, then you will feel free and not pressed down.

Strength And Encouragement

1 Kings 19:9-18

My Beloved, I came to Elijah and called him to My mountain and he stayed in a cave fearful for his life. The wicked Queen Jezebel had sent her men to search him out and find him and kill him. He was very afraid. I came to him, but he did not find Me in the landslide or the earthquake or the fire, but he found Me in the stillness-in the quiet. He heard My Voice calling him, and he knew it was Me. He came out of the cave to hear Me. He told Me that He was afraid, and I told him that I would keep him safe and no man could touch him just like I had kept the other 7000 people who did not worship Baal safe. I strengthened him with My words and gave him direction as to what to do. I showed him the way ahead clearly, and he listened to My voice and did what I told him to do. He was promised that I would wipe out the wicked in the land of Israel. Come to Me and find Me in the quietness and hear My Voice. Come to Me and know who I AM. If you are having trouble hearing My voice, then stop and wait and prepare yourself to hear Me. Repent of all your sins and wait on Me to speak with you. I will come to you and we will commune together. I AM looking for a faithful people who come to Me day after day and want to hear My voice and do My will. I AM faithful and just. I will show Myself faithful to you and you will rejoice in knowing Me.

2Kings 6:8-23

My Beloved, I sent My prophet to Israel to protect My People. I told My prophet what their enemy was doing at all times, so My People were never overtaken. I frustrated their enemy until they took their whole army and surrounded the camp of Israel. I AM stronger than any army or any enemy. I made a mockery of this enemy. I brought My angels to strike them blind and confuse them, and they ended up surrounded by the enemy's camp. When their eyes were opened they could not believe where they were. Instead of killing all their enemies, Israel gave a great feast for them and sent them home establishing peace with their enemies. I AM in charge of every situation. I give to you what I want you to have and I take from you what I don't want you to have. I give and I take. I heal and I wound. If you are in a dark place, then call on My name and My angels will come minister to you. They will heal you and support you, so you can get on your feet and become strong and mighty. At times, My People need some extra help, and I do not mind sending those people help. Call on My Name and I will bring you the help you need. Do not ever be afraid, because I will deliver you from all trouble no matter how big it seems. If you have caused the trouble, then you must pay the price. If you have not caused the trouble, then I will deliver you from the trouble and set you free from your oppressor.

Strength And Encouragement

2 Kings 8:1-6

My Beloved, I found a faithful woman who loved Me and wanted to follow in My ways. Elijah came across her path and she saw him as a man who followed Me, and she made a place for him to stay and be comforted in her house. She wanted the man who served Me to be close to her and tell her about Me. I gave her a child, because of her goodness towards Elijah. I told the woman through Elijah that famine was coming for 7 years, so she should leave and not suffer loss. I will tell My faithful children when to leave their house if the land is going to be punished. I will deliver you from the wrath of My judgment on the land and send you to a safe place, so you will not suffer loss. When the woman returned, she went to the king to restore her land. I gave her favor with the king and he restored her land and gave her money for all the crops that she lost during the time she was away. I take care of My faithful children. I take care of those who love Me and want to serve Me. I will bless you and care for you. Think of your home as a temporary dwelling. Do not decorate it and cling to it as your prize possession. Open your ears, because I will call you to leave your home and go live in another place. Do not love your house and your land more than Me. Be ready to leave at a moment's notice, so you can escape judgment that is coming on the land. If you choose to stay, then you will suffer loss and must walk through the same judgment as the wicked. Think on these words.

1 Chronicles 16:8-12

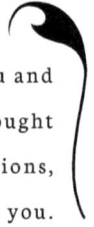

My Beloved, give thanks to Me for all the things that I have done for you and your family. I delivered you from the hand of slavery in Egypt and brought you to a new land filled with good things. I have scattered you to the nations, but I have not forgotten you. I AM always with you. I AM always beside you. I know your every thought and your every breath. I know you, because I made you. I formed you with My Hand and breathed into you the breath of life. I know you and I know your weaknesses. I know how to help you become strong. I will bring adversity to you, so you will have to push against it and trust in Me to help you and you will become stronger. Remember that this life is temporary and you are here to become strong, so you can rule with Me and help those around you. You are not here to be self centered and without purpose. You are here to follow close to Me and obey Me and do as I tell you to do. If you do not listen, then you will be cut off and thrown aside. You will lose the blessings that you had stored up for you, if you turn away from Me and want to go your own path. I will help you know the way to go. I will light the path before you and you will see My fingerprints as you go along the path. I love you, so do not give up hope. I AM always with you. I will never leave you-not for a moment.

Strength And Encouragement

1 Chronicles 16:13-22

My Beloved, I told My People to keep My covenant. I told them to follow My commandments. I told My People to follow in My ways of loving kindness and tender mercy. I told My People to be kind to those around them, and let them see the light of My presence. My People went into exile, and they have gone from nation to nation and people to people. They have traveled great distances and ended up in the far corners of the earth. My People have never been forsaken or neglected. Whenever they are, I AM there with them and care for them and love them. I know where all My People are no matter where they are scattered among the pagans. Their light is very evident. Their lives leave a trail of love and compassion. They are My priests and they minister to Me as My Hands and Feet. They are My servants. They obey Me and love Me and given generously to others. You must continue in the ways of your ancestors who walked with Me into the Promised Land. You must be pure hearted and strong in faith. You must be able to not look at the physical, but believe in Me. My People went into a land of giants and believed that I would protect them and help them overcome and gain the Land that I Had promised them. This same faith must be in you, so you can be strong and mighty for the last days. Teach your children to walk in faith, and be ready for the days ahead.

1 Chronicles 16:23-36

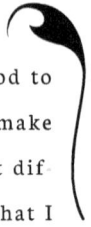

My Beloved, praise Me for My wondrous works. Praise Me for I AM good to My People. Sometimes you cry over your troubles, but your troubles make you strong and mighty. You will become so strong that you will look at difficulties in the face and stand firm and not be shaken. You will know that I will care for you and bring only good things to you. What you think is a good thing may not be a good thing for you in My eyes. You cry and moan over your situation, but you do not realize that this is exactly what you need. You must be an overcomer. You must trust Me in all that you do. You must love Me with all your heart and overcome the weaknesses within you. Life may be difficult at times, but your sin and your weaknesses magnify the difficulties. You should take a step back and look at all that I have done for you in the past and how I have always been faithful. You never lacked for anything. You always had good things. I take care of My Children. They never go without food or water. They may have to move from place to place, but it is My Hand that moves them. I show them that wherever you go I AM leading you. Just like My People in the desert, they did not know where they were going, but they trusted Me to get them there. They trusted Me to show them the way. You must trust Me to know that wherever I take you will be a good place, and you will have all you need. Do not grow weary and give up, but trust in Me. I will never let you down.

Strength And Encouragement

1 Chronicles 29:9-19

My Beloved, all things come from Me. Whatever possession that you have came from Me. I put everything into your hands and you are blessed by Me. I also take from your hands and give you what is suitable for you. If I give you too much money, you could so astray and not serve Me. If I give you too many possessions, you could become proud and not humble. If you are given too little, you could become bitter and resentful that you serve Me and I do not bless you. I know what you need and how much you need. If you are longing for riches, then stop. You may be praying for something that you really do not need. You may be praying for a curse instead of a blessing. You may not know what is best for you. Pray that you will receive what is good for you. Sometimes you do not see things as a blessing, because it is not what you want. Do not long for the things of the world. You are a temporary resident. You are here so briefly. You are here to be tested to see if you are worthy of entering My Kingdom of Light. You are here to be tested by fire to burn away all the fleshly desires, so you can reflect Me and be a light to the world. If you want to serve Me, then focus on your temporary residence. If I want you to do something, then I will provide the means to do it. I will never leave you lacking or without. I will bless you greatly, because I love you so much.

2 Chronicles 6:14-35

My Beloved, a house cannot contain Me, yet I chose to live among My People. When the Temple was finished, My People were filled with joy. I brought fire down from the heavens and lit the altar and filled the Temple with My Presence. The people bowed down and worshipped Me. Their hearts were bent towards Me. I promised to live among them as long as they kept My laws and obeyed Me and did not serve other gods. My People were loyal to Me for a long time, but then they turned aside from Me and spilt the kingdom and divided My People. A divided house cannot stand and it was destroyed. The Temple was destroyed and My People were driven all over the world. Most of My People are in exile and I have mercy on them, because they do not have a teacher to tell them about Me and My ways. They have no one to teach them My laws. I have mercy on them, but soon I will call them back and I will bring them back to the Land and I will pour My spirit upon them and they will be taught by My spirit. Already I AM opening the eyes of My People, and they are learning about Me by My spirit. They are learning about My laws and how to keep them. My People are separating. Those who really love Me will long to come back to the Land and serve Me, but those who are blinded will stay in exile with their children and be destroyed during the judgment that is coming on the land. Seek Me with your whole heart, so that you will not sin against Me and you will be counted worthy to be called back to My Land.

Strength And Encouragement

2 Chronicles 6:36-42

My Beloved, My servant Solomon prayed for you before you were yet born. He prayed that when your ancestors sinned that if you turned from your sins no matter where you are in captivity that you would call on Me and I would hear your prayers and help you. Solomon wanted Me to hear you from My exalted Temple and look down upon you with favor. I honored his prayer. I made a way for you to come to Me and draw near to Me. You can come very close to Me or you can take a step away from Me. That is your choice. Every day you make steps towards Me or away from Me. You must listen to My Voice and trust in Me. The path ahead may be dark, but you will have to trust Me to guide you. Others around you may not take the same path that you take. You will want to be righteous, but they will not want to be righteous. You will rise above them and shine like a light. Solomon had a vision for My People. He knows that the Land was their strength and they needed to live on the Land. If you do not live in the Land, then you do not know My presence on the Land. Rejoice and be glad that you can go there soon with all your family that loves Me and wants to serve Me. You will live in My presence once again.

2 Chronicles 7:12-22

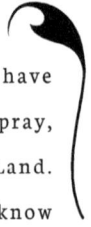

My Beloved, I told My People that if they sin and realize that they have sinned and repent and turn to Me and humble themselves before Me and pray, that I will hear their prayers and listen to their pleas and restore their Land. If they see famine or war or sickness come upon the Land, then they know that they have sinned and they must turn from their wicked ways and seek My face and repent humbly before Me. If you see evil fall upon the place where you live, then pray for the people there to repent and come to Me. I may tell you to leave that wicked place and go to another place, or I may tell you to stay and pray for the people there. If you are in the midst of judgment, I can still provide for you there if I have asked you to stay and be a light to the people there. If I have placed you in a dark place and you struggle there to walk in righteousness and teach your children how to walk in righteousness, then I will add to you 100 times the reward because you are faithful to Me even in a dark place. If I have asked you to leave and you do not go, then the darkness will consume you and you will suffer loss. You must hear My voice and do as I ask you to do. I will put you in the place that I want for you to grow and prosper. I will give you what is best for you. You may not understand what I AM doing, but you must trust Me to do what is best for you. Do not become bitter, but rejoice that I love you so much and want to give you only the best.

Strength And Encouragement

2 Chronicles 20:13-22

My Beloved, the battle is not yours, but it is Mine. If you come to Me and ask Me to help you, then I will bring you deliverance no matter how many are against you or how powerful they are. I will bring you deliverance. I will come to you from heaven and bring My angels to fight on behalf of you. I will bring weapons from My storehouse and I will rain down upon the wicked ones that come against you, and they will be destroyed in front of your eyes. No man can stand in My Wrath. If someone has taken what is yours, then I will fight on behalf of you and give back to you what has been taken. You do not have to be afraid, but you must trust Me with your whole heart. You must know that I AM just and fair, and I will bring back to you what has been stolen from you. If your enemy takes from you or attacks you and wants to take away from you, then I AM there in your midst to guard over you and I will restore you. I will restore My People to Israel, and their Land will once more come back to them. Their enemies have rejoiced over My Land long enough. I will restore My Land to My People, and they will sing and dance and rejoice and know that I have redeemed them. I will make merry with My People and healing will fall on the Land and it will be restored. All the curses will be broken, and My People will cultivate the Land and it will prosper and give My People abundance. You must rejoice that I have chosen you to come to My Land and be at one with Me. Not all will come back to My Land. Only the faithful will come singing and dancing and rejoicing before Me.

Isaiah 9:6-7

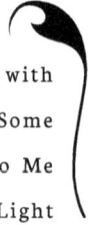

My Beloved, I sent My son to you -an extension of My arm. I walked with you and talked with you and taught you the way to live in My laws. Some received it and some did not receive it. Some wanted to draw close to Me and they became My disciples. Some did not want to draw close to the Light of My Presence. They remained in the darkness and will be lost on the Judgment Day. They will go to eternal destruction in the Lake of Fire and will be no more. I AM such a loving and kind Father that I wanted to come down to Earth to walk with My Children and talk to them. I saw who wanted to follow Me and I notated their righteous seed. I know who My Children are. Inside of them is the seed of righteousness that will blossom and bloom when they hear My words. They will know that they are Truth, and they will turn from their wickedness, repent, and follow Me. Only the righteous will be able to follow Me. The rest of the world will not understand. They will seek demon gods and fall into destruction. They will be judged on Judgment Day and will be found worthy of death and not eternal life. Only My Children who love Me and seek Me and call on My Name will enter My Kingdom and serve Me for eternity.

Strength And Encouragement

Isaiah 25:1-10

My Beloved, I will keep all My promises. I will bring all My Words to pass. I will show the nations that you are My People. I will show the nations that I AM mighty and they should serve only Me. All the other gods are lying and deceiving to gain power, but they are not gods at all. I AM the only Elohim and I AM the One who all men will bow down to and worship. I will bring all My Children to My wedding feast at the last day. They will see Me judge the nations and see the wicked receive their reward and be thrown into the Lake of Fire. They will see My Wrath fall on them, and they will cry out for mercy but there will be no mercy. Their time of judgment has come, and My children will be glorified. My children will receive their places in My kingdom and no longer will they have to suffer under the weight of their flesh. All their tears will be wiped away, and they will rejoice in being in My presence all the day. There will be no more time. There will only be eternity. Time will slip away and My children will not count the hours and minutes, but will experience the eternal present with Me. They will be free from all their enemies, and rejoice in victory all the day and praise Me all the night. I have spoken and I will bring it to pass.

Isaiah 26:1-12

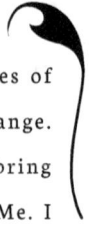

My Beloved, I AM the Rock of Ages. All men who cling to Me in times of trouble, I will save them. I AM firm and unbendable. My Words never change. My promises to My People are never broken. I AM Truth and Light. I bring revelation of who I AM to My People who love Me and want to serve Me. I bring strength to My People who serve Me and want to walk in My ways of loving kindness and tender mercies. My People will arise from the ashes and will once more be a mighty nation, and all the nations will fear them. They will be a faithful People who cannot be made to falter. They are unbendable and strong. They will not waiver. They will keep all My laws and walk in My ways and do what I tell them to do, because I AM faithful to them to protect them and care for them and show them the path of righteousness. I will keep their pathway straight, so they know where they are going and what they are doing. They will see ahead and not be afraid. They will know that I AM with them and will bring to pass all My promises to them. I will bring them back to My Land and fill My Land with abundance once again. I will restore My People. I will restore My Land. I will make all things new and fresh, and My People will rejoice and be glad in My presence.

Strength And Encouragement

Isaiah 33:14-24

My Beloved, who can live among Me with My devouring fire? Who can stay in My presence and speak with Me? Who can walk with Me and talk with Me? Only the righteous with an upright heart, one who tells the truth and does what is right in My eyes not harming others, but loving others and treating them fairly in all they do and say. These are My righteous, and they will hear My secret things and will listen to My voice and walk in My ways and never falter. They are My faithful people who love My laws and love My Words. They meditate on My words and find the Truth in them. They are My beloved ones who desire to be intimate with Me and cling to Me and rest within Me. These little ones will be strong and mighty and never bend to temptations. They will turn from evil and always seek what is good and right in My eyes. These little ones I have My Hand on, and they feel the guiding of My spirit. They seek Me with all their hearts and are true to Me in all their ways. No man can harm them. No one can touch them. No one can take from them. Only I give and I take from them, and I do so only to bless them and keep them safe from harm. You may not understand My ways, but you delight in Me and love Me and trust Me to do what is best for you. You are My chosen ones. You are the ones who will reign with Me forever.

Isaiah 40:18-31

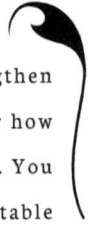

My Beloved, I will be your strength when you grow weary. I will strengthen you and nourish you and make you able to weather the storm no matter how large it is. I will renew your strength and make your feet firmly planted. You will be a man of war and not be easily moved. You will fight and be stable and not give up an inch. You will want to serve Me with your whole heart and not give way to sin. You will want to make a way for Me, so those around you can see the Light of My presence within you by the loving and kind deeds that you do. If you love Me, then you will love others and do good things for them. If you love Me, then you will want to bring joy to others and not be concerned about yourself. I AM the only true Elohim, and I watch over My People to preserve them. If you are one of My righteous seed, then you will want to walk in righteousness and not give into sin. You may become weary, but you will call on My Name and the storm will not overtake you, but you will be anchored firmly. When the storm passes, you will still be anchored in Me and not lose ground or be washed out to sea. You will know that I AM with you, and I will never let go of you. You will rejoice and be glad that I hold you in My arms of love.

Strength And Encouragement

Micah 6:8, 7:18-20

My Beloved, I AM the only one who can forgive you for your sins. I AM the only one who can have compassion on you. You ask Me what I want you to do. I want you to love others and have compassion on them. I want you to walk in justice treating others fairly. I want you to stay pure before Me by keeping My laws and not disobeying Me. It is very simple what I ask you to do. I want you to think of others before you think of yourself. If you are humble before Me, then you will obey Me and give to others. If you are arrogant and want your own way, then your life will be hard and you will stumble and fall. Even if you fall, I AM there to pick you up and brush you off and show you the way to go once again, so you can get on the right path and stay there. You may be bruised and broken from your sin, but the path ahead is clear and as long as you stay on the path of righteousness, then you will have a good life and not lack for anything. You will be given treasures in the life to come. As you go along your path in this life, keep your eyes open for those in need and talk with them as you walk along your path. Keep them close to you and encourage them to remain faithful and do what is right. I will stay near to you and help you as you are a light to others. Even if you live in a dark place, you will still be able to light the path for others and show them the way to go. I will give you a double portion of strength, so you can be strong and help those who are weak become strong also.

Nahum 1:1-7

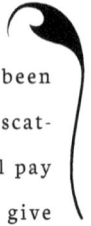

My Beloved, I avenge those who wrong My Children. My Children have been driven out of their Land with a strong unmerciful hand. They have been scattered to all the parts of the world. I will redeem My Children, and I will pay back those who have wronged them. I will restore their fortunes. I will give to their children a good inheritance. I will open the eyes of My Children in exile and bring them the Truth. They will see clearly and teach their children the way to walk. They will be upright and strong and unbending. They will not grow weary in doing what is right, even though those around them want to walk in darkness. If you see others around you saying, "Come to us and have fun with us. We know how to enjoy life", do not believe them. They do not know life unless they know Me. They do not know how to enjoy life unless they know Me. Be strong and be brave, because I will redeem you and bring you home to Me once again. I AM slow to anger with My Children, but once they turn away from Me for so long, then I must punish them and rebuke them and put them on the path of righteousness once again. If you love Me, you will want to only please Me and obey Me. Look into My eyes. What am I asking you to do today?

Strength And Encouragement

Habakkuk 3:17-19

My Beloved, even if things are doing wrong all around you, rejoice and know that I AM still in charge of your life as long as you continue to call on My Name and desire to serve Me. If you see others that you love having difficulties, I have not deserted them. Call on My Name for them, and I will deliver them. You must praise Me even when you do not understand what I AM doing in your life. You must continue to trust Me in all things. You must continue to believe that I will only do what is best for you. Sometimes you cannot see the path ahead, and you may become discouraged, but you must have faith in Me every day and know that whatever lies ahead is what is best for you. The purpose for your life is to be counted worthy to enter My Kingdom of Light. You are tried and tested here to show that you are worthy to be called My own, My Child, My bride, My beloved. You must show yourself faithful to Me here on this earth before you can enter into My Kingdom. Only the overcomers will enter and become heirs to the throne. Only those who love Me will enter the gates of My Kingdom. If you want to spend eternity with Me, then do not try to figure out your future, but trust Me to guide you day by day and you will do well.

Zephaniah 2:3, 3:18-20

My Beloved, if you live in exile and you are grieved because you cannot celebrate the feast days in Jerusalem or with others who want to celebrate and keep My feasts, then you will be spared the coming judgment on your land. I will call you away from here and take you to another place, so you can be spared and free from My wrath. Keep your eyes and ears open and listen and see what is coming ahead. I will tell you to be ready and leave, so you can escape My wrath on the land where you live. I have sent warnings already, but soon I will send My poured out wrath and destroy the land where you live with judgment. If you will listen and be guided by Me, I will take you away from here. Do not be afraid, but be strong and bold and brave and trust Me with your whole heart. I will take you to another place, and then call you back home so you can dwell on My Land and have your treasures restored. You will become a nation of believers who walk n righteousness and love Me with all your heart. You will obey Me and keep My laws. You will teach your children the right way to live and walk in My ways. You will be called a righteous people who want to serve Me, and I will bless you greatly. I will restore your fortunes, and you will have houses filled with treasures.

Zechariah 10:6-10

My Beloved, I know you are grieved, because you are in exile and far from your home. I know you want to come home, and you long to live on the Land of your ancestors when they served Me with their whole hearts. I know you grieve when you cannot celebrate your feast days with Me on My Land. I know you want to sing and dance during your feasts days with your other brothers and sisters. I know you grow weary in exile. My promise to you is true. I will deliver you from exile and bring you home to the Land that I promised your ancestors. I threw them out of My Land, because of their wickedness, but I will remember you and how you want to keep My laws and walk in My ways. I will bless you and deliver you from the bondage of exile, so you can dance and sing once more on My Land. The day is soon when I will call for you and you will come. Open your ears and listen. I will tell you the day to come to My Land. You will see the open door and come to My Land. You will be placed in a good place, and you will be in My presence. You will know that you are blessed, because I AM so close to you. Come to Me My People. Come to Me My beloved ones. Come to Me and dwell in My presence.

Zechariah 14:1-9

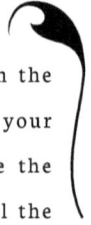

My Beloved, I will gather all the nations together against Jerusalem in the last days. The city will be captured and one half of it will be taken by your enemies. I will arise and stand on the Mount of Olives. I will divide the mountains and make a way for My Children to escape. I will destroy all the nations that have made war against My People. I will destroy all of them, so My People can live in peace. I will come and live in the midst of My People. I will be their king. I will reign over them. I will feed them the bread of life and they will rejoice in My Presence. They will love Me with all their hearts and want to draw near to Me and serve Me. They will be faithful children not like their ancestors. They will be bold and brave knowing that they will not falter, because their love for Me is so strong. They will long to only serve Me. In the midst of Jerusalem a new fragrance will arise. The sweet smell of My People praising Me in spirit and truth will ascend to Me. I will cover My Presence over My Land and My People will rejoice in My closeness. No nation will come against My People. No one will want to come close to My Presence. They will fear Me and know that I AM the only Elohim. I AM the only King. I AM the only One who creates. I AM and I AM.

Strength And Encouragement

Zechariah 14:10-21

My Beloved, in the last days I will arise and protect Jerusalem from her enemies. Now she fights daily with her enemies not knowing when they will attack and descend upon them like locusts. In that day I will fight against their enemies. I will destroy the curse that has been on Jerusalem. I will destroy the curse that has been on My People. There will be peace in Jerusalem. I will destroy all those who come against her. Their eyes and tongue will be dissolved in their heads. Their flesh will fall away from their bones. They will disintegrate before your eyes. I have made weapons of warfare for My People, and they will use these weapons in the last day to conquer all their enemies. The nations will not be able to stand against My People. They will have no power against them. They will turn on each other and battle against each other in their confusion. They will know that I AM and there is no other. The world will know who I AM and all the enemies of My People will be destroyed. It will be a day to rejoice and be glad. I have conquered all your enemies, and now Jerusalem will have peace at last. Peace will be on My People, and all will know that My Presence dwells in Jerusalem for My People who love Me.

Malachi 3:16-4:6

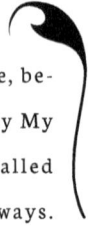

My Beloved, you are My own special treasure. You are called by My Name, because I have adopted you and given you My Name. No one else is called by My Name, but My Children, My own unique special treasure. No one will be called by My Name unless he loves Me and serves Me and wants to walk in My ways. A child listens to his father's voice and honors him and obeys him unless he is wicked. A wicked child will disobey his father and rebel against his wisdom and advice. A wicked child will want his own way and not want to hear the voice of his father. My children love me and want to hear My words and listen for My voice. If you love Me, you will want to please Me. I have recorded in My books all your days and all your deeds. I have you balanced and tried. You will be found worthy to enter My Kingdom or you will be counted unworthy and not enter My Kingdom, but be thrown into the Lake of Fire. Few are My Children who love Me and want to serve Me. Many want to go the way of the world. Only My special children who have the seed of righteousness will be found worthy. They will seek Me and find Me and want to walk in the ways of their ancestors who loved Me.

Strength And Encouragement

Job 38:1-18

My Beloved, who are you that you can question Me in what I do for you? Who are you? Have you formed the earth? Have you made man? Have you created anything at all? What is it that you can do without Me? There is nothing that you can do apart from Me. I hold your breathe in My Hands. I know the number of your days of life on this planet. I know the path you will take for your entire life. I know all the people you will touch by your loving kindness. I know how much you will give to others and how you will give My Truth to others. If you love Me, you will not question Me. You will trust Me. You will want to have faith in Me and listen for My voice to guide you. You will want to listen for My wisdom that I will give you, if only you ask Me to do it. You should not ever question My will for you. If I take away from you, it is because it will benefit you. If I give to you, it is because it will benefit you or others. I do all this to form you into My image and make you ready to reign with Me in My kingdom. If you are My child, you will be humble before Me and you will want to submit yourself to Me and do whatever I tell you to do knowing that I will only bring good things to you. What you think is a good thing may not be a good thing for you. Only I know what you need, so do not question My judgment but accept My will for you every day.

Job 40:1-14

My Beloved, do you hold the key to wisdom? Do you hold the key to the storehouse of knowledge which is locked and only unveiled to those who are worthy to enter My kingdom? Do you tell the angels what to do every day? They are my servants and they only respond to My voice. I AM looking for a people who will only respond to My voice and will respond quickly and obediently wanting to please Me. I AM looking for a people who want to walk uprightly and never turn from My path of righteousness. I AM looking for a people who want to separate themselves from the things of the world, because they do not want to be like the world. They want to be set apart and remain set apart before Me. They are anointed by My presence and they know Me and are intimate with Me. They long for Me and desire My presence. They seek Me daily and often. They cut off the things of the world from coming into their home. They remain pure before Me and they sit quietly and listen for My guidance. If you do not like to do any of these things, then you must search your heart and see if there is sin within you. Repent from your sin, so you can sit quietly in My presence and enjoy the Light that comes from Me. I will bring you revelation knowledge from My storehouse of knowledge. I will allow you to peek inside and see hidden things, because I love you so much.

Strength And Encouragement

Ruth 1:16-18

My Beloved, I will call you to come to Me, and you may be in any nation in the world. You may be scattered to a land far away from your home, but I AM calling you to return to your Land that I have given you. You may have to leave the only land that you have ever known, but you will desire to hear My voice and obey Me. You will want to leave and cling to Me just like Ruth could not leave her mother-in-law. Naomi had showed Ruth a better way to live through serving Me. You will see a better way to live and will want to come to the Land of your ancestors. You will want to walk in My ways and do My will. Ruth did not want to be left behind in her country and serve her pagan gods. You had met Me and knew My ways, and she could not depart from My ways and live as the pagans lived again. She wanted to go with Naomi to her Land and her people. Ruth had seen Truth and embraced it. You must embrace Truth and receive it and cling to it and never want to leave Truth. You will want to obey Me and My ways and not cling to the things of the world or even look into their darkness. If you love Me, you will want to return to My Land and be with your people. You will sing and dance unto Me and keep all My feast days. You will rejoice together and be at peace at last in My Land.

Lamentations 3:21-26

My Beloved, it is good to wait on Me patiently and allow Me to move on behalf of you. If you call on My Name and ask Me to do something for you, then you must believe that I will do it for you. If what you ask will not benefit you, then I will tell you that I will not do this for you. Otherwise whatever you ask for from Me, I will give to you. You may have to wait on Me for a while before I answer your prayer. I will give you what you ask in the time that is right for you, so you can know that I AM faithful and will give you all good things. If you call on My Name often, then we can reason together and I will show you what is good for you and what is not. I AM all you have. I AM the One you should cling to. I AM your Elohim and there is no other. If you remember that I AM your Father and I only bring you good gifts, then you can realize that I will hear your prayers and let you know if this is good for you. You may pray for others and not know their needs like I do. I will let you know what others need, so you can help them. Most of the time all they need is your love to encourage them and heal them. Love can heal many wounds that will make them stronger and stronger. You never know who needs your love, so love all men and do not judge them or be prejudice towards them. You do not know their heart. Only I know the hearts of men.

Strength And Encouragement

Lamentations 3:34-42

My Beloved, the courts of men can make errors in their judgment, but I never make any errors in judgment. I know the hearts of men. I know the sins they are hiding inside. I know what they are thinking. I know when their heart is turned towards Me, and when it isn't. If you love Me, then I will know it and I can guard over you even in the courts of men. I will make sure that justice comes to you. I hold the heart of the judge in the palm of My Hand. Even the cruelest judge I can change his mind and have mercy on you. You must not judge others, but allow Me to continue to judge them and pass the punishment on them that I desire. If the world falls around you, I will take care of you because I AM your Elohim. I AM the One who will cover you from the rocks and will give you water in the desert. When destruction comes to your land, I will tell you in advance so you can leave and escape destruction. I will send you back to your home-My Land-the Land of your ancestors. You will rejoice and be glad that you have returned at last with all the other people who love Me and want to keep My feast days. You will no longer yearn to be back at your old home, but you will be at peace and rest in the new home that I have made for you.

Ecclesiastes 3:1-17

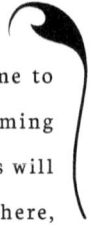

My Beloved, there is a time for everything- a time to punish and a time to reward-a time to curse and a time to bless. Everything is in my perfect timing before I weight the scales and balance the deeds of men, so the righteous will be able to enter the Kingdom of Heaven. They must be tried and tested here, so they can be found worthy of entering the gates of My Kingdom. How do I balance the scales? How do I make things justified in My eyes? Only a wise Elohim would be able to do this. I have laws and if they are broken the person must pay the penalty for breaking the laws. If the person does not know that he has broken a law and broke it unintentionally, then his penalty is light but he must still pay the penalty. If he broke the law in rebellion to Me, then he must pay the full penalty of breaking My law. How does a man pay the price? He may have the penalty taken off his flesh by causing him pain and suffering through a disease or accident, because he has caused others pain and suffering. He may have his wealth taken away, because he has to make restitution to those he has taken from. He may have his pride afflicted, because he has been prideful and arrogant and looked down on others. Now others will look down on him, and he will feel the pain of this suffering. He may have to watch his children suffer or his children may go into rebellion, because he went into rebellion as a child and did not obey his parents. However you treat others is how I will treat you, and this is how your punishment will come to you. If you walk in righteousness, then you will be blessed and good things will come to you in the right season.

Strength And Encouragement

Ecclesiastes 4:9-12

My Beloved, cling to Me and I will guide you along this path as you walk alone. I will provide for you friends-brothers and sisters-along your path that you can stand with and pray with and support each other. I will provide you a mate, so you can be as one with him/her and hold him/her and love him/her. I will provide for you children to hold you and need you, so you can guide them in the path of life. If you do not listen to what I say, then you will be alone and lonely and have no one close to you. You will suffer because of your sins. If you are obedient to Me, then I will bless you with all good things-a mate, children, a family, and friends that believe in Me. If you want to go your own way, then you will end up lacking and without what you need to be happy. Do not complain against Me when you are alone. Remember your sins and know that I promised to give you good things, if you listened to My voice. If you will turn aside from your sins, then I will return to you what has been taken from you. You will rejoice that you have turned aside from your sins and want to walk in righteousness. If you wonder why others have so much sadness, then look at their life and see that the sins in their life have kept them from many blessings. If you want to comfort those in grieve, just love them and I will help them see clearly. Your only purpose in this life is to love others, and help them when they are in need.

Ecclesiastes 5:2-7

My Beloved, be very careful before you make a promise to someone. Make sure you can keep that promise. If you tell someone that you are going to do something, then they are expecting you to do what you say you will do. They will suffer disappointment, if you do not follow through with what you say you will do. If you make a promise to Me that you will do something if I do something for you, then you must follow through with your vow. It is better to trust Me to do what is best for you, than to ask Me to do something for you and you promise to do something for Me in return. This puts you in a very difficult situation. If I give you what you want, then you must fulfill your promise. If you do not fulfill your promise, then you will have to pay the consequences. If is better to trust Me to give to you what is good in My sight. When others break their promise to you, you are sad. Forgive the person, so I can forgive the person and set them free from their sins. I will still punish them for what they did not do for you. I will take into account what suffering they have caused you and make sure what punishment I give is equal to the suffering that it caused you, so they can learn from their sins. You must guard over your mouth at all times. Stop and think before you speak. Let your words be seasoned with salt and light. Do not allow your words to be filled with hatred or anger. If you speak in anger, you will regret your words later and want to take back the words you have already spoken. You must be silent until you have fully thought through what effect your words will have on others, and this will please Me.

Ecclesiastes 5:10-20

My Beloved, do not love money or the possessions that money can buy. They will flee from you. I will take all your money away, if you love money more than Me. If you love money, then you will not love others. You will not give away your money to the poor. You will want to store up your money and see it grow with interest. You will want to see how much money you can make and brag about your wealth. You will want to buy expensive possessions and brag about the possessions that you have. I can take them all away in a moment. I AM in control of your life and I will give you only what I want you to have. I will give to you freely, if you love Me and want to serve Me. A righteous man works hard every day and makes money for his family, so they can have food, clothes, and shelter. A righteous man gives to the poor, and he helps those in need of his help. A righteous man will not love money, but he will work hard to make money. A hard worker sleeps well at night because he is satisfied with his life. A wealthy man will over eat his expensive food, and he will toss and turn in his bed at night. He will have no peace. He will look for peace and not find it. Think about what you want from your life. Do you want to leave an inheritance for your children, so they will honor your name? Do you want to be righteous before Me? Do you want to be at one with Me? Make the right decisions and I will bless you.

Ecclesiastes 11:9-10, 12:13-14

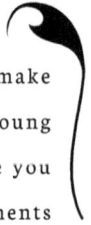

My Beloved, if you are young, then you need to look at your life and make decisions for your future. Do you want to just have fun while you are young or do you want to plan for your future and your family that I will give you if you delight in Me? If you listen to My words and obey My commandments instead of following your friends and seeking your own pleasure, then I will bless you with abundance. I will make sure that you are rewarded, because you did not follow the crowd to party and folly. If you keep yourself pure and do not fall into sexual sin, then you will be a blessing to the mate that I give you. You will want to please only that person and not desire to go after other people for sexual pleasure. If you keep away from the crowd that runs toward darkness, then you will be filled with Light and know the way to go. You will be able to see the world in a different light. You will guard over your body and keep away from sin. You will want to walk in righteousness even at an early age. You will know that I have you in the palm of My Hand, and I will keep you safe and always provide for you. Youth is fleeing and soon you will have the responsibilities of an adult. Look ahead and see the value of preparing for the future.

Strength And Encouragement

Esther 4:1-14

My Beloved, I put Esther in a position of authority and gave her favor with the king. When her people were persecuted, she was in a position to talk with the king and persuade him to turn this vengeance aside and allow her people to stand up and fight to protect themselves. Esther was afraid that the king would dismiss her if she came to his chamber and kill her, but I gave her favor in his eyes and he accepted her to come before him and speak with him. He never once thought of killing her. He knew that if she came to speak with him that if must be important. He knew there must be a traitor in his midst. The king was a wise man and he watched over his kingdom carefully. When he learned of Haman's desire to kill all My People he was astonished that Haman had been so deceitful. He was furious, and did not want a man with such deception to continue to live in his kingdom. What would be his next plan? The king hung the wicked Haman and saved My People. Esther called out to Me through praying and fasting for 3 days, so I would hear her voice. She sought Me to give her wisdom what to do. She arose peacefully from her fast knowing that I would give her passage and favor with the king. She was placed in her position for such a time as this. Since she stood up and was bold and brave, I rewarded her. The memory of her life can be read by My People and they can rejoice in her bravery and be inspired to stand up and be brave when challenged. Will you be bold and brave when you need to be? Will you stand up for your faith and make the right choices? I will reward those who are courageous.

Daniel 2:14-23

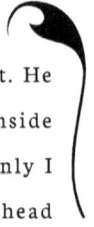

My Beloved, Daniel was a humble man. He sought Me with all his heart. He sought Me and I gave him hidden treasures. I allowed him to peek inside the storehouse of secret things-the hidden things and see the future. Only I can see the future, because I know all things. No created being can see ahead unless I reveal it to him. Others can see the past, but only I can see ahead. If you look to other sources to see ahead, then you will fall into deception. No horoscope or card readings can give you an accurate reading of your future. Others may guess at the future, but only I can give accurate details of what is about to happen. I unveiled the future to John, and he wrote it down so all My Children can see what was coming ahead. I never leave My People without a vision for the future. I always speak through My Prophets and tell them what to expect in the future, so they can be prepared. I have told you that I will call all My Children home to My Land and give strength back to the Land again. The Land calls out to Me to be cleansed of all the sin on it. I will cleanse the Land and call you home, so you can rejoice and be glad once again. I know that you grow weary in exile, but I will hold you up and keep you safe until I bring you and your children home again. Be bold and brave and listen to My Voice, and come when I tell you that it is time to come. Do not try to come sooner than I want you to come, or you will be caught up in the destruction of the Land. I will bring you home in a time that you can reap and sow the Land and be prosperous and rejoice, so wait until you hear My Call.

Matthew 4:1-11

My Beloved, I was put to the test on Earth and I overcame and was counted as victorious. I was tested by the Evil One. He came to Me three times to test Me. He came with deceit, but I could see his deceit clearly. He came to Me at a time when my flesh was weak, but My spirit within Me was strong. I saw his darkness and his lies pouring out of him. I knew that he came to kill Me and find Me unworthy to overtake the Kingdom once again. He asked me to make bread, but I stood on the Words which bring life, and he was paralyzed and could not break through to Me. He came again and I also used the Words that bring life, and he could not break through to Me. He came again, and I rebuked him and told him to leave so he had to leave Me. My angels came to minister to Me and bring Me food. He is wicked in all his ways. He will bring you lies to your door. You must rebuke him and turn away from him. You are to have no conversation with him or any of his demons. You are to quote My Words of life to him, and he will not be able to break through and harm you. You will be safe in My arms of love no matter what the enemy tries to do to you. Be prepared, because the days are growing darker and you must know My Promises and trust Me in all you do and say.

Matthew 5:1-16

My Beloved, I came to Earth to walk among you and see My People. I found My People, but they were down trodden with rules from the religious leaders. I wanted to restore My Words and give them meaning and life once again. I showed My disciples how to walk in My ways and what is Truth and Light. I told My disciples to be a Light to the world and let them see their good works and loving kindness to all men. I gave them a good example of how to treat others. My disciples walked in My footsteps, because they heard the Truth and it adhered to their inner man and fed them manna-the bread of life. I AM the Bread and I AM the Truth and I AM the Life. No one comes to salvation except through Me. I told My People to have mercy on others and to make peace with all men. I told My People to expect the evil ones to persecute you and treat you harshly. I will deliver you from the hands of your adversary. I AM calling My People to come back to My Land. Listen to My Voice and come when I tell you to come.

Matthew 5:17-20

My Beloved, I came to fulfill or complete the law, not to break the law. The prophets told My People that I was coming. They wrote all their words down, so My People could know My Plan for them and know how they must repent and draw close to Me. My People have been reading My Words from the prophets and waiting for My Words to come to pass. Now the end of the age draws near, and the signs are unveiling themselves. The prophets could see in part, but you will see clearly. You will see the hidden mysteries. You will see clearly how My Promises will unfold. Do not be afraid of the future. As long as you are guided by My Spirit, you will know just what to do. Some say that I came to put an end to My Laws, but My laws never end. They were put in place for eternity. My Laws established the earth and created everything that is in it. My Laws are supreme to all living things. There are no other laws but Mine. If a man adds to My Laws, then he is worthy of punishment. Have My Laws passed away? No they are firm and unending. I judge the universe on My Laws. All the foundations stand on these laws. Rejoice and be glad that I have given you so much.

Matthew 5:21-26

My Beloved, I told My Children not to murder someone, or even hate someone so that you think about killing him. I have told you to love others, because this is the foundation that all My Laws are based upon. If you cannot love others, then you cannot love Me. If you love only yourself and try to serve only yourself, then you will be subject to My Wrath, and you must pay the penalty of your wickedness. I tell you to love others, and do not hate your brother. Forgive your brother who has harmed you and settle things with him. He must pay you restitution, if he has wronged you. If he doesn't want to pay you restitution, then I will deal with him. Forgive him and I will bring My lashes on his back and bring him lower and lower until he repents and restores what he has taken from you. Many come to you and want things from you, but give to only those who I say to give to, so you will not be grievous against your brother. I will guide you and tell you when to give to your brother, so he will not harm you but bless you. If you are angry, then repent of your anger and allow Me to heal your heart, and forgive the person so you can be freed from sin. Bitterness and unforgiveness are sins that can wreck your life and cause you great pain. If you forgive and let go, then I can heal you and comfort you. If you are stuck in unforgiveness, call on My Name and I will help you overcome and be able to forgive the person, and be released from the bondage of unforgiveness.

Strength And Encouragement

Matthew 5:27-32

My Beloved, keep pure and do not look on the bodies of others and desire them. If your eyes want to look lustfully on the bodies of others, then cut out your eye, so that you do not sin. Do I really mean to cut out your eye? No, I mean for you to cut your sight off to sin no matter what it takes. If you will look at your mate whom I have given you and look at his/her love for you and how this person serves you, then you can rejoice that I have given you a mate to walk along with you on this journey of life. Do not look at the faults of your mate, but look at all the good things that your mate does. Some people have no partner to walk with them. Some have chosen to walk alone. My desire is for you and your mate to walk together hand in hand. If you break the marriage covenant with your partner, then repent and ask your partner to forgive you, so you can renew your vow of marriage and walk uprightly in My Presence. If you say that you cannot live with this person anymore, then repent and love this person, so you can remain pure before Me. Call upon My Name and I will restore your love for your mate once again. Do not make your partner fall into sin and fall into adultery. If you do this, then I will hold it against you. Repent and walk in the covenant that you have been given, and you will do well and be blessed.

Matthew 5:33-48

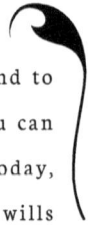

My Beloved, I told you to keep your vows and your promises to Me and to men. I do not want you to make a vow or promise to others unless you can keep it. You do not know what tomorrow will bring. You only know today, so do not make vows that you will do this or that, but say, "If Father wills it, then I will help you." If you make a vow or promise and cannot fulfill it, then go to that person and ask forgiveness. If the person will not forgive you, then you must make restitution to him, so you will not be held accountable for your sin. If a man is mean to you, then love him back. If he asks you to do something out of meanness or hatred, then do it in love and let him see how you serve Me in love. Show him mercy and I will deal with his heart. If a man continues to show you unkindness, then continue to love him and cast fire upon his head. He will be destined for the Lake of Fire, if he does not repent. The main reason you are here is to be tested to see if you are worthy to enter My Kingdom. To be found worthy, you must love others and serve Me with all your heart. Do not be sad if someone hates you. I will deal with the person, and I will punish him for his sins against you. I AM faithful to care for you. I know when someone is harming you. When he has been weighed in the balance, he will be lacking and My Hand will smite him, because he has harmed you. Do not take revenge into your hands, but allow Me to give the proper punishment to the man. Only I know what will break the man and bring him to repentance. If you seek revenge, then punishment has been cast on him by you and this is all the punishment that he will receive. You have authority to punish those who harm you, but if you put that authority in My Hand, then I will punish him in a way that will make him repent. Trust Me to punish those who harm you.

Matthew 6:1-18

My Beloved, I told My disciples not to parade around like the religious leaders of the day who blew trumpets when they gave large gifts to the Temple and gave their gifts to the poor. They gave large gifts, so they would be recognized in front of the people and bring honor to their name not Mine. I told My disciples to give in secret and not tell others what they are doing, so I could give them a reward. If you tell others about your faithfulness to Me, then you have lifted up yourself, and you have received your reward. I want you to give to Me and not tell others about what you are doing, so I can bless you by My Hand. If you will come to Me and pray in private and let me know what you need, I will give it to you. Of course I already know what you need before you even ask. I taught My disciples how to pray. I told them to praise Me and thank Me for all My many blessings that I have given to them. I told them to ask Me to forgive them for their sins, but only if they had forgiven the people who had wronged them. You cannot be forgiven by Me, if you have not forgiven others for their wrongs against you. I told them to ask for what they needed for today trusting Me to provide what they would need tomorrow. You never have to worry, because I will give you everything that you need. I love you. You are a treasure to Me, so I will guard over you and keep you close to Me all the days of your life.

Matthew 6:19-24

My Beloved, do not love money and desire to only make money. Do not put money before Me and your family. If you are a slave to money, then you will not be a slave of Mine. If you love money so much that you work all the time and you love to spend your money on yourself, then you have lost My will for you. I want you to give to others and take care of those in need. I know that you are angry when others do not work and are cared for by the government and yet they want you to help them. I say to you not to help anyone if they choose not to work. These people are not My People. If someone has fallen into a bad time, and he cannot find work but he wants to work and benefit his family, then this person is the one you should help to get on his feet so he can provide for his family. Those that want someone to help them, and they do not want to help themselves are not My Chosen People. My People work hard and benefit their family and those in need of help. You will know when to give, because I will tell you by My Spirit. Guard over your heart, so you are not longing for money. Accept the money that I have given you and know I give you only what you need. I will give you the job I want you to have. I will bless your business, only if you give to others and are not stingy. You must follow what I tell you to do, and then all will go well with you.

Strength And Encouragement

Matthew 6:25-34

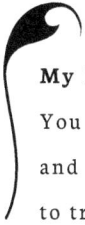

My Beloved, do not worry about the future. Do you have enough for today? You will have enough for every day. You will be given food, clothing, shelter, and all you need, so you can be formed into My image. You are on this planet to transform you into My image-a glorious child who will be given authority over other peoples. You will rule over others under My authority. You will teach them about Me and My love for them. You will be My priests spread among the universe. You will be glorious like fire and light. You will be pure and righteous before Me. You are My beloved, so know that I will care for you at all times. Nothing can harm you. No man can touch you. You are in My Hands and I will lift you up above the circumstances and take you to another place. I am almost ready to pull My Children from all over the world and take them to My Land once again. I will bring you singing and dancing to My Land. The rest of the world will not understand your joy, but I will know what is in your heart and I will rejoice over you. I will bless you greatly. As the rest of the earth will fall under great tribulations, you will remain at peace and rest in My arms of love.

Matthew 7:1-6

My Beloved, do not judge those around you in an evil way. Do not cast evil words on others and criticize them for what they do. Do not embarrass them with your words. Build up your brother and give him encouraging words. Help him to find the right path. If you want to judge him harshly and not help him, then this is sin. If you rebuke your brother for his sin and help him by encouraging him to go a different way and live a righteous life style, you have done well. If you think that you can cast your angry, bitter words on others and not be held accountable for them, then you are wrong. If you are critical and harsh and not kind to your brother, then you make him fall under self criticism and self condemnation. If you build him up and pray with him for strength and walk beside him and not give up on him, then you have done well. If you see someone that is not a believer and you try to tell him the Truth, he will trample the Truth under his feet and blaspheme My Name. Do not cast what is pure and righteous before any unclean man and have him bring you down with his words of treachery. I would rather you not say anything to him at all. Choose your words wisely and always speak with love and be careful to whom you give My words of Truth. Be wise as a serpent, but harmless as a dove.

Strength And Encouragement

Matthew 7:7-14

My Beloved, ask Me for help and I will help you. Ask Me to guide you along your path, and I will guide you. Ask Me to provide for you, and I will provide for you. Ask Me to show you the Light and Truth, and I will bring it to your house. If you will seek Me, you will find Me. You will find righteousness and be able to walk in it. If you come and knock on My door, then you will be able to come in and be intimate with Me. Do not desire the things of the world, but desire Me and the things of the spirit. Only I can give you good gifts. Only I can show you the way into My Kingdom of Light. Love those around you, and treat others the way that you would like to be treated. My way is the way of love. If you love others, then you love Me. If you are selfish and want only what you want, then you do not know love at all. You are not worthy to enter My Kingdom. You are not My servant. My servant gives generously to those around him, and walks in the way of Light. If you want to keep all I have given you, then you are selfish. If you want to give to others, then you are generous and will be blessed. Many times you have a chance to give to others, so open your arms of love and give generously. I will help you overcome and not be so fleshly. Call on My Name to help you overcome and I will help you. You will have to walk a hard road and be tested before you can be found worthy. You have to walk on the narrow road and be righteous in all you do and say. You cannot walk down the way of the world and expect to find Me. Be strong and be brave, and walk down the narrow path to peace and contentment.

Matthew 7:15-27

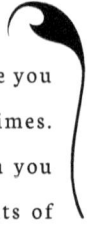

My Beloved, you must walk in Truth, and you must bear good fruit before you can enter My Kingdom. You must be ready to do what is right at all times. If you love yourself, you will not want to love Me. If you love Me, then you will want to please Me and want in the way of righteousness. The fruits of the spirit are love, peace, joy, and a spirit of giving to others. You must want to see others be happy and at peace. You will go to great lengths to see your brother walk in righteousness and be at peace. If you see your brother and he needs you to stand beside him, then walk beside him for a while until he can stand alone. The world is hard and many times you need your brother to walk beside you and encourage you. You need to lean on him for awhile. I will give you strength to stand, but an encouraging word will heal a man's spirit. If you think that you want to walk alone, then think again. Two men are stronger than one, and three men cannot be easily broken apart. You can stand alone only if you have the strength to do so, but I have given you others to help you in your journey. If you display your fruits to all men, they will see your fruits and they will be encouraged to walk in the fruits of righteousness. If you are blooming with good fruit, I will bless your fruit and you will produce even more. Think on these words and do not falter. Be like the man who built his house on a rock-a firm foundation. He never moved, because he knew who he believed in. Believe only in Me and you will never be moved.

Strength And Encouragement

Matthew 10:16-30

My Beloved, be on guard. The enemy is all around you. He is watching to accuse you and turn you over to evil men. The enemy wants to harm My People, but I care for My People even in exile. Even in exile I watch over you and keep you safe. You are precious to Me. You are My Treasure, so I tenderly care for you. Do not fear man. What can he do to you without My permission? Fear Me and what will happen to you if you do not walk in My ways and serve Me with your whole heart. Fear Me and walk in righteousness. Serve Me, and love Me, and teach your children to serve Me and love Me. If you do not serve Me, then you will search for another master to serve. What master will you serve? Money, power, fame, yourself? Who do you serve? You must serve only Me and walk in My ways of love and devotion. You must be guided by compassion and mercy. There are many all around you that need to learn about Me and My love. If you walk in love, then you will not have to speak a word to them, but your joy, peace, and happiness in Me will touch them and allow them to see Me. Watch carefully over the example you leave for others. Deny your flesh and think of what you need to leave for others. If you are faithful to Me, then I will be faithful to you, and deliver you from exile, and take you to your Land-the Land of your ancestors.

Matthew 10:31-42

My Beloved, honor Me before men, and I will honor you before men. Lift up your voice and tell others about how much you love Me. You do not have to tell them anything else. Just tell them about all the blessings that I give you and about the Truth that I have brought to you to set you free from the bondage of sin. You do not have to tell them about all the things you know. Most people are only interested in love and joy and happiness and how to receive it. They can learn later all the laws that I have given you as I direct them by My Spirit. You must be careful about whatever you do and say. Someone is always watching you and judging you for how you live your life. You must be on guard to walk in love all the time and never give up. You should always want to do what is right. Do not grow weary in walking in righteousness, because I will bless you for your endurance. The end is coming soon when I will take My Children back to My Land. You must be counted worthy to enter My Land, just like My People in the Wilderness could not enter until they were found faithful to Me. You must be found faithful, and I will guide you into My Land of Promise.

Strength And Encouragement

Matthew 12:25-37

My Beloved, others know you by your fruit. What fruit are you bearing? Are you displaying love on your tree of life? Are you displaying peace? Are you displaying joy even in the midst of troubles? What do you display to others? If you are fearful and worrying and complaining, then how can you display fruit that others would want to have? You want to show others that the life you live is worth living. You want to show others that you have something that they do not have. You want to show others that you have peace, because you have allowed Me to guide you. You want others to see your joy and ask you why you are happy all the time. You can testify that I dwell in the midst of you and bring you joy, peace, and happiness. The greatest commandment is that you love others. If you love others, then you walk in My Ways and know who I AM. You cannot know Me, if you do not love others and forgive them for their wrongdoings. If you want to walk in the Light, then love those around you. Do not judge them harshly, but have mercy on them, and then I will judge them and I will convict them and bring them to repentance. Love them in the midst of their sin, and they will see your good works and love you also. The words that come out of your mouth show what kind of person you are. Guard over your heart and mouth, and I will bless you greatly.

Matthew 13:1-9, 18-23

My Beloved, everyone has a chance to hear the good news: "I have come to deliver you from sin through My blood that I shed for you". If any man hears the Truth and receives it, then he will inherit the Kingdom of Light. Some men hear the words of Truth, but they allow the world and its glitter to overshadow the words of Truth and they turn away quickly from the path of righteousness. Satan tries to make the world seem bright and happy, if you sin. Some learn the words of Truth, but they allow worries about life to over-take them and destroy the words of faith within them, and they turn quickly away from the path of righteousness. No man comes to Me except that he has faith in Me. Some men are turned away quickly from the way of righteousness when I ask them to deny themselves and follow Me. They love themselves so much and the pleasures of the flesh. They are blinded and do not want to walk towards Me, so they turn towards wickedness. Flesh is temporary and its plea-sures are temporary. If you do not want to give up the pleasures of the flesh and you want to indulge in the things of the world, then you will have no part with Me in My Kingdom. I know My Children and I know who loves Me. My Children call on My Name all day long. They want to be intimate with Me and know Me. They want to walk in righteousness and never stray from the path of Truth. My Children are loving and kind and giving and would never hurt anyone. My Children are a Light to the world that no man can put out. The seed of righteousness within them is firmly planted and is growing strong and mighty. No man can tear out the root of righteousness within them. They confess their love for Me and never waiver even in the darkest of days. They are light and love and a treasure to those who can see all their good works. Rejoice that I love you so much, and give you such good gifts from My Heav-enly Kingdom.

Strength And Encouragement

Matthew 15:10-20

My Beloved, you have been given My Laws and they are not burdensome. They are life to all who keep them. My People have been given many man-made laws that are a heavy burden and do not bring life. They cause confusion and dissatisfaction. I told My disciples that the law that the religious leaders created to wash their hands up to their elbows was not what kept them clean. What comes out of a man's mouth is what keeps them clean, because whatever is in his heart is what comes out of a man. You can tell how clean a man is by the things that he talks about. If a man loves the things of the flesh, then he will bring forth the uncleanness of his flesh by the words that he speaks. If a man remains silent, then no one knows that is in his heart. A fool rattles on and on and exposes his sins. A wise man is silent, and no man can judge him. If you desire the things of the flesh, then your sins will be exposed to others as you speak. Watch over your tongue and guard yourself, so that you are not judged by your words and what you say and do. If you guard you eyes and ears, then you will guard over your life. Only look on things that are clean and listen to things that are clean and pure. If you delight in sinful movies and music and find your happiness in this, then be warned. You will reap what you sinfully do, and trouble will fall on you. The more you indulge into wickedness, the harder it will be for you to set yourself free. Do not think that since you are young that you can change when you grow older. All the wickedness that you are exposing yourself to at this present time will linger into your adulthood and cause you much grief. Be wise and keep yourself clean, so you can draw close to Me and experience My awesome power and might in your life.

Matthew 16:24-27

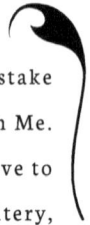

My Beloved, if you desire to follow Me, then you must pick up your own stake and follow Me. You will have to deny your flesh and walk in oneness with Me. If you love the pleasures of your flesh, then you cannot love Me. If you love to lie, indulge in carnal sex, boast in pride, steal from others, commit adultery, and you think that no one will see what you do, then you are wrong. I see all things. I see your drunkenness and your lustfulness. I see you gossiping and slandering others. I see your jealousy and your greed. I see your selfishness and I know that you want to only serve yourself. You have set yourself up as a god. You have made yourself an idol. You dress yourself and put jewels on yourself and you decorate your home like a temple. You indulge yourself at any moment. You do not want to work, but you want to indulge yourself in the things of the world through its movies, TV, music, and clothes. You see the idols of the world and you want to be just like them. You do not despise them, but you envy their lifestyle. You do not realize that you are lost in your wickedness. You draw closer to the shadows and are lost in the darkness around you. Your time is running out to turn towards the Light and love Me with all your heart. I have warned you many times, but soon the time of grace with be over and you will pay for all your sins and be destroyed in the Lake of Fire. You will wonder what you did that kept you so blinded. You are wicked and your heart longs for wickedness. You have no place in My Kingdom of Light. You must deny your flesh or you serve the world. You must do as I say and walk in My Ways, or you will never enter My Kingdom of Light. Rejoice that you can see so clearly and can reign with Me eternally.

Strength And Encouragement

Matthew 18:21-35

My Beloved, forgive those who wrong you. Forgive those who hurt you. Forgive those who plot against you to harm you. Forgive those who take from you and steal what is yours. They will receive the full payment of their sins. If you will forgive, then I will forgive you. If you continue to be unforgiving and you are revengeful, then I will not forgive you. I will forgive you only if you forgive others. I will break the darkness from you, so you can see clearly. If you call on My Name and ask Me to help you learn how to forgive others, then I will show you how to love others and look past their sins and look at them the way that I look at them. You will not hold their sin against them, but you will set them free from the sins against you. As a result of this, you will be set free through your forgiveness. No man can draw close to Me if he holds unforgiveness and bitterness in his heart. He must forgive all men just like I forgave all men who have come to Me and asked Me to forgive them and want to serve Me as a bondservant. Since I forgave your debt of sin, then you became My servant and work for only Me. I AM the legal owner of you, and I tell you what to do, so you can walk in righteousness. If you will listen to My voice and obey Me, then you will have a life filled with peace, joy, and happiness. I want you to be happy here while you walk in the flesh. As long as you listen to Me and obey Me, then your short time here will not be miserable. You will be blessed by My Hands and draw closer to Me. Do not think that I will forget you in this life. I send you blessings everyday and only want good things for you. Lift up your eyes, if you are straying today. I will take your hand and bring you back to the good things in this life, because I AM the Life.

Luke 18:1-14

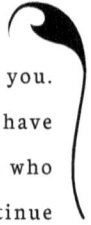

My Beloved, do not stop praying. Do not think that I do not want to hear you. Do not think that I will turn a deaf ear to you. I AM fair and just. I will have mercy on you even while you are on exile. I will deliver you from those who oppress you. I will deliver you from all evil people that hate you. Continue to pray without ceasing. Certainly I will bring good gifts to you, because I love you so much. Sometimes you may be battling in the spirit and you must continue in prayer and have endurance before your prayers will break though the curses that have been placed on you or your community. You may have to fight against darkness in your area to overcome and have your prayers become as fire before Me. You must never give up, because I will see your faithfulness to pray and fast and I will deliver you from your troubles. I will bring salvation to those who you battle for and do not want to lose to the evil one. I have placed it in your heart to pray for the person, and your grip will not let go of them. You will be given great rewards for your faithfulness to pray for this person. Do not become haughty as you pray, but remain humble repenting of your sins and staying pure before Me. I want to listen to the prayers of a righteousness man. I want to listen to someone who praises Me, and knows that he is not worthy of entering My Kingdom. Only through My mercy and grace you can enter into My courtroom and enter your pleas before Me and know that I have heard you and I will move on behalf of you. View all men as equal in My sight. All men have sinned and gone astray from the Truth. Only through My love have you been saved from your transgressions and brought to a place where you can commune with Me. Rejoice in this!!!

Strength And Encouragement

John 1:1-14

My Beloved, in the beginning I AM and always will be. In the beginning I made the world and the entire universe. I made all things and placed them on the earth. In the beginning I spoke and it came to be. In the beginning I spoke and it was filled with light. There was darkness and light. I filled the darkness with light. I brought life to the darkness. I spoke and I created beings to fill the earth. I looked into them and they were evil, because they did not know Me. They did not desire to know Me, so I washed them all away except one man and his family. One man wanted to know Me, so I saved him and placed him on dry land and started his family as the new people on this earth. All the others were washed away. All life on earth was replaced by this family, and the animals that they brought in this little boat. I protected this family and I brought forth a pure righteous seed onto the earth, but once again the evil one produced evil seeds and brought murder and bloodshed to the earth. I came to the evil ones and I brought confusion and scattered them to all the earth, so their plans would be brought to nothing. This was a long time ago, and I am still in control of all life on earth. Soon I will come and destroy this planet with fire, and cleanse it of all unrighteousness. I will create a new heaven and earth, and My Children will flourish in it. I will walk among My People and teach them My ways, then I will send them out across the universe and they will rule over the nations. I will fill all the universe with life and love for Me. The universe will sing and rejoice over My loving kindness and tender mercies. I will reign supreme and no one will stand against Me.

John 10:1-16

My Beloved, there is only one way to enter the Kingdom of Light and that is through Me. I call My Children and they come to Me. I know who has the seed of righteousness within them. I know who will love Me and want to serve Me. I can see ahead, and I know those who want to love Me. I know all things. There is no time within Me. I have given you time, so you can count the days and seasons and know when My feast days are coming, so you can celebrate with Me. I have given you time, so you can count the days until My return and know the timing. I have given you time to count the days of your being and know when your existence is over. Everyone on earth counts time, yet I do not count time because I AM and have always been. I use time only as a marker for you, so you can know what I AM doing and when I will do it. There is nothing hidden from you. It is all in My scriptures. In the last days I will bring forth the Truth from My scriptures, so only the faithful can see the Truth. Only those who I call My Name can come to Me. They know My Voice and follow Me as a sheep follows his shepherd. He feels safe in the shepherd's voice and knows that he can trust Him. If you love Me, you will want to hear My voice and follow Me knowing that I will lead you to a safe place with green meadows where all your needs will be provided for you. If you are afraid, then you do not know My Voice. If you are fearful, then you do not know your Shepherd. You need to cling to Me, and do not look at what is going on around you. The world is dark and full of evil, but I keep you in a pen with all My Children and I keep you close to Me and guard you from others who would harm you. I will bring all My sheep from all over the world back to My lush green pastures, and you will graze at My feet and know Me and have peace in all your days.

Strength And Encouragement

John 15:1-17

My Beloved, I AM the Vine and you are the branches. If you call on My Name and commune with Me and I with you, then you are connected to the Vine and you will bring forth fruit that only comes from the Spirit. You will walk in love and peace and joy. You will have compassion for others. You will have mercy on others. You will love those around you, and be an example for them. You will be a Light shining in the darkness. Others may hate you, because your Light exposes their sins. They do not want to come out of the shadows and see their life as it really is. They do not want to stop their sinning, but they want to indulge in the pleasures of their flesh. My People deny the flesh and put it in its place. They walk in the Spirit, and do not allow the flesh to overtake them and turn aside from the path of righteousness. Their hearts are pure before Me. They want to serve only Me, and they do not love the gods of this world. They love only Me. If you want to bear fruit and be connected to Me, then you must focus on Me and allow Me to guide you. You must not have your eyes set on the things of the world. The world wants to make you think that everything it has to offer is good for you, but really it blinds you and keeps you from serving Me. I want you to come closer to Me and hear My voice, but you must deny your flesh. Pray and fast and deny your flesh, so you can bear much fruit and be a Light to those around you. This is My commandment that you love others, and then you will walk in the things of Me.

Acts 2:1-41

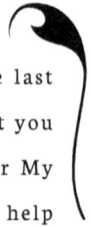

My Beloved, I promised My People that I would send My Spirit in the last days. You are in the last days and have been in the last days since I left you and returned to My Throne. I left you with My Spirit, so you can hear My Voice and know Me. You are not alone, but you have the Comforter to help you and bring you peace. You have My Presence to overtake you and deliver you from all things. There is nothing that you cannot do as long as you ask Me to help you, and walk in My will for you. Some of you are sick and you are under the care of doctors. You want Me to heal you, but you do not believe that I will heal you. You call on doctors and not on Me. You do not wait on Me to heal you or show you the natural way to heal you. Some of you are in sin, so I cannot heal you. You are covered in curses from your ancestors. You have not broken through the curses, so you cannot receive the benefit of My love for you. You must arise! You must fast and pray and walk close to Me, so I can show you what to do. You want to walk in My ways, yet the world is always at your fingertips. You are close to the world and want to be close to Me. Lift up your eyes and separate yourself from the world, and then you will be able to be healed. When My Spirit came to My People on Pentecost, they were waiting for Me to come to them just as I had said that I would. They believed that I would come back to them and I did. They expected Me to walk in the door, but instead I sent My Spirit to them so that all can be filled and hear My Voice. Even those very far away from Jerusalem -even those who live in exile-can hear My Voice and be guided by My Spirit. My prophet said through My Spirit that I would come, and I came. My prophet said that I would pour My Spirit on My People, and I did. My prophet said that I will return again to you, and I will. Be strong. Be brave. You will overcome.

Strength And Encouragement

Romans 8:26-39

My Beloved, when you are weak, I AM strong. I will give you strength to overcome, if you call on My Name. I have given you My Spirit to intercede on behalf of you. Allow My Spirit to intercede on behalf of you, and I will hear the pleadings of My Spirit within you and work in the midst of you, and you will receive the gifts that you need to help you overcome. If you are weak, I will help you stand up and be strong once again. A man may fall, but he can always get up and stand up and walk once again. I will take his hand and walk with him and take him through the darkest days, and he will become as a Light before Me. If a man wants to walk in My Presence, he must turn his face to Me and listen to My Voice so he can walk in My Will. If he walks in My Will, then I will give him only good gifts. Sometimes My Will for him may lead him through the testing of his faith. You must know that the testing of your faith will make you stronger, and you will be able to overcome because you have trusted in Me and believed in Me. I have shown you My faithfulness and you have become stronger, because you have seen Me work on behalf of you. If you lift up your voice in praise and adoration and do not complain in My Presence, but thank Me for all My wondrous works, then you will see My Hand working before your very eyes. Nothing can harm you, because you are Mine. No enemy can harm you. No man can harm you. You are held in My Hands. I chose you from the beginning. I knew what you would become, and I was pleased with you. Before you were ever born, I knew you and you smiled in My Presence and I rejoiced over you. I wrapped you in flesh and I sent you to earth and tested you in My Presence, and you show your worth daily. You show that I AM the only One that you serve. Nothing can stop you as long as you trust in Me to care for you. You may live in exile, but you live in My Presence and are led by My Hand.

Romans 12

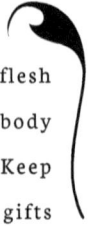

My Beloved, I want you to be a living sacrifice constantly denying the flesh and pleasing Me by the scent of its' burning. I want you to keep your body sacred and guard over it carefully. Keep yourself pure and righteous. Keep yourself in tune with Me always listening to My voice. I have given you gifts that you must use to lift up the body of believers and encourage them. Do not lift up yourself with these gifts, but use them to strengthen others in the faith. If you love Me, you will love others. Do not repay others for their sins against you. Do not seek revenge, but love your brothers and I will repay them for their sins against you. I will see that they repay every amount owed to you. I will tear them down and build you up, because you were faithful to trust Me to deliver you from this one who wanted to wrong you. Watch over your brothers, and rebuke them if they fall into sins. Encourage them if they fall and want to get back up and serve Me. If you can help your brother, do it cheerfully, and then I will bless you. Many will cross your path with needs. How many will you help? If the people of the world cross your path show them your love, so they can see My Hand upon them through your love. If your brother in need crosses your path, then make sure you help him at every turn get back on the path of righteousness. You are My Light. You are My Hands and Feet. You are the one I work thorough to help others. You must listen to My Voice and hear My Words and do as I tell you to do, then you will please Me and be a living sacrifice of your flesh before Me. I will reward you greatly for your good works.

Strength And Encouragement

1 Corinthians 3:8-17

My Beloved, do you know that you are My Temple? I live within you. Since you are moving around through many people, My Spirit within you can touch many people along your path. I will speak to you and tell you what to do when one of My Children cross your path. Be on guard, so you can see them and help them or encourage them. You are My Temple, so live uprightly. Live and walk in faith, so you can always know who I AM and what My Will for you is. If you will continue to seek Me, then you will find Me. You must love those around you and help them with all their needs. If you do not have money to give them, then help them find a job or a place to stay or food to eat. If you have money to help them, then give to them generously and I will bless you. I am always looking for ways to bless My Children. I watch carefully over you to see that you are doing. I have sent you angels to help you and show you the path to take. In the dark days ahead, angels will lead you out of darkness and into a place where you can feel My Spirit. The days ahead will grow darker, and you must listen to My Voice now while you still can, so you will know My Voice and not be deceived by the Evil Ones who try to take over the world. They will use strong deception to overtake you, but I will give you the ability to see clearly. You are my beloved, and no one will harm you. I will destroy the evil before your eyes, and you will rejoice that I love you so much. Keep yourself pure in all areas of your life-food you eat, clothes you wear, people you associate with, music you listen to, and books you read. Govern your eyes and do not watch things that are not clean. You must be clean before Me, because I will bless only My Children who want to stay clean and pure before Me.

1 Corinthians 13:1-14:1

My Beloved, seek Me in all you do, and you will know that I AM love. If you walk in the things of Me, then you will walk in love. I AM merciful and compassionate. I want you to be merciful and compassionate to others. I want you to look past the flesh and look into the heart of the person who is not kind and caring. What has brought this person to this place in his life? Seek Me concerning them and pray for them and I will reveal hidden things about them so you will know how to pray for them. You will see your mercy and compassion grow, and you will love them even if they do not do things that are right in My eyes. Even if this person wants to harm you, you will forgive him and put him in My Hands and love him in spite of his sins against you. Your love will heap coals of fire upon them and bring shame to them and they will be humbled by your love for them. They will expect you to seek revenge on them and try to harm them, but you will love them and your love will humble them. You will see through My eyes and not the eyes of the world. You must not view people the way the world views them. You must love them in spite of their sins against you. If you are wealthy and powerful and have authority but you do not have love, then you will lose all you have and suffer loss and pain. If you walk with the elite of the world and think that you will be able to walk through the last days without being touched, you are deceived. You will be wiped away with all the unbelievers who want only to serve themselves and not Me. Only those who walk in love for Me and those around them will be saved from the Lake of Fire. I will destroy those who do not love others. I know that your flesh may get hurt and you may feel pain from others' words or actions, but I will heal you if you forgive them and love them in spite of what they have said or done to you. This is a sign of a true believer in Me. You trust Me to punish the person, and you do not take actions into your own hands by retaliating with harsh cruel words or actions. You will walk hand and hand with Me, and you will inherit the Kingdom of Heaven on earth.

Strength And Encouragement

Ephesians 5:1-20

My Beloved, imitate Me how I lived when I walked on this earth. I was loving and kind and showed compassion to many. I spoke the Truth and was honest with all men. I told them to repent of their sins and walk in love. I told them to turn away from man-made laws and walk in My laws, so they could walk in freedom and not the bondage of man-made laws. I told My People to love their brothers and be good to them. Be good to those who are not good to you. Be kind to those who are not kind to others. Your love can change them. Your example of righteousness will be a Light to the world, and open the eyes of the blind. You are a Light. Do not keep your Light covered, but be an example of love and kindness to all men no matter who they are. Love will not be rejected. Love from a pure heart will not be turned away. Only the cruel will reject your loving kind deeds. I will deal with these wicked ones. I will destroy them, and they will no longer be remembered. They will no longer be a threat to any of My little ones. I guard over you and protect you. I keep you safe from all those who want to harm you. I keep My angels around you, so you can remain safe and at peace. You are My beloved, and no one will harm you. The days will grow darker, but I will help you overcome. You must reframe from entering into the sins of the flesh-adultery, fornication, gossiping, stealing, worrying, killing others with your words, rejecting others. You must enter into the Spirit, and love the unlovely and trust Me in all things. There is no need to ever be afraid or worry about anything. If you trust Me, I will give you all that you need. I will bless you in all areas of your life. Even the area that you struggle with the most, I will help you overcome and be strong. You do not have to fear. Let there be no fear in you, but only faith in Me, and I will greatly bless you.

Ephesians 6:10-18

My Beloved, the Evil One is everywhere trying to turn you away from Me. He is looking for your weak areas, so he can war against you. Your flesh is weak, but you must be strong in the Spirit. You must pick up your weapons of the Spirit and use them. Do not grow weary in battle, but make yourself strong by staying in My Presence. If you are calling on My Name all the day and praying and asking Me to help you, I AM near to you at all times. You must walk in Truth and righteousness. You must have faith to believe in Me to help you. You must walk in peace and longsuffering with those around you. Do not get angry with your brother, but talk out the problem and find peace, even if you have to compromise what you want as long as you do not compromise walking in the Truth. If you stay in My Truth and walk in righteousness, I will keep you in a strong tower. You will not be able to be penetrated. You will stand firm and not waiver. If you do waiver and you do fall, get up quickly and do not look back. Repent of your sins, and do not go that path again. Change what you are doing and how you think about things. Read My Words and meditate on them, so they can wash your mind clean. You will see your heart changing as you read My Words and begin to put My love into action. There are many around you who watch what you do. You must be a loving and kind example everyday to all those around you. You must not be angry, bitter, resentful, but forgiving, kind, and caring to others. The Evil One focuses on your hurts and tries to magnify them, so you will fall further into sin. Do not allow the enemy to get a foothold, but forgive the person before you go to bed at night. Go to the person and talk out the problem, so you can find a solution and not harbor bitterness against the person. If the person will not talk to you, then forgive the person and put that person in My Hands and I will deal with the person. You must trust Me that I know his heart, and I will punish him according to his works. I love you and I want you to have a happy, peaceful life. Cling to Me and I will help you walk in that peace.

Strength And Encouragement

Philippians 4:4-9

My Beloved, rejoice in Me and be thankful for all the things that I have done for you. Even if you do not understand why some things are happening in your life, accept My Will for you, and walk in the task that I have given you. You may feel burdened and overwhelmed, but call on My Name and I will give you strength. I will help you overcome even today. Rejoice and be thankful in all things knowing that I only give good gifts to My Children that love Me and call on My Name. If you are always calling out to Me to help you, then My Presence is upon you and you will have peace. Do not be fearful for the future, but trust Me with all your heart and I will help you. Do not look at man and be afraid, because I can change the heart of a man overnight. I know what every man fears, and what motivates him. I will bring on him his fears, if he does not trust in Me. I will bring peace to the man who clings to Me. Think about only those things that are pure and righteous. Think about things that are loving and kind that you can do for others. Be forgiving and have compassion and mercy on others, like I have compassion and mercy on you. If you love others and are kind and caring to others, then I will have mercy on you and kindness will be poured out on you. If you think on good things, then you will have peace. If you are anxious and worrying about what is going on around you, then you do not trust Me. If you trust Me, then you will walk in peace and I will protect you and all your love ones and all your possessions. If you are afraid and worry about the future, then you do not know Me. Fear opens a door for the enemy to come and steal from you. He will steal your peace, and even all that you have. You must rejoice and be glad everyday and know that your heavenly Father will only bring you good things. You must trust Me, even though you do not understand why something is happening. Wait to see the end result, and then you can look back and see how I was with you the whole time, and how I changed you from glory to glory.

Colossians 3:1-15

My Beloved, put aside your old fleshly nature and walk in the Spirit. Let your spirit rise up and overtake the flesh, so you can walk at one with Me. If you deny your flesh and you walk in purity, then you will be at one with Me. Put aside the flesh with its lust and wicked desires. You must focus your thoughts on the things of the Spirit and not on the things of the world. Do not look at the things of the world and want to be a part of these things, but desire the things of the Spirit and walk in these things...love, compassion, mercy, peace, longsuffering. Be patient with others and forgive them when they sin against you. People are not perfect, and they do make mistakes. Be merciful to them, and I will be merciful to you. There are some men who hate Me, and they will hate you. I will protect you from these men, and you will not be harmed by them. I will raise you above them, so they cannot touch you. Rejoice and be glad that I love you so much. Rejoice and be glad that I will bring you only good things. If you do not know what direction to take, then seek Me and I will guide you. Follow My peace. If you have asked Me to guide you and you have peace about going forward, then you should walk in this peace. If you are still uncertain after you ask Me to guide you, then wait until I give you peace to go forward. If you do not have peace about going forward and you do not understand why and you want to go forward, then continue to seek Me and I will show you the reason why you should wait. I know the future, and I know what is best for you. I will give you peace, if you are walking down the right path. If you have no peace and you know that something is not right, then stop and seek Me and I will guide you. I AM faithful to guide all those who call on My Name. I will send you a message, and you will hear My Voice and begin to trust My Voice. You will know that I love you and want only the best for you. Think on these things, and rejoice that I love you so much.

Strength And Encouragement

James 1:2-25

My Beloved, rejoice when you face temptation and testing, because you will overcome and be rewarded for your victories. I will give the crown of eternal life to those who overcome the world and all its temptations and want to only serve Me. There are many who have fallen away from the faith. Do not be concerned about these, and do not allow these to keep you from going forward. You must walk in the things of Me and not the world, or you will have no life eternal. You will not receive the rewards that I have for you in My Kingdom of Light. If you love Me, you will want to follow Me and do only what I ask you to do. You cannot hear the voice of your Master and ignore it. You must follow through with His commands. You must want to do what I tell you to do like a humble servant. If you read My Words and know what I AM asking you to do, then you must walk in these commands. A faithful servant keeps My commandments and wants to do what I ask him to do. If you hear My Words and then do not obey Me, then you are a rebellious servant and you will receive many lashes. You will continue to be lashed until you turn aside from your rebellion and follow Me. I may ask you to sell your house and leave your job and separate from the unbelievers in your family, and follow Me. I may ask you to go to a place and live that you have never known before. You may have to be like Abraham who left his home and went to a new place and walked in faith. You may have to be like Jacob who left his home and went to a new place and served Me in a new land. You may have to be like the widow who heard the voice of the prophet that famine was coming to the land and fled to another land. If you listen to My voice, then you will hear Me when I tell you to do something. It may be hard for you to do or it may be easy for you to do. What is most important is to obey Me, and I will guide you to a good place where you will have peace, and your enemy will not torment you. Great darkness is coming to the nations. I will bring My People back to My Land and care for them tenderly during the darkest of days.

James 3:1-18

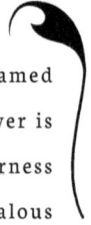

My Beloved, the tongue is a wicked member of your body that must be tamed by My Spirit. You cannot tame it yourself. You cannot bridle it. Whatever is in the heart will flow through the tongue. If you carry jealousy or bitterness or selfishness, then it will flow out through the tongue with bitter jealous words. You will curse others and not bring blessings to those around you. If you want to walk in My Spirit, then you must humble yourself and not brag or boast about your selfish desires, but brag and boast about what I have done in your life to bless you. Your tongue should be praising Me and giving Me the glory for all the wonderful things that I have done for you. If you praise Me and bless others, then I will bless you. If you complain and spread gossip or belittle and criticize your fellow man and do not bring encouragement or strength through your words, then you will suffer for your words. I will bring judgment on you, because you have brought death instead of life with your words. Your heart will be pierced, and you will be driven to repentance. You will see clearly that I desire for you to walk in righteousness and spread love to all around you. Speak words of love and have compassion and mercy for others. No one is perfect. They all make mistakes. Go to your brother and reason with him about his actions that have hurt you. Pray together over what has happened. Try to find peace with that person, then you can have peace in your life and have happiness. If you are afraid to go talk to this person, then send a letter or a message through a friend that you trust. Try to open the door of communication. Once you begin to reason with the person, you will feel released from this burden of sin. Even if the person will not want to make reconciliation, at least you have tried to work things out with the person. I will count this as righteous, and bless you for your good deeds.

Strength And Encouragement

James 4:1-10

My Beloved, lift up your petitions to Me with humble hearts. What is the motive of your prayers? To get more? To help others? Is your greed keeping your prayers from being answered? Are you praying for the things of the world? I want you to be prospered, but can I trust you that when I prosper you that you will not desire the things of the world and fall into the ways of the flesh? My Children, I love you so much and I want you to follow Me. Sometimes I do not give you much, so your focus can be on Me, and you will not turn away from Me. If you love Me, then you will want to serve Me and give to others. Do you want to serve Me? Do you want to give to others? If you desire to make more money and spend it on yourself, then your motives are wrong. Do you need a brand new car or house? Do you need fancy clothes and shoes? Do you need your house to be decorated like a temple for yourself? What do you really need? You need a house filled with love and compassion for others. You need food to fill your stomach and clothes to cover your body. You need shoes for your feet and money to pay all your bills. Get out of debt, and then you can give to others. Your life should be simple and not filled with many possessions. If you have many possessions, then you do not know what to do with all of them. Cleanse your house, and give to the poor all that you really do not need. Cleanse your house and your life of unnecessary possessions. Do not long for possessions, but long for the ability to give to others, and then your prayers will be answered, and you will prosper greatly.

1 Peter 1:1-9

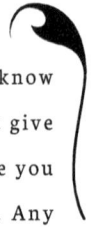

My Beloved, Peter wrote to those scattered in exile. He wanted them to know the Truth. You live in exile and this message is for you, so you will not give up when you suffer difficult situations. When you have people persecute you and say mean things to you, rejoice because your rewards will be great. Any time others are mean to you and you stand firm in the faith, then your faith is growing stronger. You become unbendable and cannot waive even in the darkest of days. Stand firm and be strong, because I love you so much. I will deliver you in the Last Days from those who persecute you and cause you trouble. The enemy roams the earth looking for those who he can torment and cause to fall into sin and not be counted worthy on the Day of Judgment. I want you to be found as a faithful servant on the Judgment Day. I want to say to all those who look on that you have been found worthy of entering My Kingdom of Light. I want you to rejoice on the Day of My Coming instead of hiding from Me in sin. Repent of all your sins, and walk in righteousness. Walk in the ways of peace, love, and kindness with those around you. The pagans do not understand you, but love them anyway and they will see your Light and not be able to ignore it. If you see clearly, you will know that these days are temporary and you will not live here long. You will be tested by fire, but you will overcome and emerge a glorious creature ready to rule with Me in My Kingdom of Light. Rejoice and be glad that I love you so much and have chosen you to be My Own.

Strength And Encouragement

1 Peter 2:1-12

My Beloved, you are the living stones that I am carving laying the foundation of My Kingdom of Light. You are chosen by Me to be My Servants that you will be the ones who hold fast to the Truth and teach the Truth to the nations. You are chosen by Me from the darkness and brought into a great Light. You were not a people, and I made you My People. You were lost and forgotten, and I redeemed you and made you My own. You should turn away from hatred and malice and any such fleshy desires, but turn to Me and walk in loving kindness. I will have mercy on you and help you become strong, so you can walk into My Kingdom. You will be counted worthy on the Last Day. You will be able to rule with Me in My Kingdom. You do not realize that you are being chiseled into the stone that will be the anchor of the foundation in My Kingdom. On you I will build a stable Kingdom that will not waiver. You will emerge glorious from your fleshy bodes ready to serve Me whole heartedly. You must not give up, but you should realize that you are temporary aliens on this planet and your mission has not even begun yet. You are in the process of transforming into a being of Light. Put aside all darkness from you and cling to what is pure and righteous, and then you will do well. Then you will be able to commune with Me and hear My Voice and walk in My ways. You must put aside all fleshy desires, and follow My Voice to love others and not yourself. Be kind and loving and not greedy and selfish. There are those around you that will try your flesh, but rejoice because you will overcome them with your love and compassion. You will not allow your flesh to overcome you so that you walk in hatred or malice. Be strong and be brave. You are an overcomer!

1 Peter 3:8-17

My Beloved, put evil far away from you. Do not repay evil for evil, but repay evil with good. In this way you will break the circle of hatred, and you will dissolve the hatred of the person. Who can fight against pure love? No one can continue to fight against a man who loves him. Allow your love to overcome all obstacles. You may have to suffer for a season and if you do, then rejoice because I will reward you for loving those who hate you. I will give you great rewards. You were placed in this world to love others and not to hate others. How can the world be different if you hate as the world hates? You are here to change the world by your love for others. You are My Hands and Feet, and you walk among the people and spread My Love to others. You must always remember that you are My Servant, and you walk in a dark world. There are many who are wounded and hurting, and they need your love and compassion and encouragement. They need you to care about them and show that they are important. Many voices are calling out asking for someone to listen to them and show them love. Look for those who are calling to you, and give them love and bring them a little bit of happiness in this troubled world. You are My Ambassadors, and you speak on behalf of Me. You should always speak kind and loving words to those around you, and let them know that I AM always with them if they call on My Name. Be strong and brave, and do not give into the evil one and allow hatred and bitterness and resentment into your heart to grow and transform you into a person filled with hate. You will never be happy unless you forgive the person and allow Me to deal with his heart. Forgive and do not allow the enemy to have any place inside of you, so you can hear My Voice and follow My plans for you.

Strength And Encouragement

1 Peter 4:12-19

My Beloved, you must know that you will suffer in this life. You will suffer even if you are doing what is right in My Sight. You will suffer, but you will be rewarded for showing yourself faithful even if others are cruel to you. You may be mocked for bearing My Name and speaking the Truth. You may be hated, because you do not believe as others believe. You may be put to shame in front of others, because you love Me and want to do what is right. Rejoice when this happens, because I will reward you for any suffering that you may have to endure for confessing My Name. Even when others are cruel to you, their conscience will be seared because you carry My Love and My Light, and you show others the way to walk. They do not want to want in the Light or be close to the Light, so they will shun you and not want to be your friend. Continue to love those who shun you and do not hate them, because your love will pierce their hearts and they will see your good works and know they are lacking and without. You must continue to walk in righteousness no matter if no one else wants to walk the same path that you want to walk. There are others that are walking in your same path, and you will cross paths in the proper season. Sometimes I put you in a desert, and I test you and form you just like I did to My People in the desert. These people who walked forty years in the desert were transformed and became people of faith. If you walk in faith, you will also be transformed and you will become a new creature. You will be used greatly for My Kingdom. Do not be afraid when obstacles arise in your path. I will help you know what to do and how to do it. You must call on My Name, and I will show you a way out. You do not have to fear anything, but know that I AM always with you guiding you even in the darkest of days. I will arise like a Light, and open a door for you to escape. The darkness will not overtake you, but you will overtake the darkness by the Light of My Presence in you. Rejoice and be glad that you have been given so much.

1 Peter 5:6-11

My Beloved, humble yourself under My Hand as I mold you into My Glory. Humble yourself and accept what plans I have for you, even if I have called you to suffer for a season. Humble yourself and know that as a humble servant you will be rewarded greatly in My Kingdom. If you are fearful, then put away all your fear and put your cares on Me. Put yourself in My Hands. Won't I take care of you? Won't I always provide what you need for each day? Do not worry. If you worry, you cause your flesh to grieve and you harm your flesh. A man that does not worry will be happy, and he will not feel the weight of worry on his flesh. He will be happy and free from the cares of the world. Lift your eyes up to Me, and I will give you all you need. Whatever your problem is today, give it to Me. Do you think that I can handle it? Am I capable of taking this burden off of you? Why do you keep worrying about it? You must trust Me with all your heart. I cared for your ancestors in the wilderness and their clothes and shoes never wore out and their stomachs were always filled. You must trust Me to care for you. If you are thinking that you are not good enough, then repent and walk in righteousness so your conscience can be clear. You must want to overcome. Do not give into temptations, but resist all temptations and walk in what is right, and you will be blessed. I will lift you up, and you will not even want to do the sinful things that you use to do. You will want to only do what is right in My eyes. Love those around you, and be kind to all men. Even if men are not kind to you and treat you cruel, just know that I love you and I will guard over you and keep you from these people, if you call on My Name to help you. I wait for your voice and I listen. I love to hear your praises and shouts for joy. I rejoice when you rejoice. I want you to find happiness in this life. I know there will be tests to overcome, but stay focused and trust Me to guide you, and you will be victorious. Be strong and be brave and your life will be filled with victory.

Strength And Encouragement

2 Peter 3:3-14

My Beloved, there will be those who say, "When is He coming? He has forgotten about you. He is not coming back!" Do not listen to these people, but remember My Promises and know that I will return. I will destroy the earth with fire and create a new heavens and earth for My People who love Me and call on My Name. My Children love Me and want to serve Me and want to do what is right in My Sight. If you love Me, you will love others also. You will want to do what is right. If you know that I AM coming soon, then how will I find you? Will you be working faithfully for your Master? Will you not be willing at all to do what is right? I will come as a thief in the night. You will not know when it will be. You will know the season, but not the exact time. You must be trying every day to walk in righteousness, so you can be counted as worthy to enter My Kingdom of Light. If you want to walk in your flesh, then I will spit you out of My mouth. I will not want you in My Kingdom. If you love Me and walk in My Ways and give to others, then I will open a door for you to enter My Kingdom. You will walk into My Kingdom with the others that love Me. I have kept a remnant for Myself, and I will care for you tenderly. I will cover you with My Presence. You will know what to do and how to do it. Stand firm until the Last Day when I take you in My Arms and show you My Kingdom. I will give you a new name and a new home. You will rule with Me and have authority in My Kingdom. You will be a Light to the universe, because you will spread Light out in all directions. Rejoice that I love you so much, and do not allow the cares of the world to overtake you. I will give you all you need. You are people of faith and you must do what I tell you to do, then you will walk a straight path and be an example to all those around you. Even if they mock you, they will admire your good works and know that you are a people of love and compassion. You will want to rejoice that you have left the fingerprints of love on each person that you touch. Know that I will give you all that you can handle, and strengthen you, and hold you up, and lift you to a high place, so you can see clearly and know that My Hand is on you to guide you, and provide for you, and make you into My Image. Rejoice that I love you so much.

1 John 3:1-15

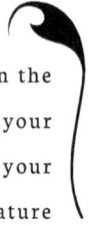

My Beloved, continue to keep purifying yourself, so you can be ready on the day of My Return. Be ready and awake. Do not fall asleep as some of your brothers and sisters have. Stay sober and awake. Continue to sacrifice your flesh and remain clean before Me, so you can emerge as a glorious creature transformed into My Image. Even the angels look on in wonder of what you will become. You will become a being of Light filled with love for others just like I AM filled with love and mercy and compassion. I will judge each man fairly on the Last Day. Those who have obeyed Me and longed for My Return will be able to continue in My Kingdom of Light, but those who are filled with hatred and exile will be thrown into the Lake of Fire and be destroyed. They will be no more. Their names will be forgotten, but your name will shine in the Light and you will be a servant always of the Most High living in the Light of My Presence and doing My Will continually. If you have My Seed within you, then you will be convicted to continue to do what is right. You will be miserable until you walk in My Ways of love and kindness. You will not want to hate your brother, but you will forgive your brother and love him. You will show him that your life is filed with love and compassion, and you will be an example to him. Your love will change him, and he will want to walk in the way of love. If you continue to sin, then you do not love Me. Only My Children who love Me will want to walk in righteousness. If you continue in your sin, then you want to walk in darkness, and My Light is not in you. Beware, because you will pay the full penalty of your sins. You will suffer under the payment of your sins, and you will cry out to Me. You can pay for all your sins on earth and not have to pay a penalty in My Kingdom. When the books are opened, you must be paid in full for your sins. You must make restitution for all the wrongs you have committed against your brothers and sisters. You must wake up and see that the sins that you commit today will bring you pain tomorrow, if you do not do what is right in My eyes. Listen and be brave to stop what you are doing, and repent and turn to Me with your whole heart, so you can be found worthy on the Day of My Return.

Strength And Encouragement

1 John 4:7-21

My Beloved, if you love Me, then you will love others. If you follow after Me and commune with Me, then you will love others and put others before yourself. If you love others, then you are a Light to the world and will bring sin into the Light. You will be an example to others of My love and compassion. If you do not love your brother who you have seen, how can you love Me who you have not seen? You must learn to forgive all men. Do not allow the enemy to build up hatred in your heart against any man, but allow your love to overtake this hatred and put it out of your heart, so you can love the person and not walk in darkness. If you fear, then you do not walk in love. There is no fear in love. There is no fear in My Presence. If you want to walk in love, then you must commune with Me and know My Voice, There will be no fear for those who know My Voice. They will call out to Me in times of trouble, and I will comfort them and drive out all fear. Their trust will overdrive their fear. If you are worried and upset over a situation or person, then lift it up to Me, and put the problem in My Hand so I can take the burden away from you. You must trust Me to take care of it and resolve the situation. You should never have fear in your heart. If you have fear, then you have no faith and you do not trust Me. Only My Children that love Me will have faith in Me, because they know who I AM. They know that I will never leave them or neglect them. I will always stand beside you even in times of testing. The testing of your faith makes you a strong warrior, so you can stand firm against the enemy at all times and never bend. You will need this courage in the Last Days. You will need to be faithful and courageous trusting only in Me to deliver you from the evil ones. I will take you to a safe place, and you will be sheltered by My Hand. Do not worry about how much money you have or your job or your family or any such thing. I can change the problem in a moment. Take one day at a time and trust Me and love others and you will do well. Focus on loving others instead of your concerns, and then you will do well. You will have victory, and be an overcomer. Rejoice in this!

Revelation 21:1-22:5

My Beloved, I opened the heavens to My servant John and showed him what will happen in the days to come. I showed him the new city that I will bring to My People who endure to the end. I will dress them like a bride in beautiful clothing made of Light and Spirit. They will be glorious beings and radiant like costly jewels. My Children who love me and want to serve Me will become beings of Light and will dwell with Me in My City of Light. There will be no darkness. The sinners will not want to come to the city, because the Light will expose their sins and only the pure can enter the city. Only those who want to walk in righteousness can enter. If you want to indulge in the things of the world, then you will not come into My City. You will be left outside. There are 12 gates with 12 names of the tribes on the gates. You will be given the name of the tribe of your ancestors, and you will walk through the gate with your tribe's name on it. You will rejoice with your brothers as you walk through the gate. You will hold a kinship with those of your tribe and will rule with them. You are My beloved children and I have great treasures to give you, if you remain faithful and endure until the end. There are many around you that want to pull you astray. Do not listen to them, but focus on Me and I will help you remain strong. Look for those around you who want to serve Me and do what is right. Look at those who are truly prue in heart-those who look at Me and My ways and want to keep My commandments. These are loyal servants, humble servants, faithful servants, and you should bind your-self to them. Be strong and do not bend. The times are dark and the enemy is seeking to deceive all those that he can. Deception is everywhere at every turn. You must recognize it, and be on guard that it does not suck you up into its trap. The enemy starts with Truth, and then twists it and gradually turns it to lies. This is why you have so many denominations. They all stem from one Truth and one Way, but the sin of man has allowed the Truth to be twist-ed and deception has come. Keep your eyes open, because the days are dark. Only the faithful will endure to the end. Remain faithful to Me.

Strength And Encouragement

Revelation 22:12-21

My Beloved, I will reward you for the things you have done. If you love Me, you will love others and give to them freely. If you love Me, then you will want to give good things to those around you. If you are found worthy to enter My Kingdom, then you will eat from the Tree of Life and live eternally. If you turn away from Me and serve the Evil One or want to live like the world does, then you will not eat of the Tree of Life. If you desire to gratify the flesh and not deny the flesh, then you have no place in My Kingdom. If you want to indulge in sexual sins, greed, selfishness, gossip, murder, theft, or anything that would make you sin against your neighbor, then repent because you are not from My Seed of righteousness. Only those who desire to help others and not hurt them or cause them pain will enter My Kingdom of Light. If you love those around you and want to help them, then I will bless you. I will judge you according to the balance between your good and bad deeds. I will open the books and weight you in the balance. If you are found worthy to enter My Kingdom, then the gate will open wide for you and the angels will rejoice over our faithfulness. You will be rewarded with great treasures. You will be rewarded by My Hand being opened wide to you. I will make you My own, and you will be given the Kingdom to rule over many nations. Across the universe My People will rule over others and show them the way to walk in righteousness. They will show them love and peace. They will show them mercy and compassion. They will teach the people how to walk in My Commandments, so the whole universe will be filled with love for Me. You are My first born, and you will be given your inheritance. You will be allowed to rule with Me and have authority over many. You will rule over angels and all the heavenly hosts. Only I will be given more power than you. You will be second only to Me. You will be loved by all the heavenly beings, because you endured to the end and was found faithful. Rejoice that you love Me so much and you have sacrificed your flesh daily, so that you may live with Me forever!